NH

Airline Economics

Airline Economics

Edited by
George W. James
The Air Transport Association
of America

LexingtonBooks
D.C. Heath and Company
Lexington, Massachusetts
Toronto

387.71
A298

Library of Congress Cataloging in Publication Data

Main entry under title:
  Airline economics.

  Includes index.
  1. Aeronautics, Commercial—United States—Addresses, essays, lectures.
2. Air lines—United States—Addresses, essays, lectures. I. James, George W.
HE9803.A4A7   387.7′1   81-47824
ISBN 0-669-04909-3   AACR2

m-R.

Copyright © 1982 by D.C. Heath and Company

Published simultaneously in Canada

Printed in the United States of America

International Standard Book Number: 0-669-04909-3

Library of Congress Catalog Card Number: 81-47824

*To Mark W. Crandall
and Stephen E. Klingelhofer,
two fine young men who believe.*

Contents

               George W. James   185

Part III   Airline Planning: The Air Transport
               Association/Stanford University Symposium   209

Chapter 10   Strategic Cargo Planning
               William M. Caldwell IV   211

Chapter 11   Marketing Planning   Robert L. Crandall   231

Chapter 12   Financial Planning for Fleet Acquisition
               Charles L. Glass   253

Chapter 13   Government Affairs Planning
               Harvey J. Wexler   261

Chapter 14   Airline Fleet and Schedule Planning
               Russell Thayer   265

Chapter 15   International Planning
               William H. Waltrip   281

               Glossary   293

               Index   301

               About the Contributors   313

               About the Editor   317

List of Figures

List of Tables

Preface

During the last decade, the shape of aviation in the United States has
undergone significant changes. No longer is aviation an infant industry,
glamorous because of its novelty. On the contrary, air transportation has
become the chief form of intercity common carriage. Millions of new
passengers have flown for the first time, and subsequently made repeated
flights. The larger carrier systems have been supplemented by an ever-
growing commuter class of service in many markets, and former
nonscheduled charter carriers have entered the scheduled market. The
general (private) aviation sector has grown substantially as well. In a real
sense, aviation has become an integral part of the American way of life.

After forty years of strict economic regulation by the Civil Aeronautics
Board, Congress in 1978 enacted legislation intended to deregulate the air
transport industry. This legislation permitted the airlines greater flexibility
than existed previously to develop their route systems and pricing policies
according to the demands of the market. In many respects the airlines have
entered a marketplace not unlike other business, despite the peculiarities of
the product sold by airlines and their centrality to the economy as a prime
transportation mode.

Moreover, the energy crises of the 1970s, environmental and consumer
concerns, the capital shortage and productivity declines experienced by the
nation as a whole have affected the airlines and their operations in important ways.

The Air Transport Association of America (ATA), a trade association
representing virtually all of the nation's scheduled airlines, has had an
almost unique vantage point during this time of change. New conditions
have bred ever-increasing demands for new and more sophisticated analyses
to help carriers understand what has happened and what will happen to the
industry and its operating environment. Moreover, the needs of its member
carriers have changed, particularly with respect to requirements for
economic data and its analysis—and ATA has served as a primary source
for meeting those needs.

ATA's Economics and Finance staff has responded to the industry's
needs by focusing on a wide variety of economic analyses, some derivative
of earlier work and others breaking new ground in the field of transportation economics. These studies, while clearly of academic interest, have
resulted from real-world concerns. Each has a particular practical purpose
and objective; taken together, they reflect the conditions in which the
airlines are operating and the efforts of this industry to deal effectively with
those conditions.

A cornerstone of this ATA effort has been the relatively recent development of a computerized airline data bank. Through the use of this bank and the ability to access and manipulate the data contained in it, the industry has dramatically enhanced its power to keep up with the changes occurring in the industry. The ATA studies contained in this anthology reflect that new analytic capacity.

This anthology is a compilation of these ATA studies and several other studies by airline analysts who serve regularly as ATA economic consultants. It also includes the proceedings of an August 1980 conference on airline planning, cosponsored by the Air Transport Association and Stanford University with the cooperation of Professor Charles Banfe.

The anthology is divided into an introduction and three principal sections.

The four chapters constituting the first section of the book deal with the economics of the air transport industry. The reader is introduced to data sources that make it possible to study the cost and revenue structure of individual airlines or of the industry as a whole. Factors in the environment that affect trends in both costs and revenues are discussed. The passenger market is then analyzed to provide an understanding of who travels and for what purposes. The effect of fluctuating travel patterns on airline economics is treated in a chapter on load factors (the percentage of seats that are actually occupied on flights). This introduction to airline economics ends with a chapter on financial forecasting in which a forecasting technique developed by the Air Transport Association is described.

The next section of the book deals with recent developments in the industry and the outlook for the future. Since fuel has become such a dominant cost element, one chapter deals with the supply and cost effects of aviation fuel. Next, in a capital planning chapter, the requirements for new capital equipment are explored and analyzed. It is shown that the industry requires about $90 billion during the decade of the 1980s for new equipment to replace obsolete equipment and to provide for expected growth in traffic. A chapter on the international aviation market details the marked changes in that market that have occurred over the past decade. Following a chapter on the changes in the U.S. aviation regulatory structure subsequent to the Airline Deregulation Act of 1978, the section concludes with a chapter that discusses the outlook for the industry over the next five to ten years.

The final section of the book is a summary of presentations by airline executives to the Airline Planning Symposium conducted in the summer of 1980. All major aspects of the planning process are treated in this final section of the book.

This book is not a treatise on the airline industry; rather, it is a collection of essays about important aspects of the industry. The book is intended to provide the student of aviation with an understanding of the structure, economics, and problems of the industry and its component airline companies.

Acknowledgments

Since this book is an anthology, many individuals have contributed to it. The most valuable contribution has been the work of Mark Crandall, a student employee of The Air Transport Association (ATA), who became the catalytic agent in helping to bring this book to its culmination. His energy, intelligence, organizational capabilities, and good sense of humor kept us all together and on time.

Preceding Mark, the focal point for the continuation of this book was the Reverend Stephen Klingelhofer, who was initially with ATA full time and then worked on the book in a part-time role while a theological student at the Virginia Theological (Episcopal) Seminary in Alexandria, Virginia. A man of many unusual skills, ranging from journalism to law, Steve kept the book going while others of us often had distracting administrative duties.

John Summerfield and Mel Brenner, two highly valued economic consultants to ATA, played significant roles in writing and rewriting many parts of the various chapters contained in the book. Their long and significant experience with the airline industry is reflected throughout the book.

No acknowledgments would be complete without recognition of those who provide the fundamental basis on which any book can be accomplished. Nedji Ellsworth worked untiringly on providing relevant and accurate data. In turn, Norma Durand, assisted by Jane Martin, typed at length on typewriters and word processors and checked and rechecked each sentence, paragraph, and chapter. They did so with patience and a charming attitude throughout.

Finally, I would like to acknowledge with grateful thanks the cooperation of Professor Charles Banfe of the Stanford University faculty. Professor Banfe, a retired Pan American pilot, working with ATA, arranged the first joint university and airline industry seminar on long-range planning at Palo Alto, California, in 1980. Airline executive participation in this seminar is reflected in chapters 10 through 15, which set forth many of the ways in which planning is carried out by individual U.S. carriers.

Introduction

The term *airline industry* is subject to a wide variety of interpretations. Several hundred American companies engage in the carriage of persons or goods by air. The largest of these earns revenues of several billion dollars a year, while the smallest may operate a single plane only several hours a week, carrying an occasional passenger from one place to another. This book deals only with the larger end of this spectrum.

Broadly defined, the airline industry consists of a vast network of routes that connect cities of the country (and of the world). Over this network, a large number of airline companies carry passengers and cargo on scheduled service. The network of scheduled service is supplemented by flights that are chartered for individual trips, and by private airplanes flown by individuals or by companies for their own purposes and to conform to their own schedule preferences.

To clarify the structure of the industry at the outset, it is useful to define the industry as its regulatory agency, the Civil Aeronautics Board (CAB), classifies it. Prior to 1981, airlines were classified by the CAB as follows:

Trunk Airlines, consisting of American, Braniff, Continental, Delta, Eastern, Northwest, Pan American, Trans World, United, and Western.[1]

Local Service Airlines, consisting of Frontier, Ozark, Piedmont, Republic, Texas International, and USAir.

Intra-Alaskan Airlines, consisting of Alaska, Kodiak-Western Alaska, Munz Northern, Reeve, and Wien Air Alaska.

Intra-Hawaiian Airlines, consisting of Aloha and Hawaiian.

All-Cargo Airlines, consisting of Airlift International and Flying Tiger.

Supplemental Airlines, consisting of Capitol International, Evergreen International, Rich International, Transamerica, World, and Zantop International.

Other Certificated Airlines, consisting of airlines formerly classified as commuters but recently certificated by the CAB.

All the airlines listed here are certificated by the CAB and thus are subject to control of routes and rates as set forth in the Federal Aviation Act.[2]

Table I-1 shows some of the operating results of each of these groups of airlines for the year 1980. Examination of the table shows that the trunk airlines have dominated the industry.

Table I-1
1980 Traffic and Revenues
(Thousands)

	Emplanements	RPMs	Cargo RTMs	Total Operating Revenue
Trunks	213,856	221,206,069	4,950,747	$26,776,514
Locals	51,490	21,601,529	133,265	3,676,410
Intra-Hawaiian	5,981	770,199	3,521	200,935
Intra-Alaskan	1,874	1,324,502	47,113	293,636
All cargo			1,907,208	890,104
Other certified	23,548	9,277,645	27,209	1,821,241

In addition, several hundred commuter airlines fly regularly scheduled service but are not under the control of the CAB. Another group, air taxi operators, also free of CAB regulation, do not fly regularly scheduled service.

In 1981, the CAB, recognizing that the structure of the industry had changed radically since these categories were established many years ago, established a new classification system. The new categories for certificated scheduled airlines are:

Major Carriers, consisting of those airlines with annual revenues in excess of $1 billion.

National Carriers, consisting of those airlines with annual revenues between $75 million and $1 billion.

Large Regional Carriers, consisting of those airlines with annual revenues between $10 million and $75 million.

Medium Regional Carriers, consisting of airlines with annual revenues of less than $10 million.

In addition, the CAB changed the classification of supplemental airlines to charter airlines. Commuter airlines and air taxi operators not certificated by the CAB retained their old classifications.

Because historical data employed in the chapters of this book precede the new classification system, the old classification system of trunks, locals, and so on, form the basis of discussion in this book. Whenever the term *airline industry* or *U.S. scheduled airlines* is used in this book, it excludes the supplemental airlines, commuters, and air taxi operators. When narrower categories are employed in the description of airline activities, that fact is noted in the context of the chapter.

The Contribution of Air Transport to the Economy

Like any other industry, the air transport industry makes a direct contribution to the economy through its employment and revenue generation and an indirect contribution through its purchase of goods and services from supplier industries. But the contribution of air transportation goes far beyond these forms. Air service is generally purchased as a means toward some other end and hence makes such contributions as:

1. Enhancing the efficiency of business and government activity by expanding the potential geographic radius of personal contact, communication, and supervision of activities.
2. Enriching life styles by broadening opportunities for vacations, educational travel, and visiting friends and relatives.
3. Supporting travel-related industries such as hotels, rental cars, and travel agencies, and promoting economic development of entire regions (for example, Hawaii).
4. Improving communications by rapid delivery of mail.
5. Aiding in commerce by providing speedy delivery of cargo from supplier to user in cases involving potential perishability, need for rapid response, inventory reduction, and the like.

As a measure of the direct contribution of the U.S. airline industry, consider the following statistics concerning the 1980 level of operations:

1. Gross revenues in excess of $33.5 billion.
2. Employment of nearly 340,000, many in technologically skilled occupations.
3. Payroll of more than $11 billion.
4. Carriage of 297 million passengers an average of 857 miles each.
5. Carriage of 7.1 billion ton-miles of freight and mail.

Air transport is a dominant factor in intercity passenger movement. Air travel accounts for 85 percent of all intercity common carrier transportation within the United States. Despite widespread ownership and operation of automobiles in this country, airlines accounted for about one-seventh as many intercity passenger miles as did private automobiles in 1980.

To provide these services, the airline industry is a large-scale consumer of goods and services. For example:

1. Its outlay for fuel exceeded $10.1 billion.
2. It spent over $900 million for passenger needs.
3. Materials used for aircraft and engine maintenance cost over $600 million.
4. Air carrier airports were paid over $500 million in landing fees and over $500 million in rental fees.
5. Over $3.2 billion were spent on new equipment and facilities, thus contributing in a substantial way to the dominant position of the U.S. aerospace industry in the world.

The Contribution of Air Transportation to
Efficient Conduct of Business

Business and government organizations take for granted the ability of
managers, executives, technicians, troubleshooters, or salesmen to reach
any point in the world within twenty-four hours. The ease and speed of
movement make it possible to keep in close touch with remote activities with
minimum loss of time away from home base. This mobility has permitted
efficient decentralization, geographic diversification of corporate activity,
and broadening of market outlets.

To visualize a world without modern air transportation, consider the
world of 1940, when surface transport was still in its prime and air transport
was in its infancy. On the high-density rail line between Washington, D.C.,
and Boston, a trip required about seven hours each way. If any meaningful
time were to be spent at destination, an overnight in a hotel was a virtual
necessity.

A New York-Chicago trip of 750 miles took seventeen hours each way
in 1940 on the fastest rail routing. It took longer to get from New York to
Chicago in 1940 than is currently required to fly between New York and
Cairo.

Trips from the Midwest to California were even more substantial adven-
tures in the era of surface travel. A 1940 railroad advertisement proudly
boasted that the crack Super-Chief took "only" thirty-nine and three-
quarters hours from Chicago to Los Angeles. The traveler had a choice of
leaving on Saturday or Tuesday. The 7:15 p.m. departure on Saturday
delivered the traveler to his Los Angeles destination at 9 a.m. on Monday.
The hapless New York-Los Angeles passenger had to add the seventeen
hours of New York-Chicago travel time to the thirty-nine and three-
quarters hours of Chicago-Los Angeles travel time, plus most of a day in
Chicago between trains. And these were the prime routes on the best trains!
Overseas travel presented even more severe problems to the business
traveler. A representative 1940 steamship schedule from San Francisco to
Hong Kong shows three weeks in each direction.

Today, domestic round trips like those mentioned above can be accomplished in a day, allowing time at destination for conduct of business.
Overseas trips are now also routine and can be almost as short and easy as
domestic trips. Trips that were once limited to highest priority needs now
can be treated as routine.

The new mobility is evident in the volume of passenger traffic presently
moving by air in key long-haul domestic markets. Table I-2 indicates the
average number of passengers each day on principal transcontinental routes
in the summer of 1980. Considering only these eight key routes, there were
more than 10,000 passengers traveling on an average day.

Table I-2
Number of Passengers Traveling Daily on Main Transcontinental Air Routes, Summer 1980

Route	Number of Daily Passengers
New York—Los Angeles	4,754
New York—San Francisco	3,234
Boston—Los Angeles	464
Boston—San Francisco	385
Washington—Los Angeles	485
Washington—San Francisco	390 (estimated)
Philadelphia—Los Angeles	388
Philadelphia—San Francisco	234
Total, selected markets	10,334

**Impact of Air Travel on
Personal and Pleasure Travel Patterns**

The impact of the air age on personal and pleasure travel has been at least as great as that on business travel. With limited vacation time, a lengthy trip by surface mode is a substantial obstacle to travel. Air service has not only brought revolutionary improvements in the quality of travel, it has combined this quality with discount fares. When adjusted for inflation, fares now available on long-haul air trips bring the cost of such travel to a very favorable relationship to the rail prices that prevailed in 1940.

A combination of speed and economy has altered the concept of personal travel. In 1940 it was the rare wealthy individual who could take a vacation in Europe. Now such travel is commonplace at nearly all levels of income. In 1940, the travel section of the Sunday *New York Times* featured almost exclusively resorts within a radius of a few hundred miles of New York—that is, in upper New York State, New England, Pennsylvania, and Canada. A current travel section of the Sunday *Times* has relatively little emphasis on such close destinations. Instead one finds heavy emphasis on such destinations as Europe, Hawaii, East Africa, and India.

Entire regions have developed into strong tourist-oriented centers because air transport has made them effectively accessible for vacationers from many locations. The economic development of such areas as Florida, Hawaii, Puerto Rico, Las Vegas, Phoenix, and San Diego can be credited to the access provided by air transport. In Hawaii, for example:

1. Between 1940 and 1980, the number of visitors increased from just over 25,000 to 4,000,000 annually.
2. Tourism accounts for 53 percent of the total state income in Hawaii.
3. Surveys by the Hawaii Visitors Bureau show that 99.9 percent of all visitors arrive by air.

Impact on Volume of Travel

Changes in speed, convenience, and comfort of travel have brought about large changes in the amount of travel, as shown in table I-3. Between 1939 and 1979, the population of the United States expanded by 68 percent. In the same period, intercity travel on commercial carriers increased by more than 640 percent. Table I-3 shows little change in the amount of surface inter-city travel, whereas air travel expanded at a tremendous rate.

By 1979, for trips over 2,000 miles, air accounted for 93 percent of all business-related trips, and for nearly 80 percent of all personal trips. Only 0.3 percent of international trips by U.S. residents were by surface transportation.

The Travel Infrastructure

Increased mobility, facilitated by air travel, has brought a large growth in travel-related industries; for example, hotels, car rentals, travel agencies, and restaurants. It is estimated, for example, that foreign travel to the United States had an economic impact of nearly $20 billion in 1978. Table I-4 shows the breakdown of receipts, payrolls, and employment from this source of travel alone.

Air Transportation of Freight and Mail

Cargo (a term that includes both freight and mail) is carried in passenger aircraft as well as in planes dedicated solely to carriage of cargo. As the net-

Table I-3
The New Dimension of Domestic Travel Mobility Created by Air Speed and Economy

	1939	1979	Percent Change
Intercity common carrier passenger-miles (millions)			
Surface	33,000	38,000	+15
Air	1,000	214,000	+21,300
Total	34,000	252,000	+641
U.S. population (millions)	131	220	+68
Passenger-miles per capita	260	1,145	+341

work over which cargo can be flown has expanded and as the system has become reliable, many companies have found air to be the preferred method of cargo transportation. Improved physical security and less exposure to damage are part of the reason for a preference for air transport. Reductions in inventory costs made possible by faster delivery are also a factor. Door-to-door next day delivery has become a standard part of the air freight business in much of the United States domestic market. As a result, air freight traffic has grown at an average annual rate of 10.3 percent over the last several decades.

Reliability of air transport plus demands of business for rapid communication have caused the U.S. Postal Service to use air as the standard method of moving mail. As recently as ten years ago, a premium postage rate was charged to send a letter by airmail. Now all first class mail routinely moves by air. And competition from small package air carriers in recent years has led the Postal Service to inaugurate Express Mail, with a guarantee of next day delivery to selected cities.

Growth of air cargo has facilitated decentralization of American industry by making it possible to move materials and to communicate among geographically dispersed segments of an organization almost as effectively as if they were in the same location.

Air Transportation and National Defense

To aid in a possible national emergency, many airlines have committed a portion of their fleets to serve in the Civil Reserve Air Fleet (CRAF). During

Table I-4
Economic Impact of Foreign Visitor Spending in the United States, 1978

	Receipts (millions)	Payroll (millions)	Employment (thousands)
Transportation	$ 1,254	$ 273	37
Food	1,597	426	95
Lodging	1,077	278	46
Entertainment	1,151	319	48
Incidentals	1,501	212	31
Direct	6,580	1,507	256
Indirect	5,698	1,774	165
Induced	7,218	1,846	150
Total	$19,494	$5,127	571

Source: U.S. Travel Data Center.

Note: Details may not add because of rounding.

normal peacetime periods, this commitment gives the participating airline an advantageous position in bidding for peacetime military transport business as required by the military departments. In the event of an emergency, these committed fleets can be called to active duty by the Military Airlift Command (MAC), to be used as best serves national defense requirements. Since the principal wartime transport shortage would be in cargo-carrying capability, the Air Force is particularly interested in cargo or passenger aircraft that can be rapidly converted to cargo configuration. A program recently undertaken by the Department of Defense seeks to induce airlines to modify wide-body passenger aircraft to convertible passenger/cargo configuration to provide that capability. Existence of these national defense programs provides the military establishment with a huge wartime airlift capability at a negligible peacetime cost. For the military to provide a similar capability by procuring and flying comparable aircraft in peacetime would be vastly more expensive.

This brief introduction to air transport's role in the economy makes it clear that aviation is an essential part of the economy, and that it makes valuable contributions to society as well. An important industry like the airline industry should be well understood; the remainder of the book provides an introduction to the airline industry with this objective in mind.

Notes

1. Two other trunk carriers, Northeast and National, were merged into other trunks in recent years. Mergers have also reduced the ranks of other categories of carriers.
2. See chapter 8 for discussion of the Act.

Part I
Background on Industry
Economics

1

8750
6150
5210
US

Airline Revenues, Costs, and Productivity

David A. Swierenga and
Mark W. Crandall

Introduction

The most fundamental aspect of any industry is its cost and revenue structure. The difference between costs and revenues is of course profit (or loss); though simplistic, the key to profitability is to find ways to increase revenues and/or to control costs.

The first two parts of this chapter present in detail the sources and magnitudes of airline revenues and costs. The data in the chapter must be analyzed fully if the economics of the airline industry are to be understood.

Following the material on revenues and costs, the third part of the chapter discusses trends in airline productivity—the measure of how efficiently airlines transform inputs into outputs or costs into revenue.

Revenue

The bulk of air transportation revenues comes from the carriage of passengers. For the U.S. scheduled airlines 84 percent of revenue comes from scheduled passenger service, and another 2 percent comes from charter passenger services.[1] Cargo services, including freight, mail, and express, account for 10 percent of revenue. Public service revenue, which subsidizes the operations of a few regional carriers, amounts to only 0.3 percent of total operating revenue for U.S. airlines. Table 1-1 shows the revenue breakdown for 1969 and 1979.

As can be seen in the table, scheduled passenger revenue increased on average more than 12 percent per year in the period 1969-1979. Cargo revenue increased about 11 percent per year. Within the cargo category, freight revenue posted large gains, while mail and express revenue increased more slowly, holding down the overall cargo increase.

The small increase in express revenue and the actual decline in charter passenger revenue can be attributed to structural changes in the industry. Express revenues on scheduled airlines have suffered because a growing segment of express freight is being handled by nonscheduled airlines specializing in express freight. Charter revenue has declined as widespread discount fares on scheduled services have cut the historic price advantage

3

Table 1-1
Operating Revenue—U.S. Scheduled Airlines
(Millions of Dollars)

	1969	1979	Percent Change (Average) Per Year
Passenger	$7,646	$23,311	11.8
Scheduled	7,120	22,792	12.3
Charter	526	519	(0.1)
Cargo	974	2,850	11.3
Freight	648	2,336	13.7
U.S. mail	288	461	4.8
Express	38	53	3.4
Public service Revenue	40	84	7.7
Other	131	1,012	22.7
Total	$8,791	$27,257	12.0%

Source: CAB Form 41.

of charter travel and hence reduced the size of the charter market. Thus some of the increase in scheduled passenger revenue represents that which in the past was charter revenue.

Although passenger revenue has increased sharply since 1969, prices have risen at only a modest pace. The average air-coach price per mile for U.S. domestic travel in 1969 was 5.3 cents. This price increased to 8.3 cents by 1979—a 4.6 percent annual increase. During that same time span, inflation in the United States, as measured by the Consumer Price Index, increased by 7.1 percent per year—a rate more than 50 percent higher than the rate of increase in air fare. Figure 1-1 shows the trend in air fares compared to the Consumer Price Index.

Part of the increase in passenger revenue was because of higher prices, but the major influence was increased volume. Traffic increased at approximately 7.6 percent per year between 1969 and 1979.

Costs—Functional

One way to examine airline costs is to look at each of the separate functions that an airline must perform to provide air transport services. The primary function is flight operations. All other functions support the process of pro-

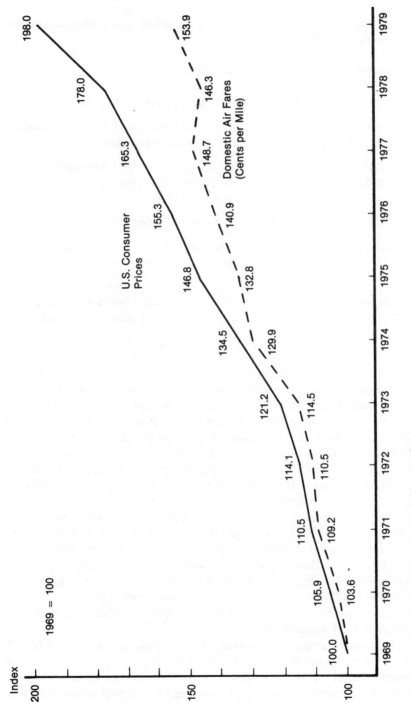

Index

200

150

100

1969 = 100

U.S. Consumer
Prices

Domestic Air Fares
(Cents per Mile)

198.0

178.0

165.3

155.3

146.8

134.5

121.2

114.1

110.5

105.9

100.0

153.9

146.3

148.7

140.9

132.8

129.9

114.5

110.5

109.2

103.6

1969   1970   1971   1972   1973   1974   1975   1976   1977   1978   1979

Source: U.S. Depart. of Commerce; CAB Form 41 data.

Figure 1-1. U.S. Consumer Prices versus Domestic Air Fares—U.S. Scheduled Airlines

viding air service. The following is a brief description of each of the major functions performed.

Function	Description
Flying operations	In-flight operation of aircraft
Maintenance	Repair and upkeep of aircraft and other property and equipment
Aircraft & traffic servicing	Handling aircraft and passengers while on the ground—generally the operations at terminals
Passenger service	In-flight passenger services
Promotion and sales	Functions of developing an air transport market, and reservations and sales
Administrative	General corporate functions, such as purchasing, legal, accounting, and payroll

In addition there is a functional category not included in this list: depreciation and amortization is a cost center used to accumulate the decreasing value of aircraft and other property and equipment as it grows older.

Table 1-2 shows the functional costs generated by the U.S. scheduled airlines. Note here that increases in total costs, like increases in total revenues, are because of both price and volume changes. Since total traffic has increased dramatically since 1969, some of the increase in cost is because of increases in the number of flights and the number of employees necessary to serve passengers. But traffic increases (measured in revenue passenger miles) need not change all factor inputs to the same degree. For example, if average load factors rise, then more revenue passenger miles can be generated without incurring proportionally higher costs for flight operations. At the same time, higher costs would be incurred in other categories where reservations agents, baggage handlers, and the like are hired to handle the additional passengers. Cost increases from year to year must be analyzed to determine which of the many factors influencing costs are responsible for the increases.

The largest category of expense, flying operations, accounted for 37 percent of all operating expenses in 1979, and is the fastest growing category. Rapid escalation in the cost of flying operations is principally because of increases in the cost of kerosene used to fuel jet aircraft, and

Table 1-2
Operating Expenses—U.S. Scheduled Airlines
(Millions of Dollars)

	1969	1979	Percent of 1979 Total	Percent Change (Average Per Year) 1969-1979
Flying operations	$2,469	$ 9,925	37%	14.9%
Maintenance	1,302	3,025	11	8.8
Aircraft and traffic servicing	1,490	4,619	17	12.0
Passenger service	831	2,651	10	12.3
Promotion and sales	1,035	3,464	13	12.8
Administrative	408	1,068	4	10.1
Depreciation and amortization	868	1,678	6	6.8
Other		612	2	
Total	$8,403	$27,042		12.4%

Source: CAB Form 41.

salaries for flight crews. In 1969 jet fuel cost about 11 cents per gallon. By 1979 this figure had grown to about 58 cents per gallon.[2] Other major expense items included in flying operations are aircraft insurance costs, and wages and benefits for the flight deck crew.

The maintenance function includes maintenance of both aircraft and of other property and equipment. The major maintenance effort is for aircraft and engines, and this category includes the cost of the maintenance work force and materials used. In addition, if work is performed for the airline by another company, costs of these outside maintenance services are included here. For example, many airlines have engine overhauls performed by other companies because of the large capital investment required to do that job. Airlines must also maintain rather large fleets of trucks, tractors, and baggage carts, and they must maintain their buildings. Most terminal buildings, however, are maintained by airport authorities and only limited maintenance needs to be performed there by the airlines.

The aircraft and traffic servicing function includes such activities as airport and ticket counter operations, baggage handling, and flight check-in.[3] Also included are costs associated with landing and parking aircraft at the terminal and the routine cleaning and maintenance between flights. Some of the costs included are wages and benefits for ticket and baggage agents, aircraft fuelers, and some mechanics. Landing fees and terminal rental charges are included here, as well as servicing supplies. Also included in this function are the costs of loading and unloading cargo from the aircraft.

The passenger service function includes charges for the activities that relate to the safety, comfort, and convenience of the passengers while in flight and when flights are interrupted. The major items of expense are the wages and benefits of flight attendants, and the cost of food served on the aircraft.

The promotion and sales function account for 13 percent of all operating expense and include all advertising costs for radio, television, newspaper, magazine, and billboard. A major cost included in this category is compensation for reservations agents. Other compensation costs included are for the sales force, whose major functions are operating ticket offices and calling on travel agents, and for advertising personnel. Travel agency commissions are included in this category, as are rental expenses for reservation computer systems.

The promotion and sales category is one of the fastest growing (second only to flying operations), and it is also one of the most volatile. Increasingly complex fare structures and large increases in passengers served have meant that the airlines receive more reservations calls and reservations inquiries are longer and more involved, and therefore more costly. The advent of reservations computers has revolutionized sales and promotion, and the recent deregulation of travel agent commissions is causing important changes in commission rates. Likewise, sales and promotion has increased in importance as the airlines have expanded into the new markets that are open to them since passage of the Airline Deregulation Act of 1978.

The administrative or overhead function generates 4 percent of total operating expenses. Most of the costs in this function are employment costs. These employees handle accounting and payroll functions, insurance, legal, budgeting, and planning. These jobs in general support the employees who work in other more direct functions. This function also includes utility charges, office and computer rentals, office supplies, and charges for bad debts.

Interest expense is not in any of the functional categories discussed so far because it is not considered an operating expense; it is deducted from operating profit when calculating net income. However, interest is a major cash expense. In 1979 interest expense amounted to $619 million, or about 2.3 percent of the total of all the functional costs. It is a major cost to the airline industry because the industry is capital intensive, and a large part of the funds used to purchase equipment is provided by banks and insurance companies.

The importance of this cost item can be gauged by the experience of 1979, when the airlines posted modest operating profits of $215 million. Subtracting the $619 million in interest expense would have made for a net loss of about $400 million had there not been offsetting gains from sales of aircraft, nonairline income, and a change in the tax laws which allowed the airlines to recoup taxes from other years.

Table 1-3 summarizes the income statement of the U.S. scheduled airlines for 1979 and 1969, and includes the revenue and cost figures from tables 1-1 and 1-2.

Table 1-3
Income Statement—U.S. Scheduled Airlines
(Millions of Dollars)

	1969	1979
Operating revenue	$8,791	$27,257
Operating expense	8,403	27,042
Operating income	388	215
Interest expense	(283)	(619)
Sale of aircraft	12	237
Other nonairline income	31	411
Taxes	(95)	165
Net income	53	409
Profit margin on sales	0.6%	1.5%
Return on investment	3.3%	7.0%

Source: CAB Form 41.

Costs—Items

Another way to examine the cost structure of the airlines is to look at costs item by item, rather than functionally. For example, we could examine labor costs as an item. Labor costs are included in each of the functions listed at the beginning of the functional cost section of this chapter, but labor cost can also be examined as a single item ignoring the functional distinctions.

Labor and fuel are two major items of expense which, taken together, make up over 60 percent of operating expense. Of the remaining cash expense items, no single one comprises more than 5 percent of total operating expense. Table 1-4 shows some of these items of expense for trunk and local service airlines, which together account for about 95 percent of the total U.S. scheduled service.[4]

One advantage of looking at costs on an item-by-item basis is that a measure of inflation for each can be developed. It is possible, for instance, to look at labor costs in terms of the number of employees to determine whether compensation costs have increased because there are more employees or because wage rates have increased. One is a measure of changes in the volume of inputs to the production function, and the other is a measure of the inflation of cost for those inputs.

The Air Transport Association (ATA) has regularly prepared an analysis of airline costs for each of the items shown in table 1-4, with the exception of the *Depreciation* and *Other* items. Depreciation is a noncash ex-

Table 1-4
Operating Expense Items—Trunk and Local Service Airlines
(Millions of Dollars)

	1969	*Percent*	*1979*	*Percent*
Labor and related expense	$3,430	40.9%	$ 9,743	37.5%
Fuel	1,036	12.4	6,178	23.8
Commmissions—travel agents	208	2.5	1,242	4.8
Passenger food	300	3.6	839	3.2
Landing fees	156	1.9	480	1.8
Advertising and promotion	239	2.9	395	1.5
Maintenance materials	289	3.4	576	2.2
Depreciation	837	10.0	1,576	6.1
Other	1,562	18.6	4,303	16.6
Interest on long-term debt (capital)	321	3.8	620	2.4
Total operating expenses and interest	$8,378		$25,952	

Source: CAB Form 41.

pense, and so is not included in the analysis. Other is composed of a large number of small items, including insurance, utilities, communications, rent, and outside services. Because of the small magnitude of each individual item, it is convenient and a fair approximation to use the implicit GNP deflator as a measure of inflation for those items. A discussion of the airline cost index follows.

Labor and Related Costs

One key to profitability is cost control, and labor costs are the largest single item of expense for an airline. In 1979, labor costs, including related expenses for pensions, insurance benefits, and payroll taxes, made up 38.5 percent of total operating expense.

Table 1-5 shows the trend in labor costs for the trunk and local service airlines. Employment in 1979 was 330,393, which was only 12.7 percent above the 1969 level. During that time, however, total labor costs nearly tripled to $9.7 billion. Average compensation costs for full-time airline employees including pension and insurance benefits increased from $11,700 in 1969 to $30,033 in 1979, which represented an average annual increase of 9.9 percent. The actual inflation in compensation was slightly higher than 9.9 percent because, during this time span, there was an increase in the number of paid but not worked hours for vacation, sick leave, and the like.

Table 1-5
Labor Cost Index—Trunk and Local Service Airlines

	Total Cost (Millions of Dollars)	Average Number of Employees	Average Compensation per Employee	Cost Index (1969 = 100)
1969	$3,429.89	293,151	$11,700	100.0
1970	3,841.25	290,231	13,235	113.1
1971	4,060.94	281,016	14,451	123.5
1972	4,479.31	278,468	16,085	137.5
1973	5,010.33	289,231	17,323	148.1
1974	5,396.68	288,433	18,710	159.9
1975	5,764.24	281,082	20,507	175.3
1976	6,427.05	283,350	22,682	193.9
1977	7,363.94	290,881	25,316	216.4
1978	8,428.42	302,189	27,891	238.4
1979[a]	9,742.94	330,393	30,033	256.7

Source: CAB Form 41.
[a]Adjusted for the United Airlines Strike.

Fuel Costs

Like everyone else, the airlines have suffered enormous increases in fuel prices. Unlike some other industries, however, the airlines are unable to substitute less-expensive or more-plentiful fuels for their primary fuel—kerosene. Consequently, conservation and efficiency have become two keys to cost control for this crucial item. Table 1-6 shows fuel cost and consumption trends for the trunk and local service airlines. Note that while fuel consumption increased 15.3 percent between 1969 and 1979, more efficient use of fuel permitted an 84.2 percent increase in passengers carried during the same period.

The remaining individual items listed in table 1-4 are briefly discussed here. For each, a method used to determine cost inflation is explained:

Traffic Commissions—Passenger. This item includes amounts paid to travel agents for passenger sales and to other airlines for international passenger sales (see table 1-7). Commission costs per revenue passenger-mile are computed to generate an index. As larger volumes of business are done through travel agents, this cost per passenger mile increases even though the commission rate may remain unchanged.

Passenger Food. The cost of complimentary food and beverage service is compared to the number of passenger miles (see table 1-8). The average cost

Table 1-6
Fuel Cost Index—Trunk and Local Service Airlines

	Total Fuel Cost (Millions of Dollars)	Gallons Issued (Billions)	Cost per Gallon (Cents)	Cost Index (1969 = 100)
1969	$1,036.10	9.278	11.2¢	100.0
1970	1,057.21	9.639	11.0	98.2
1971	1,104.32	9.628	11.5	102.7
1972	1,142.95	9.699	11.8	105.4
1973	1,315.53	10.305	12.8	114.3
1974	2,233.67	9.215	24.2	216.1
1975	2,657.43	9.133	29.1	259.8
1976	2,994.90	9.466	31.6	282.1
1977	3,587.24	9.894	36.3	324.1
1978	3,998.38	10.189	39.2	350.0
1979	6,178.21	10,698	57.8	516.1

Source: CAB Form 41.

per passenger-mile is compared to the 1969 average to compute an index. Costs are computed on total revenue passenger-miles, because there are no readily available statistics on the number of passengers that receive food service.

Landing Fees. Landing fees are charges paid to airport operators for landing aircraft (see table 1-9). They are normally based on the weight of the aircraft landed. Landing fees are compared to the aircraft weight landed to compute a cost per ton landed, and an index is then computed. Standard

Table 1-7
Traffic Commission Cost Index—Trunk and Local Service Airlines

	Total Cost (Millions of Dollars)	Revenue Passenger-Miles (Billions)	Cost per RPM (Cents)	Cost Index (1969 = 100)
1969	$ 208.19	140.84	0.148¢	100.0
1970	246.16	143.19	0.172	116.2
1971	275.49	145.58	0.189	127.7
1972	337.34	161.51	0.209	141.2
1973	394.56	172.26	0.229	154.7
1974	475.78	171.98	0.277	187.2
1975	543.88	170.64	0.319	215.5
1976	702.04	189.25	0.371	250.7
1977	805.15	203.43	0.396	267.6
1978	971.03	233.81	0.415	280.4
1979	1,241.87	259.85	0.478	323.0

Source: CAB Form 41.

Table 1-8
Passenger Food Cost Index—Trunk and Local Service Airlines

	Total Cost (Millions of Dollars)	Revenue Passenger-Miles (Billions)	Cost per RPM (Cents)	Cost Index (1969 = 100)
1969	$299.56	140.84	0.213¢	100.0
1970	328.02	143.19	0.229	107.5
1971	330.48	145.58	0.227	106.6
1972	387.70	161.51	0.240	112.7
1973	436.92	172.26	0.254	119.2
1974	455.52	171.98	0.265	124.4
1975	484.03	170.64	0.284	133.3
1976	539.45	189.25	0.285	133.8
1977	607.34	203.43	0.299	140.4
1978	702.40	233.81	0.301	141.3
1979	839.14	259.83	0.323	151.6

Source: CAB Form 41.

weights are used for various aircraft types. This index can also be computed by using aircraft capacity rather than gross weight.

Advertising and Promotion. This cost category includes all expenditures for items such as direct mail, radio, TV, newspaper space, publicity releases, and promotional materials (see table 1-10). In-house labor costs are not included, because they are already accounted for in the labor cost index. These advertising and promotion costs are compared to overall revenue ton-

Table 1-9
Landing Fees Cost Index—Trunk and Local Service Airlines

	Total Cost (Millions of Dollars)	Aircraft Weight Landed (Billions of Pounds)	Cents Per 1000 Pounds Landed (Cents)	Cost Index (1969 = 100)
1969	$156.19	556.77	28.1¢	100.0
1970	183.62	569.00	32.3	114.9
1971	225.94	592.02	38.2	135.9
1972	248.61	623.67	39.9	142.0
1973	289.14	664.79	43.5	154.8
1974	311.26	623.13	50.1	178.3
1975	340.16	634.30	53.6	190.7
1976	396.74	663.88	59.8	212.8
1977	429.88	681.50	63.1	224.6
1978	434.96	687.59	63.2	224.9
1979	479.73	670.80	71.5	254.4

Source: CAB Form 41.

Table 1-10
Advertising and Promotion Cost Index—Trunk and Local Service Airlines

	Total Cost (Millions of Dollars)	Ton-Miles (Millions)	Cost per RTM (Cents)	Cost Index (1969 = 100)
1969	$239.21	18,652	1.283¢	100.0
1970	221.41	18,610	1.189	92.7
1971	222.87	19,184	1.183	92.2
1972	250.65	20,955	1.194	93.1
1973	257.20	22,151	1.161	90.5
1974	249.29	22,077	1.129	88.0
1975	260.18	21,706	1.199	93.5
1976	277.33	23,835	1.164	90.7
1977	321.64	25,537	1.260	98.2
1978	346.42	28,648	1.209	94.2
1979	395.21	31,302	1.263	98.4

Source: CAB Form 41.

miles to calculate a cost index. A revenue ton-mile combines both passenger and cargo traffic, with a passenger and his or her bags treated as 200 pounds. No statistics are available on the actual quantity of advertising, such as minutes of radio or TV time. If we assume that over time there is no change in the effectiveness of advertising and promotion, cost per revenue ton-mile is an appropriate measure of inflation.

Aircraft Maintenance Materials. This category is a measure of materials cost in the maintenance function (see table 1-11). Materials costs for maintenance of airframes, engines, and other aircraft parts (mainly avionics and interiors) are included. These costs are compared to aircraft available ton-miles (a measure of aircraft use) to compute an index.

Interest on Long-Term Debt-Capital. The capital cost index is a measure of the cost of long-term liabilities (see table 1-12). An effective interest rate is computed by taking interest expense as a percent of long-term debt. This interest rate is related to the 1969 rate to compute an index number. Since 1978 the imputed interest on capitalized leases has been added to interest expense, and the long-term liability for capitalized leases has been added to debt, so that since 1978 the index numbers reflect these capital costs as well.

There are two major changes that are being considered for the capital cost index. It does not now include equity costs or depreciation costs. Depreciation has been excluded because it is a noncash item. Because depreciation is excluded, the index can show capital costs deflating as interest rates fall, even though aircraft prices may continue to inflate. Excluding these items also understates capital's total part in the cost equation.

Table 1-11
Aircraft Maintenance Materials Cost Index—Trunk and Local
Service Airlines

	Total Cost (Millions of Dollars)	Available Ton-Miles (Millions)	Cost per ATM (Cents)	Cost Index (1969 = 100)
1969	$288.86	40,873.2	0.707¢	100.0
1970	273.58	41,935.9	0.652	92.2
1971	257.81	44,682.5	0.577	81.6
1972	306.57	45,829.9	0.669	94.6
1973	349.04	48,647.2	0.717	101.4
1974	384.85	46,146.6	0.834	118.0
1975	400.82	46,417.7	0.864	122.2
1976	450.93	48,750.9	0.925	130.8
1977	513.77	51,700.0	0.994	140.6
1978	526.95	53,243.5	0.990	140.0
1979	575.78	57,495.1	1.001	141.6

Source: CAB Form 41.

In 1979 capital costs represented 2.6 percent of cash operating expenses. Adding depreciation increases the capital portion of cash operating expenses to about 6.3 percent, and reduces the portion of labor, fuel, and other items. Further, if depreciation were calculated on the replacement cost rather than on the purchase price, the capital share would be even greater. Equity costs are difficult to measure and include in this index, since net income, dividends, or retained earnings are not normally thought of as items of expense, and growth in market value is affected by general economic trends as well as airline profitability.

The Cost Index and Total Airline Inflation

One important use of item-by-item inflation measures is in developing a measure of total airline cost inflation. By first disaggregating total airline costs, then measuring inflation item by item, and finally reaggregating, it is possible to estimate a total airline cost inflation rate with reasonable precision.

Figure 1-2 compares the trend in airline costs with the Producer or Wholesale Price Index since 1969. The Producer Price Index is a measure of the inflation in factor prices faced by businesses in the United States.

It is clear from the figure that airline costs have been increasing at a faster pace than costs for other U.S. companies. In the ten years since 1969, the average annual rate of cost inflation for the airlines has been 9.6 percent, compared to 8.3 percent for U.S. industry. Although airline costs have

Table 1-12
Capital Cost Index—Trunk and Local Service Airlines

	Interest on Long-Term Debt (Millions of Dollars)	Average Long-Term Debt Outstanding (Billions of Dollars)	Average Book Interest Rate (Percent)	Cost Index (1969 = 100)
1969	$320.76	$5.173	6.201%	100.0
1970	358.60	5.431	6.603	106.5
1971	355.93	5.677	6.270	101.1
1972	329.09	5.252	6.266	101.0
1973	389.24	5.498	7.080	114.2
1974	434.36	5.519	7.870	126.9
1975	399.04	5.426	7.354	118.6
1976	363.84	4.996	7.283	117.4
1977	334.74	4.468	7.492	120.8
1978	534.29	6.355	8.407	135.6
1979	619.79	7.215	8.590	138.5

Source: CAB Form 41.

been increasing more rapidly than costs of U.S. companies in general, we have seen from figure 1-1 that the airlines have held price increases well below the rate of increase in overall consumer prices. The airlines have been able to hold the line on prices because of high growth in productvity.

Airline Productivity

The traditional approach to measuring productivity used by the U.S. Department of Labor and most other analysts is output per employee. This statistic of labor productivity tells us how much output can be created on a per-employed-worker basis, but at the same time ignores capital and other inputs to the productive process. From a macroeconomic perspective this is a useful measure even with its shortcomings because, for the total economy, capital-intensive and labor-intensive industries are aggregated, and output per worker represents our national potential for creating goods and services on a per-capita basis.

On the microeconomic level of the individual firm, however, output per employee is a poor measure of a company's facility in transforming inputs into outputs. A change in capital intensity caused by factor substitution causes an immediate change in output per employee, even if there is no change in the firm's overall productivity. For example, an increase in capital intensity would increase output per employee even if the firm used its available capital equipment unproductively. What is needed for analysis of an individual firm or an individual industry is a measure of "total

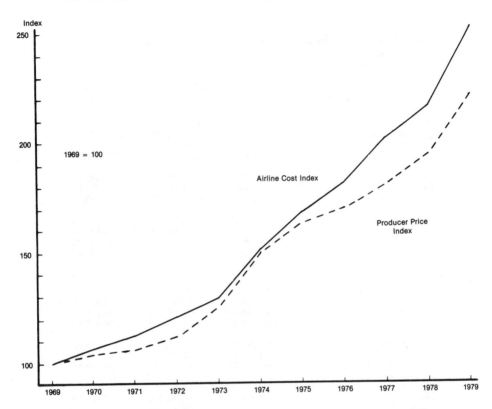

Source: U.S. Depart. of Commerce; CAB Form 41.

Figure 1-2. Producer Price Index versus Airline Cost Index—Trunk and Local Service Airlines

factor" productivity, which relates all inputs to all outputs and hence measures the efficiency of the firm's production.

To arrive at a measure of total factor productivity, it is necessary to sum all airline inputs and outputs. Outputs increasing more than inputs over time indicate productivity gains. Weighted index numbers for employees, fuel gallons, weight landed, and so on could be summed to measure input, and similarly weighted index numbers of passenger miles and cargo ton-miles could be added to measure output. The Air Transport Association (ATA) productivity study, however, used constant dollars to measure changes in input and output. This allows easy comparison between various factors of input and output.

Table 1-13 summarizes the revenue and cost data used to calculate total factor productivity for the airline industry. These data are for trunk and

Table 1-13
Productivity Input-Output Summary Report—Trunk and Local
Service Airlines

	1972	1979	1979 (In 1972 Dollars)
Output-Revenue			
Passenger—First	$ 2,067,857,774	$ 4,554,975,894	$ 3,224,701,700
Passenger—Coach	7,093,371,473	17,341,725,690	12,031,377,990
Passenger—Charter	282,981,338	340,213,306	174,716,915
Total Passenger	9,444,210,585	22,236,914,890	15,430,796,605
Cargo—Schedule	1,034,216,013	2,110,617,473	1,251,568,244
Cargo—Charter	57,756,609	8,820,209	4,212,235
Total Cargo	1,091,972,622	2,119,437,682	1,255,780,479
Other air transport	116,659,093	160,712,234	97,112,152
Transport related		875,164,603	528,827,931
Subsidy	64,484,364	72,388,922	72,388,922
Total output (revenue)	$10,717,326,664	$25,464,618,331	$17,384,906,089
Inputs—Cost			
Wages and salaries	3,886,206,791	7,970,160,842	4,585,382,113
Insurance and pensions	441,724,457	1,319,971,736	521,195,997
Payroll taxes	157,028,035	460,667,998	185,279,266
Total labor	4,484,959,283	9,750,800,576	5,291,857,376
Aircraft—owned	776,207,554	1,082,479,472	1,081,980,000
Aircraft—leased	326,121,640	287,403,654	167,104,875
Facilities and equipment owned	145,185,704	219,136,325	198,619,000
Facilities and equipment leased	276,269,642	420,159,435	211,613,918
Phantom profit	133,992,742	899,501,562	
Interest—debt	273,814,114	383,086,109	232,688,269
Interest—leases		198,936,814	126,770,037
Landing fees	248,916,179	479,726,132	270,444,924
Total capital	2,180,507,575	3,970,429,503	2,289,221,023
Fuel	1,142,953,007	6,178,211,793	1,231,531,012
Maintenance material	306,566,802	575,789,540	272,333,811
Passenger food	387,960,086	839,151,874	458,354,491
Other supplies	202,627,471	426,652,659	199,951,246
Passenger commissions	338,148,691	1,244,876,365	1,118,458,904
Advertising	250,863,499	396,017,010	208,482,113
Insurance	178,482,034	219,401,270	543,214,764
Communications	146,028,549	306,457,814	263,562,945
Utilities	40,166,201	104,403,211	48,905,756
Personnel expenses	205,441,449	488,712,590	242,402,835
Outside services	463,473,083	1,128,302,620	690,448,688
Other operating expenses	272,389,653	1,171,952,145	706,165,099
Other nonoperating expenses	(51,757,248)	(625,651,201)	(378,056,687)
Total goods and services	3,883,343,277	12,454,277,690	5,607,754,978
Net profit	202,507,055	358,028,235	360,643,225
Phantom profit	133,992,742	899,501,562	
Total profits	68,514,313	(541,473,327)	360,643,225
Total inputs	$10,617,324,448	$25,634,034,442	$13,549,476,603
Income taxes	$ 100,002,212	$ (169,416,123)	$ (169,416,123)
Total costs	$10,717,326,660	$25,464,618,319	$13,380,060,480

local service airlines, which in 1979 generated more than 93 percent of U.S. scheduled airline total operating revenues. This table contains in compact form all of the revenue and cost items discussed in this chapter.

From this table it can be seen that total revenue increased from $10.7 billion in 1972 to $25.5 billion in 1979. This increase, however, was composed of both price and volume changes. Taking out the $8.08 billion that represents price changes from 1972 to 1979 leaves $17.4 billion in total outputs. This represents a volume increase of $6.67 billion, or 62 percent in the seven-year span of time.

The table shows that inputs, including profits, increased $15.0 billion, of which $12.1 billion represented inflation and $2.9 billion volume increases. The volume of inputs increased 27.6 percent, while outputs increased 62 percent. Dividing the ratio of output change (1.622) by the ratio of input change (1.276) gives the productivity change of 1.271, or 27.1 percent over the seven-year span of time. On a compound basis that is a 3.5 percent annual growth in total factor productivity.

An interesting by-product of this productivity analysis is the phantom profit figures shown for 1972 and 1979. To put all inputs into 1972 dollars, the value of all aircraft purchased prior to that date had to be restated in 1972 purchase prices and depreciation recalculated on this 1972 replacement value. In 1972 that resulted in estimates for depreciation that were $134 million higher than the amounts actually recorded. Had depreciation been recorded in replacement values, profits would have been reduced by $134 million and capital inputs increased by a similar amount. Making the same calculation for 1979 replacement costs shows that inflation added $900 million to that year's profit. If replacement costs had been used to estimate depreciation, there would have been a $541 million loss instead of the $358 million profit reported.

If this calculation of total factor productivity is repeated for each year, an index of productivity changes can be computed. The ATA has total factor productivity measurements dating from 1950. Figure 1-3 depicts growth in total factor productivity between 1950 and 1979. Notice that there have been two clearly defined periods of high productivity growth, the first from 1961 to 1966 and the second from 1975 to 1979.

The first spurt of productivity growth, from 1961 to 1966, was due primarily to the introduction of jet aircraft. The first commercial jets came on line in 1958, but it took several years before they were a significant proportion of U.S. airline fleets. They were vastly more efficient than earlier piston aircraft, and hence contributed to rapid productivity growth during the transition to all jet fleets.

The second period of high productivity growth, from 1975 to 1979, was more complex. The very high cost of fuel was one factor. High fuel prices forced operating changes to conserve fuel. This increased productivity because tremendous effort was made to hold this input constant while output continued to grow.

A second factor was increased use of wide-body aircraft which are cheaper to operate on a seat-mile basis than conventional narrow-body planes. Of course, the unit cost savings of the wide-bodies were translated into productivity growth only when load factors were high enough to realize the economies of scale of the large jets, because on a plane mile basis the wide-bodies are more expensive to operate than conventional aircraft.

Wide-bodies entered domestic fleets beginning around 1970, just as the economy entered a recession. So initially traffic was not strong enough to support the capacity increases of the wide-bodies, and the cost savings of the new planes were unrealized. Later, traffic resumed strong strength and

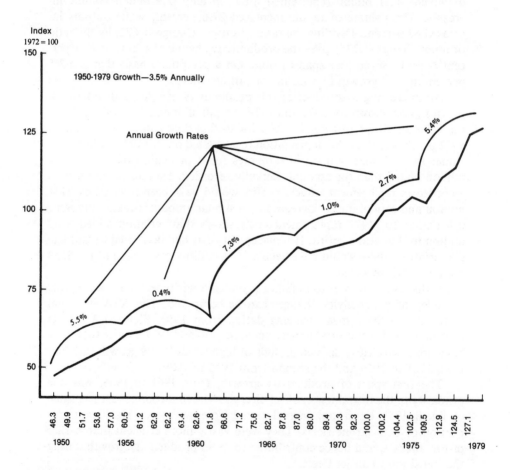

Source: Air Transport Association.

Figure 1-3. Total Factor Productivity—Trunk and Local Service Airlines, 1950-1979

began to catch up with the fleet expansion of the early 1970s, resulting in an increase in average load factors. The cost-cutting pressure of airline deregulation (1978), high fuel costs, and increased discount-fare traffic coincided to increase load factors in the late 1970s. Throughout this period the airlines continued to substitute efficient wide-bodied aircraft for narrow-bodied planes. The combination of increasing load factors, increases in seat density, and the efficient use of economical wide-body equipment is probably the key element in the productivity spurt of 1975-1979.

Notice in figure 1-4 that output per employee, the traditional measure of productivity, did not follow the same trend as total factor productivity. One of the highest growth periods in output per employee, 1966-1971, was the period of slowest growth in total factor productivity.

Output per employee and total factor productivity diverge whenever the mix of factors employed changes. The use of total factor productivity instead of output per employee allows the ATA to study productivity without this drawback presented by focusing on the productivity of a single factor such as labor. The total factor productivity measurements developed by ATA (shown in table 1-14) has permitted more comprehensive study of

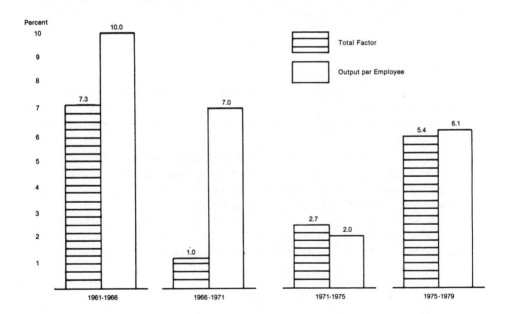

Source: Air Transport Association.

Figure 1-4. Productivity Cycle Comparisons—Total Factor versus Output per Employee (Annual Growth)

Table 1-14
Total Factor Productivity—Trunk and Local Service Airlines
(1972 = 100)

Year	Weighted Index	Year	Weighted Index
1950	46.3	1966	87.8
1951	49.9	1967	87.0
1952	51.7	1968	88.0
1953	53.6	1969	89.4
1954	57.0	1970	90.3
1955	60.5	1971	92.3
1956	61.2	1972	100.0
1957	62.9	1973	100.2
1958	62.2	1974	104.4
1959	63.4	1975	102.5
1960	62.6	1976	109.5
1961	61.8	1977	112.9
1962	66.6	1978	124.5
1963	71.2	1979	127.1
1964	75.6		
1965	82.7		

trends in airline productivity than would have been possible using only the traditional method of output per employee.

Notes

1. See the introduction or the glossary for a definition of the U.S. Scheduled Airlines.

2. Fuel prices averaged 90¢/gallon in 1980, and continue to rise in early 1981 (see chapter 5).

3. Aircraft and traffic servicing are sometimes disaggregated into aircraft servicing, traffic servicing, and servicing administration. Similarly, promotion and sales is sometimes disaggregated into two categories: reservations and sales, and advertising and publicity.

4. Trunks and locals are not exactly the same as the U.S. Scheduled Airlines discussed at the beginning of the chapter. The differences between the two are relatively minor, however (see the introduction for details).

2 The Frequency of Air Travel

K. William Horn

Total revenue passenger-miles flown by the U.S. airlines have risen significantly over the years. In 1979 the U.S. airlines carried in scheduled service 317 million passengers for a total of 262 billion revenue passenger-miles, representing an average annual increase of over 8.5 percent since 1971. At the same time, the composition of the passenger market has been changing.

Who comprises the passenger market for air transportation? Why do they fly, and how often do they fly? This chapter addresses these and other factors related to the passenger market of U.S. airlines.

The ATA Survey

Since World War II, and particularly since the advent of the jet aircraft, commercial aviation has been characterized by significant changes in travel patterns and numbers of persons who fly. The population's desire for air travel depends on demographic characteristics such as age, occupation, income, and education. Changes in general consumer patterns have important air travel implications for the airlines directly and also for airports, car rental agencies, hotels, and other travel-related industries.

The Air Transport Association (ATA) periodically conducts a survey to obtain information about the frequency of flying on commercial airlines among the U.S. adult population.[1] The survey is designed to determine the percentages of adults who fly, how often they fly, the purpose of their trips, the destination of their trips, and the demographics of the passenger travel market.

Objectives of the Survey

Specifically, in addition to demographic information, the survey seeks to determine:

How many adults have ever flown on a commercial airline?

23

How many adults have flown on a commercial airline during the last year?

How many trips were taken during the last year within the continental forty-eight states; how many trips were taken to Hawaii, Alaska, Canada, and other international points?

How many trips were taken for business purposes, and how many trips to visit friends or relatives, to sightsee, or for other purposes?

How many people took charter flights and their destinations?

Use of the Survey

The results of the survey are used in a variety of ways by the airline industry, especially for public information purposes and for market research and planning. The data obtained from the survey are used by airlines, the ATA, and other travel and travel-related organizations. For market research and planning, the survey serves as an aid to the airlines and travel-related organizations in developing market strategy, forecasting market potential, and determining advertising objectives.

Design of Research

The survey, which is currently conducted once every two years, is based on personal interviews with a national sample of about 3,000 adults, eighteen years of age and older, in the noninstitutional population (that is, not including those in prisons, hospitals, homes for the aged, and so on). As of June 1979 the total number of such adults was about 155 million, while the total U.S. population amounted to about 220 million.

A trip as defined in the current survey is a round trip; going to the main destination and returning is counted as a single trip.

Survey Results

Adults Who Have Ever Flown

Based on the 1979 ATA survey, 65 percent of all adult Americans have flown on a commercial airline (see figure 2-1). This percentage represents 101 million people, a 7 percent increase over 1977, when the last survey was conducted. In 1971 only 49 percent of adults had ever flown, and in 1962, when the initial survey was undertaken, only 33 percent had flown.

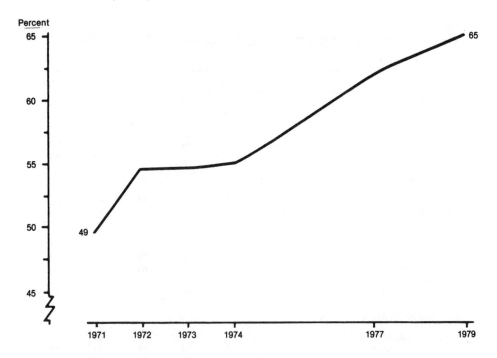

Figure 2-1. Percentage of Adults Who Have Ever Flown, 1971-1979

These statistics indicate that commercial airlines are serving an increasing percentage of the population. No longer is air transportation for a select few. The adult who has not flown is today the exception rather than the rule. Air transportation has become a common way for Americans to get from one place to another—quite a different situation from that of 1962, when only one-third of the population had ever flown.

A demographic breakdown of these results furnishes interesting information (see table 2-1). There is now little difference between the percentages of men and women who have ever flown. Adults aged 25-49 are more likely to have flown than those under 25 or over 50. Professionals are more likely to have flown than members of other occupational groups, and a considerably larger percentage of adults living in the Western part of the country have flown than adults from other parts of the country.

Adults Who Have Flown during the Year

The 1979 survey shows that 27 percent of the adult population, about 42 million persons, took a trip by a commercial airline in the previous twelve

Table 2-1
Percentage of Adults Who Have Ever Flown, by Demographic Groups
(Percent)

	1971	1972	1973	1974	1977	1979
All Adults	49%	54%	54%	55%	63%	65%
Sex of respondent						
Men	53	58	58	61	67	67
Women	46	51	51	50	59	63
Race of respondent						
White	51	57	57	57	65	68
Nonwhite	28	32	33	39	45	39
Age of respondent						
18-24 years	52	54	50	50	58	57
25-34 years	60	62	66	63	70	69
35-49 years	46	58	55	59	67	71
50 years and older	44	48	49	51	58	63
Occupation of chief wage earner						
Professional and business	70	75	75	78	83	85
Clerical and sales	66	64	67	66	74	64
Manual workers	41	45	45	49	54	57
Nonlabor force	43	45	45	46	53	58
Size of community						
1,000,000 and over	63	65	64	68	68	69
500,000-999,999	61	67	71	70	71	73
50,000-499,999	55	58	59	55	68	66
2,500-49,999	39	43	50	57	60	60
Under 2,500	35	44	38	40	52	59
Region of the county						
East	51	57	59	59	65	67
Midwest	45	51	51	50	59	62
South	39	45	43	45	53	55
West	68	70	70	73	80	81

months—an increase compared with the 25 percent (or 37.5 million people) in 1977, and 21 percent in 1971 (see figure 2-2).

Groups with the highest proportions of those flying in the past year include those in the professional and business occupational group, and those residing in the West. Although adults with family incomes of $40,000 or more are more likely to have flown in the past year than those with lower family incomes, a considerable percentage of adults with relatively low in-

Percent of Total

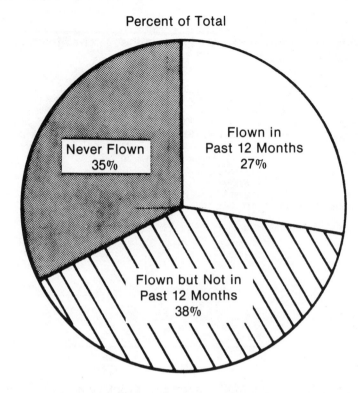

Note: 27% = 42 million adults; 38% = 59 million adults; 35% = 54 million adults.
Figure 2-2. Flying among Adult Population, 1979

comes have flown in the past year. Commercial air transportation is now so common that nearly 20 percent of all adults with family incomes between $5,000 and $10,000 have flown in the past year (see table 2-2)

Frequency of Flying

Nearly half of those who flew during the previous year took only one trip (see figure 2-3). These infrequent fliers accounted for 14 percent of all trips taken, a decrease from 20 percent in 1977. Moderate fliers (between two and twelve trips) also made up nearly half of those who flew in the last year, and accounted for about half of all trips taken. Frequent fliers, those who took more than twelve trips, represented only 4 percent of the fliers but took 36 percent of all trips—an increase from 28 percent in 1977. Thus those persons who do fly are flying more often than in the past, and an increasing percentage of total flights are made by passengers who fly frequently.

Table 2-2
Percentage of Adults Who Have Flown in Past Twelve Months, by
Demographic Groups
(1979)

Sex		Community Size		Occupation	
Men	28%	1,000,000+	29%	Professional	45%
Women	25	500,000-1,000,000	35	Clerical and sales	29
		50,000- 500,000	30	Manual workers	17
		2,500- 50,000	23	Nonlabor Force	21
		Under 2,500	20		
Race		*Region*		*Family income*	
White	28%	East	28%	$40,000+	51%
Nonwhite	16	Midwest	22	25,000-40,000	41
		South	22	20,000-25,000	32
		West	39	15,000-20,000	25
				10,000-15,000	20
				5,000-10,000	19
				Under 5,000	13
Age					
18-24	26%				
25-34	26				
35-49	28				
50+	26				

During 1979 a total of 42 million adults took about 145 million airline trips. This was an average of 3.5 trips per flier, up from 3.1 trips in 1977 (see figure 2-4).

Destination of Trips

Of all the trips taken during the year the great majority were to destinations within the continental forty-eight states. Figure 2-5 shows the percentage of trips taken to various destinations.

Purpose of Trips

One of the major purposes of the survey is to determine how many trips were taken during the year for business purposes and how many were for other reasons (such as visiting friends or relatives and sightseeing). Of the 145 million airline trips in 1979, about 80 million were for business purposes.

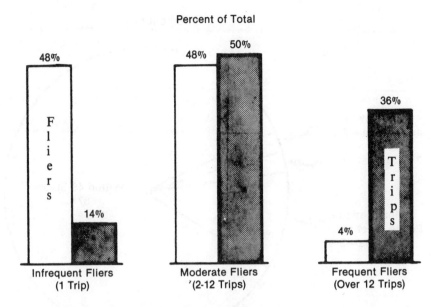

Figure 2-3. Fliers and Trips, by Frequency of Flying, 1979

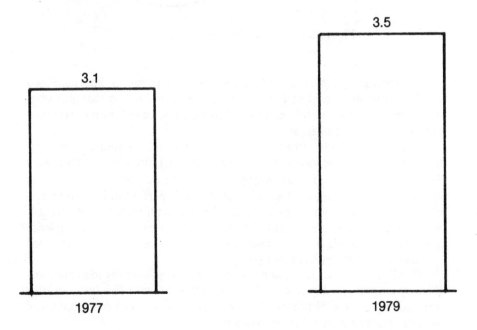

Figure 2-4. Average Number of Trips per Flier

Percent of Total

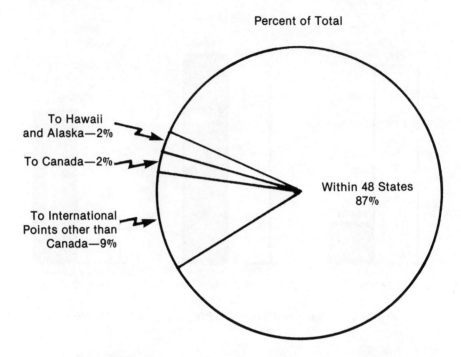

Figure 2-5. Destination of Trips, 1979

The percentage of trips taken for business purposes has increased steadily from 46 percent in 1973 to 55 percent in 1979. The changing division between business and personal/pleasure trips, based on the past four surveys, is depicted in figure 2-6.

While overall 55 percent of trips were for business, a domestic/international breakdown shows that only 31 percent of all international trips were for business, compared to 57 percent of the domestic trips. The increase in the business percentage of domestic trips from 52 percent in 1977 to 55 percent in 1979 meant that the percentage of personal pleasure trips decreased. Within that category the decline was seen in the trips for "visiting friends and relatives," while trips for sightseeing and other personal trips remained at about their 1977 percentages (see figure 2-7).

Of all the 1979 air trips, about two-thirds were taken by men and one-third by women (see figure 2-8). More than four of every five business trips were taken by men. However, the majority of trips taken for personal or pleasure reasons were taken by women.

Percent

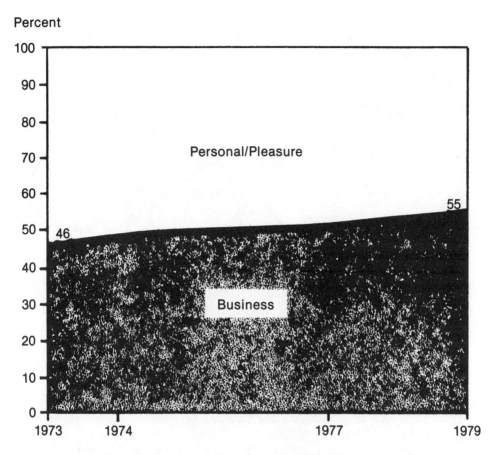

Figure 2-6. Purpose of Trips, 1973-1979

Air travelers earning less than $20,000 annually accounted for about one-third of total trips (see figure 2-9). Among travelers on personal/pleasure trips, about half had incomes of less than $20,000. On the other hand, only 17 percent of all business trips were taken by those with annual family incomes of less than $20,000, and 29 percent of all business trips were taken by travelers with family incomes over $40,000.

Air travelers in their middle years, twenty-five to forty-nine years of age, accounted for a little over half of total trips. Two-thirds of total trips were taken by persons whose head of household was in the professional and business group. The nonwhite segment of the population accounted for 5

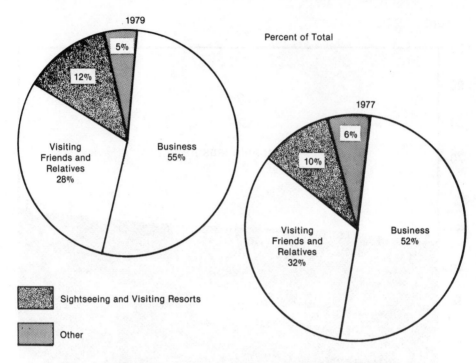

Figure 2-7. Purpose of Trips, 1977 and 1979

percent of total trips, including 3 percent of all business trips and 7 percent of all personal/pleasure trips (see figure 2-10).

During 1979 about 5 million individuals, 3 percent of all adults, made one or more charter flights. The population groups with the largest portion of charter fliers were the professional and business group and those with family incomes of over $25,000.

The following table shows a comparison by destination between scheduled and charter trips:

Destination of Scheduled and Charter Trips

	Scheduled	Charter
Within Forty-eight States and Canada	90	66
To Alaska and Hawaii	2	5
To other international points	8	29
	100%	100%

Thus the statistics showing that affluent households made the most charter trips probably reflect the greater number of international trips those households made, where charter flights are most frequent.

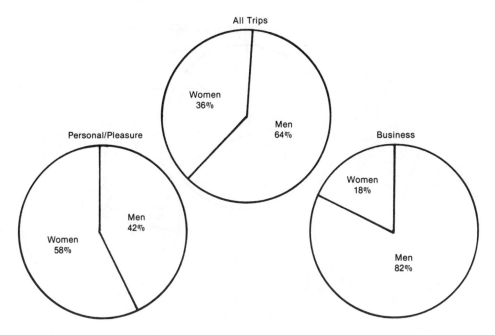

Figure 2-8. Trips, by Sex, 1979

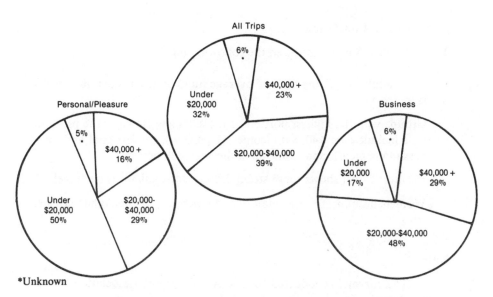

Figure 2-9. Trips, by Annual Family Income, 1979

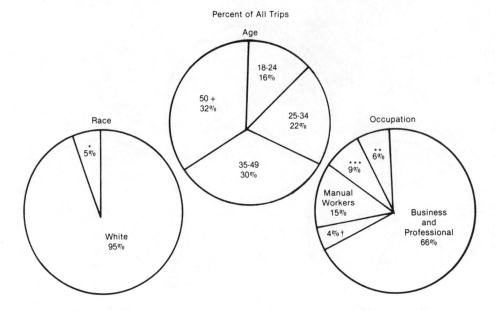

Percent of All Trips

*   Nonwhite
** Others
*** Nonlabor Force
†   Clerical and Sales

Figure 2-10. Trips, by Age, Race, and Occupation, 1979

Summary and Conclusions

The 1979 ATA Survey produced the following highlights:

More adults are flying and the average number of trips per air traveler is increasing.

Groups with the highest portion of those having flown in the previous year include over $40,000 income (51 percent), professional and business (45 percent), and residents in the West (39 percent).

Business travel shows more strength than personal/pleasure travel.

Women account for the majority (58 percent) of personal/pleasure trips.

Note

1. The survey is conducted for the Air Transport Association by the Gallup Organization.

3

The Significance of Airline Passenger Load Factors

Melvin A. Brenner

G150
US

Introduction

One of the most vital statistics in the airline business is *load factor*—the percentage of seats sold.

From a low point of 48 percent in 1971, the industry gradually worked its way to load factors in the low 50 percent range (in 1972 and 1973), to the mid-50s (in 1974 through 1977), and then jumped up to the low 60s (in 1978 and 1979). This load factor record is shown in figure 3-1.

From the standpoint of airline economics, this advance of load factors above the 60 percent level has meant better fuel economy and a more efficient spreading of cost per passenger carried, and it has permitted fares to remain lower than would otherwise have been necessary. But while the cost benefit of high load factors is a well-recognized advantage, there is another side of the coin that is less understood—that is, the relationship between load factor and service convenience. The higher the load factor, the greater the prospect that a passenger will find his or her desired flight already fully booked when seeking a reservation.

There is, in other words, a trade-off involved in high load fators—the benefit of lower cost versus the disadvantage of lower service convenience. If this trade-off is to be reasonably judged, it is important that the service implications of load factors be understood, as well as the more evident unit cost aspect. The purpose of this chapter is to explore the service implications of varying load factors.

Methodology

Most data regarding load factors relate to averages of one kind or another—averages that summarize carrier systemwide networks, and averages that summarize entire months or years.

Unfortunately, the service implications of load factors are buried in the averaging process. An individual's travel requirements are very specific, both as to destination and departure time. That on the average less than two-thirds of all airline seats were sold in 1979 provided no relief to the passenger who wanted to get from New York to Chicago on a Friday afternoon, and could not get a seat.

35

The first step in assessing the service implications of a given average load factor is to look beneath the average data, and examine the actual daily trip loads that are the components of the average figure.

Detailed data on specific daily loads became available on an industry basis for only one brief period of 1975-1976, when the CAB collected such data in connection with a special investigation of load factors. The present analysis has made use of those data. That the data are several years old does not reduce their validity for this analysis, since the relationships between loads on individual flights or days and broader averages do not change with time. To come as close as possible to simulating current conditions, we have concentrated on the individual daily data for the month of August 1975. While that was, of course, a peak season month, the load factor experienced in that month was quite close to the level that recently has become the year-round norm. Therefore, reviewing the data for August 1975 provides a reasonable basis for understanding the implications of current "normal" load factors.

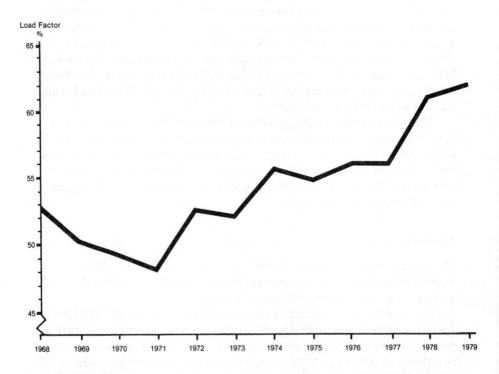

Source: CAB Form 41.

Figure 3-1. Passenger Load Factors—Trunks, Systems, 1968-1979

Limitations of Load-Factor "Averages"

Average load factors are misleading because of the time-sensitive nature of air transport demand, and the instant perishability of air transport supply. The empty seats that may have been available on a given route on Tuesday, for example, were "lost" the instant those flights departed, and cannot assist in meeting the needs of the passengers trying to get a seat on the same route on Friday. Yet when the Tuesday empty seats are statistically merged with the Friday full planes, the average load factor may appear quite moderate.

Thus the first key to understanding load factors is to recognize the extent to which air travel demand fluctuates widely above and below overall monthly averages.

Figure 3-2 shows the substantial daily variation in traffic volume on a long haul route—Chicago-Los Angeles. The peak day of the month had nearly 7,500 passengers, which was 40 percent above the average; the lowest day of the month had only 4,100 passengers, or about 20 percent below the average.

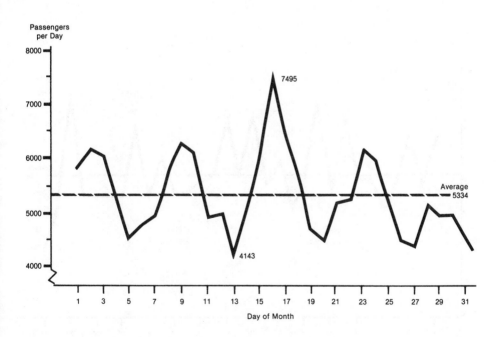

Source: CAB data.

Figure 3-2. Daily Traffic Variation, Chicago-Los Angeles Route

Figure 3-3 shows similar data for a short-haul route, that is, Dallas-New Orleans. Here the specific pattern of variation was different, but the wide amount of variation was still present. In this case, the peak day was 39 percent above the average; the low day was 42 percent below the average.

Figures 3-4 and 3-5 depict the traffic on these routes on a week-to-week basis, making it easier to examine the pattern of fluctuation by day of week. The differing day-of-week patterns are evident. On the short-haul route, where business travel predominates, Saturday is distinctly offpeak. On the long-haul route, where personal and pleasure travel is much more important, Saturday is a high day.

For the present analysis, however, the essential point is that all routes display considerable daily variation in traffic, even though the peaking by day of week differs with the nature of the market.

Limited Ability to Vary Seat Supply

The wide variation of air travel demand would present no load-factor problem if the supply of seats could be equally varied. But in scheduled ser-

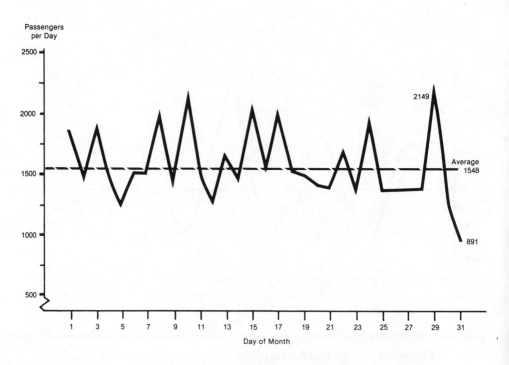

Source: CAB data.

Figure 3-3. Daily Traffic Variation, Dallas-New Orleans Route

vices this is not possible. The aircraft unit itself is obviously inflexible; if a given airline's B-727 is equipped with 130 seats, that seat supply on a particular schedule cannot be shrunk or expanded between Thursday and Friday, and changed again for Saturday.

Within limits, the total number of flight frequencies flown on a given day can be varied, and this is indeed done where feasible. On business routes, for example, it is common to reduce frequencies on Saturdays. (Between New York and Detroit, seven frequencies were canceled on Saturday—over one-third of the schedules on the route.)

But there are a number of factors limiting this effort to adjust daily seats to daily traffic. For one thing, many routes have too little frequency operated by each carrier to permit much leeway for canceling trips on a particular day without damaging the overall pattern.

Second, the day-of-week pattern of demand does not vary in a precise, predictable, or fully consistent manner (see figure 3-5, for example).

Finally, the schedule pattern on any one route is too interrelated with those of other routes (and with operational constraints of various kinds) to permit an erratically scheduled operation from day to day.

As a result of these various factors, the supply of seats is necessarily much more uniform than is the demand.

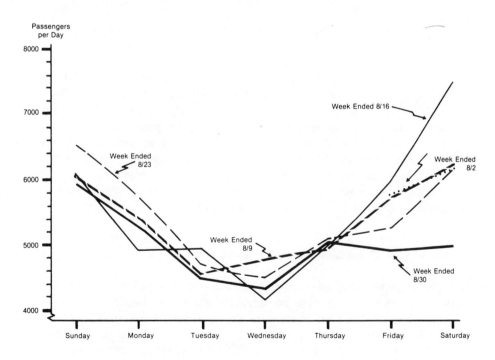

Source: CAB data.

Figure 3-4. Day-of-Week Traffic Pattern, Chicago-Los Angeles Route

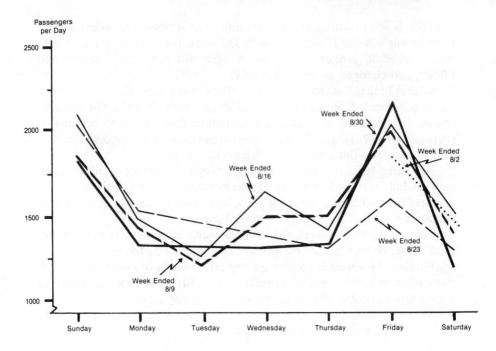

Source: CAB data.

Figure 3-5. Day-of-Week Traffic Pattern, Dallas-New Orleans Route

Figure 3-6 shows the number of seats offered each day, and the passengers actually carried, for a specific schedule on an intermediate-length segment (Miami-New York). For the month as a whole, the average load on this trip was seventy passengers, which produced an average monthly load factor of 68 percent with the equipment operated. On the other side of the coin, the average number of empty seats per trip was thirty-three. But, as can be seen in figure 3-6, at one extreme there were four days when there were more than sixty empty seats and, at the other extreme, there were seven days when there were fewer than fifteen empty seats.

Reservations Constraints Related to Load Factors

In the example just cited, though space was relatively tighter on some days than on others, there were no days on which this particular schedule departed absolutely full. There were always at least a few empty seats remaining at departure time, and the question may arise as to why there should ever have been any need to turn any passenger away from this

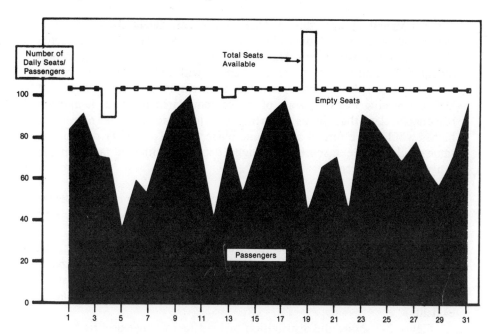

Source: CAB data.
Figure 3-6. Daily Seats and Passengers, Miami-New York Schedule

schedule. Yet the probability is very high that passengers were indeed turned away on a number of days, even though there were some empty seats at departure time.

The explanation lies in the nature of the reservation process, and the fact that a schedule can be fully booked days or even weeks in advance, and then have some of those bookings dissipate by departure time. Passengers originally holding reservations may have to change their plans at the last minute and either cancel their space too late for it to be rebooked, or simply become no-shows.

Thus the existence of some empty seats at departure time does not preclude the possibility that prospective passengers were turned away at some time during the booking process.

The importance of this factor is indicated by the no-show rate, which has recently been running at about 20 percent for most airlines—in other words, roughly one-fifth of passengers holding seat reservations failed to use them, and also failed to cancel them.

At present, this is partly offset by overbooking, which attempts scientifically to allow for the mathematical probabilities of no-shows and adjusts the seat inventory accordingly. One cannot completely correct for this factor, however, since some allowances must be made for unexpected changes in booking patterns. Hence there is still the prospect of unaccommodated demand for any flight that departs with only a few seats empty.

Based upon the no-show rate, and upon empirical evidence discussed here concerning measurements of unaccommodated demand, it appears reasonably clear that flights departing with load factors of 90 percent or higher would have turned away some passengers. To a lesser degree, the same would be true of some of the flights departing with load factors in the range of 80-90 percent.

Measuring Unaccommodated Demand

Data are not kept on the requests for airline space that are turned down, but we can get a reasonable approximation of such unaccommodated demand by comparing the patterns of passengers flying on flights where ample space is always available versus service where some amount of tightness of space is evident.

Figure 3-7 shows the distribution of load factors that occurred on individual flights, on a route that had an average monthly load factor of 43 percent (Dallas-New Orleans). Because of this low load factor, space was not tight; there would be hardly any occasion to turn passengers away, and the distribution of demand can be regarded as essentially unconstrained.[1]

In the situation described in figure 3-7 the load-factor distribution of individual flights follows the familiar normal curve, with most of the flights having load factors at the midrange point, and with the percentage of flights tapering downward about equally both to the lower and upper ends of the load-factor spectrum.

Examination of other routes with low (that is, unconstraining) average load factors indicates that data approximating a normal distribution are typical of such unconstrained situations. As another example, figure 3-8 shows the distribution of load factors for the Miami-New York (JFK) route which, in August 1975, also had a low load factor. This route had a load factor of 46 percent in that month. Note in figure 3-8 that this route also showed a normal curve for the distribution of its individual trip load factors.

In contrast, figure 3-9 shows the distribution of load factors on a route that averaged a monthly load factor of 66 percent (Chicago-Denver). Here we see a curve that still follows the normal shape at the lower end, but not on the upper end. Instead, the right-hand extension of the curve is literally cut short by the physical limit on the available seats. Thus many passengers wanting to fly this route were simply not accommodated on the flight they would have found most convenient.

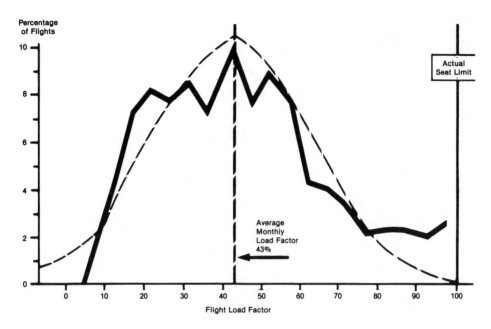

Source: CAB data.

Figure 3-7. Distribution of Load Factors, by Flights, Dallas-New Orleans Route, August 1975

By applying mathematical probability techniques, it is possible to analyze the data at the low end of the curve in figure 3-9, and construct a curve of normal demand as it would have been distributed had it not been constrained by the physical limit on the number of available seats. Figure 3-10 superimposes such a normal-demand distribution over the actual distribution plotted in figure 3-9.

Notice that the shaded area includes not only load factors to the right of the 100 percent capacity line—where there is an obvious lack of capacity—but also to the left of the 100 percent line, where seats would still seem to be available.

Airlines, of course, attempt to compensate for the no-show rate, but they can never fully compensate because they must be sure of having enough seats if a higher-than-average number of passengers honor their reservations. Hence some level of unaccommodated demand due to the no-show problem still exists (as indicated in figure 3-10).

Examination of other routes with high average load factors indicates that the truncated version of the normal curve is typical of such routes. As an example of a route with an even higher load factor, figure 3-11 shows the

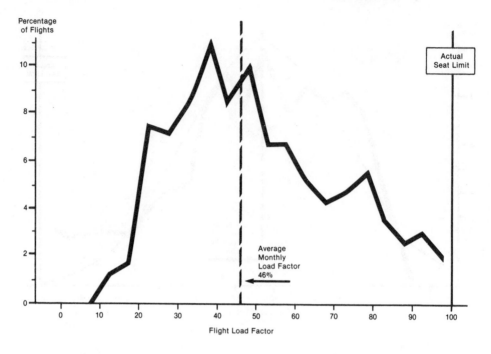

Source: CAB data.
Figure 3-8. Distribution of Load Factors, by Flights, Miami-New York (JFK) Route, August 1975

situation on the Atlanta-Washington route, which had an average load factor of 74 percent in the month analyzed. Here there is an even sharper cutting off of the right-hand portion of the normal-demand curve.

To provide a control test of the preceding analysis, different flights on the same route were compared, thus guarding against the possibility that the contrasts described here resulted from fundamental differences between the routes themselves.

The Chicago-Los Angeles route was studied, and two groups of schedules were analyzed from within this one route. On the one hand, four schedules were reviewed that each averaged very low load factors (35 percent) for the entire month. The distribution of their loads is shown in figure 3-12. It shows the same normal-curve pattern observed in the case of unconstrained demand.

The other four Chicago-Los Angeles schedules averaged load factors in the high 70s. The distribution of their loads is shown in figure 3-13. And

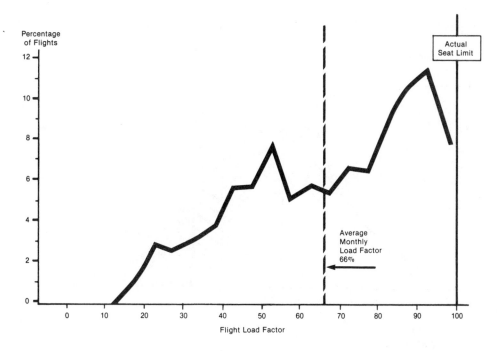

Source: CAB data.

Figure 3-9. Distribution of Load Factors, by Flights, Chicago-Denver Route, August 1975

here the same type of truncated demand curve appeared which was discussed earlier in connection with Chicago-Denver.

Especially significant is the evidence that demand constraint occurs when load factors average in the 60s—a level that is more the current norm than an extreme.

The staff of the Civil Aeronautics Board (CAB) recently prepared a study on this same point, to assess the unaccommodated demand implications of high load factors, to determine what would constitute "essential air services" for small communities.[2] That study concluded that with small planes (such as used in commuter operations) a 65 percent load factor would represent excessively tight space, and that instead essential service determinations should be based on a 50 percent load factor. Based on the analysis presented here, it appears that the CAB staff conclusions regarding small aircraft would be applicable to larger planes as well, and that limita-

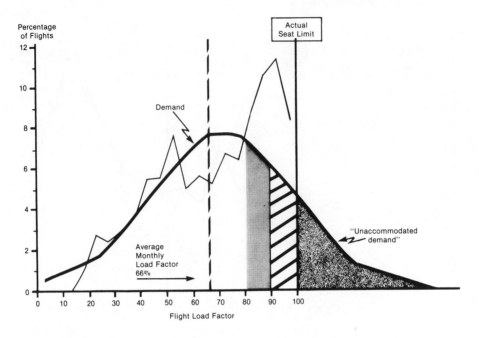

Source: CAB data.

Figure 3-10. Distribution of Load Factors and Distribution of Demand, Chicago-
Denver Route

tions in accommodating full demand show up at (or below) an average 65
percent load factor for both large and small planes.

Unaccommodated Demand on Specific Days

The preceding comments on unaccommodated demand have related to an
entire month's experience on a given route. However, this unaccommodated demand obviously becomes even more significant when focusing
on the specific days of the week that have the highest loads. A passenger
wanting to travel from city A to city B is not interested in the statistical fact
that for the month as a whole the load factor is 65 percent, and that this
means that on the average there is one empty seat for every two seats sold.
Passengers need to know more specifically whether they can get a seat on
the particular day when they need to travel, and at approximately the time
of day that fits their travel requirements.

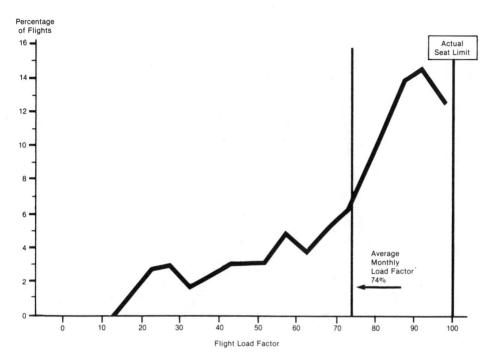

Source: CAB data.

Figure 3-11. Distribution of Load Factors, by Flights, Atlanta-Washington Route, August 1975

As we get to such real-world specifics, a seemingly moderate average monthly load factor can translate into a significant problem of space availability during peak periods.

We have already referred to the day-of-week pattern of traffic variation, and to the fact that different routes have different peak days (see figures 3-4 and 3-5). It is relevant to consider the day-of-week pattern for the Chicago-Denver route which, as noted, averaged a 66 percent load factor overall (see table 3-1). On this route the highest loads were on the weekends, with the highest individual day being Sunday with a 72 percent average load factor.

The distribution of load factors by individual Sunday flights is shown in figure 3-14. On that day of the week, over one-fourth of all flights departed with a load factor of 90 percent or higher, and over one-third departed with a load factor of 85 percent or higher. Here the distortion of the normal curve is quite extreme.

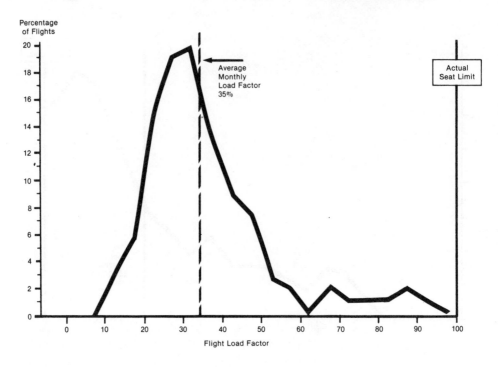

Source: CAB data.
Figure 3-12. Distribution of Load Factors, by Flights, on Low-Traffic Flights, Chicago-Los Angeles Route, August 1975

And if we look at the three most popular individual schedules on that route, we find that those schedules on Sundays departed with load factors of 90 percent or above more than three-fourths of the time.

An important point to note here is that higher load factors raise dramatically the level of unaccommodated demand. The increase in the average load factor for a heavily traveled day of the week compared with the average for all days creates an even greater increase in unaccommodated demand. This relationship is represented schematically in figure 3-15.

Pricing in Relation to Load Factor

Within recent years, the airlines have developed a new approach to promotional pricing, which has helped to improve load factors while minimizing the impact on service convenience. This has been the introduction of capacity-controlled fares, such as Super Saver.

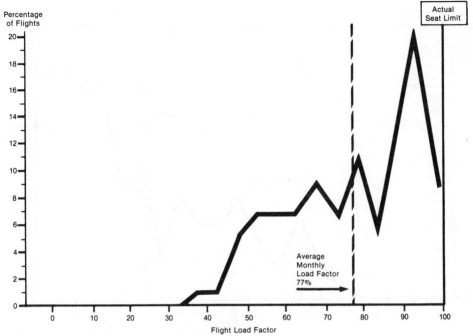

Source: CAB data.

Figure 3-13. Distribution of Load Factors, by Flights, on High-Traffic Flights, Chicago-Los Angeles Route, August 1975

Table 3-1
Distribution of Load Factors, by Day of Week—Chicago-Denver Route, August 1975

Day	Average Load Factor
Sunday	72%
Monday	68
Tuesday	60
Wednesday	59
Thursday	65
Friday	68
Saturday	68
Average	66%

Source: CAB Data.

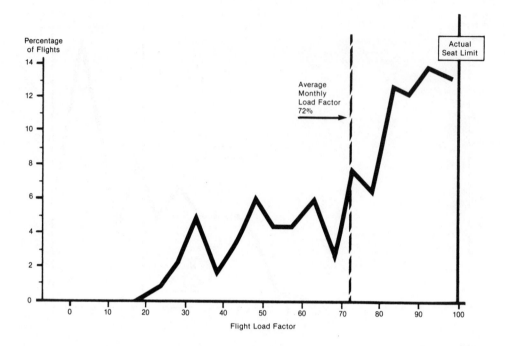

Source: CAB data.

Figure 3-14. Distribution of Load Factors, by Flights, on Sunday Flights, Chicago-
Denver Route, August 1975

Capacity-controlled fares are deep discount fares that an airline offers
for an overall percentage of total seats on a route. The airline adjusts the
percentage of seats offered on specific flights in accordance with demand at
normal fares to fill seats that would not normally be filled, usually during
off-peak hours.

In one sense, this is a refinement of a pricing concept that the airlines
have employed for many years: off-peak pricing. It has always been recognized that both the public and the industry would benefit if the empty seats on
low traffic days could be filled with passengers who would be willing to travel
on those less-popular days, in exchange for some fare reduction.

In effect, this is one way to beat the cost penalty of the industry's inherent traffic fluctuation. It permits average load factors to be increased,
thus decreasing average costs without increasing demand on the already
heavy days or subjecting passengers on those days to any greater problem of
getting space.

Off-peak pricing goes back to the earliest days of the airline industry.

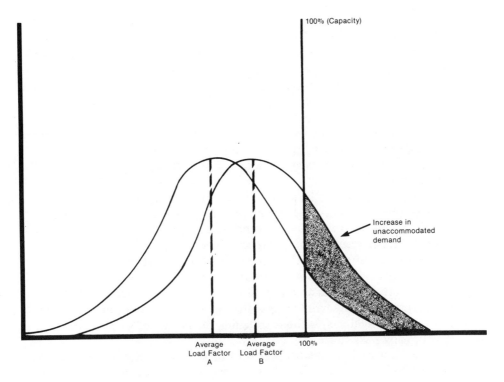

Figure 3-15. Distribution of Demand and Unaccommodated Demand for Two Average Load Factors

The first coach service, for example, was off-peak night coach.

One difficulty with off-peak pricing until recently, however, has been the fact that the timing of the peak has varied from route to route, and even from one direction to the other on the same route. In this study, we have already seen how Dallas-New Orleans had its peak traffic on Friday, Chicago-Los Angeles on Saturday, and Chicago-Denver on Sunday.   •

As another example, the peak departure hour of the day westbound from New York to Los Angeles is 5-6 p.m. Yet, if traveling eastbound on the very same route, the peak departure time is 9 a.m. because of the effect of time zones.

Until a few years ago, the definition of off-peak had to be spelled out specifically in promotional fare tariffs, and this seriously restricted the use of special fares. The wide daily variation in demand on a given route made it difficult to find a definition of off-peak suitable for an entire airline system.

The capacity-controlled fare retained the old idea of off-peak pricing, but gave the airlines the flexibility to make discounts available in specific relation to the demand fluctuations demonstrated by individual schedules on individual routes. This enabled the carriers to take advantage of new computer technology in handling reservations. With this technology, it is possible to predict the demand patterns of individual schedules, and thus predict the amount of space on future individual departures that could be used for promotional discount traffic.

At the same time, other pricing trends of recent years have moved in an opposite direction, and have reduced the airlines' ability to use off-peak pricing.

Off-peak pricing, by its nature, injects some complication into the pricing structure. In contrast, some pricing developments of the recent past have aimed for the simplicity of overall fare reductions, applied across the board, without restrictions. While such overall fare reductions have the welcome effect of reducing the complexity of the fare structure, they do require higher load factors for their viability, and cannot themselves channel traffic to off-peak times and days to achieve these load factors. Therefore this particular pricing trend brings into play the full force of high load factors on space tightness, without softening the impact of such tightness on the normally peak times.

It is impossible to predict which of these pricing strategies will prove dominant in the long run. For reasons already indicated, the outcome will have an important bearing on the service convenience aspect of future load factors.

Load-Factor Impact in Perspective

The degree to which load factors have risen sharply in recent years has been noted. In 1979, the industry's average year-round load factor represented the type of load factor that just several years ago would have been recorded only in peak season.

The key point of the preceding analysis is that increases in load factors have mixed effects. In the emphasis on fare reductions of the last few years, there has been a tendency to view increased load factors only in their favorable aspect, with little attention to the implications of space tightness.

High load factors also mean an inability to accommodate demand fully at the times of desired travel to a degree that has not been generally recognized. Systemwide load factors that look moderate in average terms contain a substantial portion of individual segments, flights, and days with very tight space.

Various specific examples have been presented in this chapter to demonstrate that, because of the inherent day-to-day variation in demand, attaining even a moderate average load factor requires that some flights have very high load factors and hence some unaccommodated demand. However, all of these examples have been specific flights or route segments during the single month of August 1975. It is now important to look at these results and assess the degree to which year-round results are similar.

Interestingly, extrapolating from this experience to the national system as a whole reveals that for any given numerical load factor the amount of unaccommodated demand would be greater than discussed herein for specific flights for a single month.

A year-round system average of, say, 65 percent, would embrace much more dispersion around the average than is the case for a single flight for a single month. And when there is more dispersion the portion of the normal curve extending out to the lower and upper extremeties is much greater than when the dispersion around the average is limited.

This is shown graphically in figure 3-16. Curve A is more representative of the demand distribution for a single flight, while curve B is more representative of the demand for an entire system. Notice that, while both

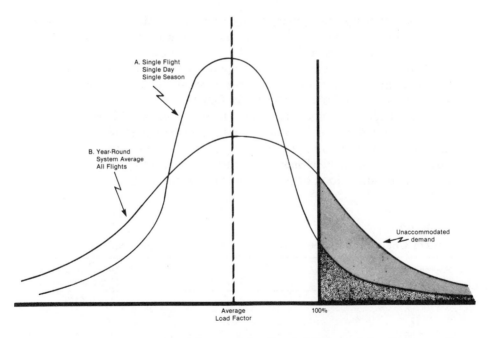

Figure 3-16. Unaccommodated Demand for Single Flight and for System at Same Average Load Factor

have the same average load factor, the year-round system curve (curve B) shows much more unaccommodated demand than the curve representing a single flight during a single season.

The Boeing Commercial Airplane Company has studied the problem of unaccommodated demand for some years. They have developed a computer program that provides the basis for the tabulation of year-round system unaccommodated demand presented in table 3-2.[3]

Thus averaging a year-round system load factor of 70 percent would mean that over the entire year about 21 percent of total demand would not be accommodated at the desired departure time due to insufficient capacity. It is clear from this table that, as average load factors rise above 60 percent, the rate at which unaccommodated demand increases accelerates dramatically. Also note that table 3-2 does not include the demand unaccommodated because of the problem of no-shows, which would increase further the extent to which passengers would be inconvenienced by insufficient seats at their desired departure times.

Conclusion

There is a tendency among many to regard high load factors as an unmixed blessing. Increases in load factors can indeed mitigate inflationary pressure in airline cost elements, and this benefit of higher load factors is important.

This chapter, however, has tried to point out that increases in load factors necessarily involve, to some degree, a penalty in service convenience, which increases rapidly as average load factors rise.

This chapter has not argued that load factors should be lower (or higher) than they are today; its intent has merely been to show that changes in average load factors have service as well as cost implications. Full consideration of both these elements is necessary for the effect of varying load factors to be understood by policy planners and the public.

Table 3-2
System Unaccommodated Demand at Varying Average Load Factors

Average Passenger Load Factor	Percent of Demand Unaccommodated
80	64%
70	21
60	6
50	2

Notes

1. Load factors data were collected on intervals of 5 percentage points. Each plot on the axis marked "flight load factor" is plotted at the midpoint of the interval; that is, 2.5 percent, 7.5 percent, and so on. The highest plot point will be for all load factors of 95-100 percent, and it will be marked on the graphs at 97.5 percent.

2. Office of Economic Analysis, Civil Aeronautics Board, *Aircraft Size, Load Factor, and On-Demand Service*, September 13, 1979.

3. Boeing Commercial Airplane Company, *Surplus Seat Management* and *Discount Fare Management*.

4

Airline Financial Forecasting

Lee R. Howard and
John R. Summerfield

1323
5210
6150
US

Introduction

Other chapters of this book discuss in detail various economic aspects of the airline business. All of these aspects, in one way or another, point toward the bottom line—profits. This chapter examines major factors that affect profits, relates economic aspects of the airline business to these factors, and discusses how the relationships are used to develop short-term financial forecasts.

Profit has been aptly described as the small difference between two very large numbers—revenue and expense. For airline managements, this statement conveys the constant message that every facet of the business must be well managed since a small increment in any of its revenues, or a small increment in any of its expenses, can result in a substantial loss. The financial forecaster is constantly aware that an error of one or two percentage points in estimating revenues or expenses can shift the profit position markedly.

Because the future will always be shaped by a vast number of factors whose magnitudes, directions, and interrelationships can be estimated only imprecisely, forecasting is extremely difficult. Yet many organizations find it essential to devote considerable resources to the task of forecasting. A good forecast can provide management with a means of profitably taking advantage of the future, or, at the worst, avoiding disaster. This chapter is devoted to short-term financial forecasting. Some aspects of longer range forecasts are covered in chapter 6.

Profit is defined as revenue minus expenses. Revenues can be measured or estimated as a product of traffic (for example, revenue passenger-miles) and yield (for example, revenue per revenue passenger-mile). Expenses can be measured or estimated as a product of capacity (for example, available seat-miles) and unit costs (for example, expenses per available seat-mile). The above relationship is referred to as the earnings equation and can be written in the following form.

$$\text{Traffic} \times \text{Yield} = \text{Operating Revenue}$$

$$\text{Capacity} \times \text{Unit Cost} = \text{Operating Expenses}$$

Operating Revenues − Operating Expenses = Operating Profit

Operating Profit + / − Nonoperating Items[1] = Net Income

A forecast of operating profit or of net income can be made directly or indirectly, through a forecast of its component parts. As an example of direct profit forecasting, suppose that an analysis of past data discloses a high correlation between changes in the Dow-Jones Industrial Average and changes in airline profits one year later. A belief that the relationship would continue may result in a good method for forecasting profits one year into the future. Unfortunately, such simple relationships are hard to find and, more importantly, belief in their stability is hard to maintain. A high correlation among two or more variables is not in itself a good basis for assuming a continuation of that correlation. There must be some real world relationship among such variables, relationships that might be attributed to cause and effect, before one should assume that the relationship provides a valid basis for forecasting. Because airline operating profits result from successful combinations of revenues and expenses, it is safer—more reliable—to forecast revenues and expenses, and their components (traffic, yield, capacity, and unit costs) than to forecast operating profits directly. We will look first at forecasting operating revenue.

Operating Revenue Forecasting

Prior to forecasting airline operating revenues, historical data must be compiled in meaningful form and thoroughly analyzed. The airline industry has a uniquely comprehensive source of statistical information known as the CAB Form 41 data. This information, supplied by the airlines, covers virtually all aspects of airline operations. Because the data are voluminous and need to be manipulated extensively for a forecast, computer time-sharing services are used.

Airline operating revenues are earned by carrying passengers and cargo. A small amount of additional revenue is generated from miscellaneous other sources. The vast majority of airline revenues, however, are from passenger travel, most of which is on scheduled operations. Table 4-1 illustrates an eight quarter history of airline sources of revenue. The need for a thorough understanding of the underlying factors affecting current airline operations can be shown by examining the changing sources of scheduled passenger revenues. In late 1979, the revenue shown in the table was produced by growth in both traffic and yield. Through 1980, traffic declined but revenue continued to grow because yield increases compensated for the traffic declines. A similar inspection of other sources of revenue such as

Table 4-1
Sources of Revenue—U.S. Scheduled Airlines
(Millions of Dollars)

	4th Q 1978	1st Q 1979	2nd Q 1979	3rd Q 1979	4th Q 1979	1st Q 1980	2nd Q 1980	3rd Q 1980
Scheduled passenger	$4,631	$4,759	$5,255	$6,128	$5,755	$6,097	$6,531	$7,228
Charter passenger	95	94	76	88	82	74	65	76
Cargo	530	488	497	547	588	559	573	585
Other	243	229	264	315	301	292	324	345
Total operating revenue	$5,498	$5,570	$6,091	$7,077	$6,726	$7,022	$7,493	$8,235

Source: CAB Form 41.
Note: Q = Quarter.

charter passenger and cargo operations would indicate varying movements in traffic and yield in those operations, each of which must be analyzed to provide accurate forecast results.

The following sections examine separately the major components of revenue—traffic and yield.

Traffic Analysis

Traffic is multidimensional. A basic breakdown is between passenger travel and cargo movement. Passenger travel, in turn, includes domestic and inter-

Table 4-2
Domestic versus International Traffic—U.S. Scheduled Airlines
(RPMs—Percent Change from Previous Year)

	Quarter	Domestic	International	System
1978	1	13.0%	12.3%	12.9%
	2	16.0	12.7	15.3
	3	17.7	16.2	17.3
	4	13.2	17.2	14.0
1979	1	16.9	15.6	16.7
	2	9.4	20.4	11.7
	3	9.1	16.0	10.7
	4	4.9	10.0	5.9
1980	1	(2.2)	6.2	(0.6)
	2	(2.5)	(2.1)	(2.4)
	3	(9.9)	(2.9)	(8.2)
	4	(7.6)	(7.0)	(7.5)

Source: CAB Form 41.

national travel, discount and full-fare travel, first class and coach travel, and scheduled and charter travel. During any period, each of these segments of total air travel has grown at a different rate; some may have declined. Table 4-2 shows the changes in international and domestic air traffic for recent years, as compared to the overall system average. It is common practice to measure passenger travel by revenue passenger-miles (RPMs), rather than by total passengers carried, to aggregate long and short trips.

Traffic is also broken down into discount and full-fare traffic. Table 4-3 shows forty-eight-state domestic trunk traffic growth rates for the past five years, along with the percent change in discount and full-fare traffic. Discount traffic data are reported only on the basis of the forty-eight contiguous states.

A substantial divergence in growth rates between discount and full-fare traffic occurred in 1978. Early in that year the CAB began to allow airlines more flexibility in pricing. This flexibility, along with easier market entry, allowed carriers to offer promotional fares at substantially reduced rates, with fewer restrictions than in the past. This airline policy has continued, producing growth in discount traffic (during 1979 and through 1980) when a recession cut deeply into full-fare traffic.

First class traffic growth lagged that of total scheduled service in 1976 and 1977 when a fixed fare differential between first and coach class service was required by the CAB. In 1978 the greater fare flexibility granted by the Board resulted in lower first class fares, thus making first class service available to more travelers. In September 1978 all restrictions on first class fares were removed by the Board. This change allowed airlines to lower the fare differential between classes of service, causing first class growth to exceed that of coach in 1979. In 1980 skyrocketing operating costs required substantial airline fare increases. First class travel, which for the most part is at nondiscount fares, absorbed the brunt of these increases and suffered most in the decline of air travel in 1980. Table 4-4 details these changing patterns.

Table 4-3
Discount versus Full-Fare Coach Traffic—Forty-Eight-State Domestic Trunks
(RPMs—Percent Change from Previous Year)

	Discount	Full Fare	Total
1976	5.1%	16.2%	13.6%
1977	0.8	12.3	8.8
1978	44.8	(1.1)	16.6
1979	14.8	2.0	8.1
1980	11.8	(23.2)	(5.4)

Source: Air Transport Association.

Table 4-4
Scheduled Service, First Class versus Coach Traffic—U.S. Scheduled Airlines
(RPMs—Percent Change from Previous Year)

	First Class	Coach	Total Scheduled
1976	3.3%	11.2%	9.9%
1977	4.4	8.6	7.9
1978	16.1	17.5	17.4
1979	20.9	11.5	12.8
1980	(16.8)	(1.9)	(4.2)

Source: CAB Form 41.

In the early 1970s, charter traffic grew more rapidly than scheduled traffic, reflecting large differences in fares. But beginning in 1977, as airlines started the move to large discounts on scheduled service, a transition occurred. These changes are charted in table 4-5. If the data included the supplemental carriers that were then totally in charter service, the drop in nonscheduled traffic would appear even more dramatic. In fact, part of the growth in scheduled traffic shown on table 4-5 represents traffic diverted from nonscheduled airlines.

Because cargo represents about 15 percent of airline revenues, historical data on the elements of that portion of the traffic are also prerequisites to a revenue forecast. Table 4-6 shows the distribution of air cargo traffic growth between domestic and international operations for the period 1978-1980.

For forecast purposes, it is also useful to know growth rates for cargo carried in freighter aircraft and for cargo carried in passenger aircraft. Table 4-7 shows how those rates changed over the three year period 1978-1980.

Table 4-5
Scheduled versus Nonscheduled Traffic—U.S. Scheduled Airlines
(RPMs—Percent Change from Previous Year)

	Scheduled	Nonscheduled	Total
1976	9.9%	22.3%	10.7%
1977	7.9	(0.1)	7.4
1978	17.4	(20.5)	15.0
1979	12.8	(27.4)	11.1
1980	(4.2)	(26.7)	(4.9)

Source: CAB Form 41.

Table 4-6
Domestic versus International Cargo Traffic—U.S. Scheduled Airlines
(RTMs—Percent Change from Previous Year)

Year	Quarter	Domestic	International	System
1978	1	13.6%	2.4%	8.8%
	2	12.0	2.3	7.9
	3	9.9	3.4	7.1
	4	8.1	(6.6)	1.4
1979	1	6.8	9.1	7.7
	2	(0.5)	7.8	2.8
	3	(1.2)	(1.0)	(1.1)
	4	(0.6)	2.2	0.6
1980	1	(3.4)	5.2	0.1
	2	2.4	3.1	(0.1)
	3	(3.0)	8.3	1.7
	4	(6.5)	(3.0)	(5.0)

Source: CAB Form 41.

Traffic Forecasting

Airline analysts have developed a number of econometric models for forecasting airline traffic. These models differ in detail but include such independent variables as Gross National Product (GNP), Disposable Personal Income, average fare level (yield), and consumer confidence. Each of the models claims a high correlation between forecast traffic and actual

Table 4-7
Freighter versus Belly Cargo—U.S. Scheduled Airlines
(RTMs—Percent Change from Previous Year)

Year	Quarter	Freighter	Belly	Total
1978	1	8.6%	9.0%	8.8%
	2	15.2	1.1	7.9
	3	15.6	(1.5)	7.1
	4	4.3	(1.8)	1.4
1979	1	10.2	4.8	7.7
	2	4.9	0.5	2.8
	3	(7.5)	6.8	(1.1)
	4	(1.8)	3.3	0.6
1980	1	(0.4)	1.1	0.1
	2	(2.9)	3.0	(0.1)
	3	5.3	(2.5)	1.7
	4	(6.2)	(3.7)	(5.0)

Source: CAB Form 41.

traffic for a given year when actual values of the independent variables for that year are inserted in the model. Forecasting errors nonetheless persist with all of these models. It appears that forecasting of the independent variables is as difficult and subject to error as forecasting the traffic directly. All such models implicitly assume the contrary; that is, they assume better accuracy in forecasting the independent variables, such as GNP and the like, than in forecasting traffic.

These comments are not intended to convey the impression that the economic variables mentioned have no influence on traffic. Clearly they do or the analysts using the models would not have found such good correlations. Figure 4-1 displays the similarity in growth patterns between air travel and real GNP during the three economic downturns between 1969 and 1980. But, as demonstrated by the data in tables 4-2 to 4-7, traffic is multidimensional and growth rates of traffic components vary widely in magnitude and often in direction. Hence a more eclectic approach to traffic forecasting is in common use in the airline industry. This approach to short-term forecasting enables the forecaster to analyze recent data that exhibit changes in the structure and operation of the industry as a principal influence on results to be expected in the near future.

This short-term forecasting method depends heavily on careful analysis of recent trends in the industry, such as those discussed earlier in this chapter. But more than historical data must be considered in forecasting, because the air transport industry is in a constant state of change.

Aircraft technological changes have had an impact on airline operations over the years, as have changes in the overall economic environment. New and innovative marketing programs are constantly being devised. And now the highly competitive environment under deregulation is motivating further experimentation in marketing programs.

Special marketing efforts also have significant effects on short-term traffic. In 1979 United Airlines, following an extended strike, instituted a novel marketing effort involving coupons. Beginning in May 1979 the airline offered every passenger a coupon that entitled the holder to a 50 percent discount on any ticket purchased for travel prior to December 15 of the same year. Other airlines soon announced that they also would honor the coupons. This promotional marketing program had a significant effect on air traffic during the months of June-December 1979, an effect that must be accounted for when estimating the traffic growth for the following year. Similar promotional programs are becoming more widespread and can be expected to increase under the more competitive environment of deregulation.

In analyzing historical data, it is important to consider the effect on traffic data of disruptive occurrences such as strikes. Between 1978 and 1980, for example, there were ten strikes of at least one month's duration.

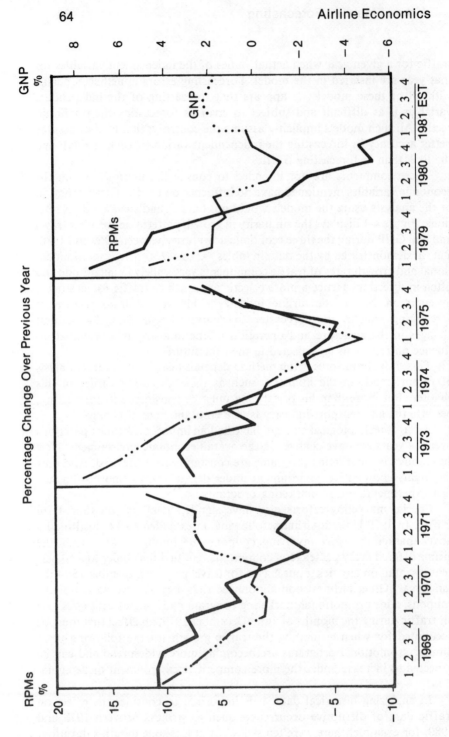

Estimated 1981 GNP consensus of Chase, DRI, Wharton, UCLA, Merrill Lynch, and Conference Board.

Figure 4-1. RPMs versus Real GNP during U.S. Recessions—U.S. Scheduled Airlines System

In addition to all these factors, fares have an effect on the demand for air transportation. Airline analysts over the years have searched for a measure of price elasticity of demand for air transportation. Unfortunately, the search has not been very successful. This does not imply that air travel demand is not affected by fares; obviously it is. However, the relationship is dependent on a specific set of conditions such as the status of the U.S. economy, length of haul (total fare), total trip cost (including ground costs), and costs of alternate modes of transportation. In addition, business travel is affected by fare changes differently from pleasure and vacation travel. Since many combinations of these conditions have prevailed over time, it has not been possible to derive a simple and enduring relationship between airline fare changes and traffic. This conclusion provides little direct help to the analyst in estimating traffic, but should demonstrate that the effect of fares on traffic demand, although elusive, situational, and changing, is a factor that must be reckoned with in short-term forecasting of airline traffic. Some ways of checking the validity of assumptions regarding the combination of traffic and fares (yield) are discussed later in this chapter.

There are no known models that will account for all of these factors and provide reliable estimates of short-term traffic growth. The analyst must, in the end, rely upon combining his or her best judgments with reasonable assumptions about the future. There are, however, numerous tools that provide significant assistance in making the judgments and testing their validity. In addition to historical data illustrated in tables 4-2 to 4-7, monthly traffic data for the air transport industry and for its individual airline companies are publicly available from published CAB reports or through one of the several time-sharing programs.

A short-term forecasting model has been developed by the Air Transport Association to permit rapid assessment of alternative inputs and assumptions, thus facilitating an evaluation of the effect of changes in the environment on airline profits. A description of that model is included in appendix 4A.

Yield Forecasting

In the earnings equation, the other major element of operating revenue is yield—the average price of air transportation per revenue passenger-mile (¢ per RPM) and per revenue ton-mile (¢ per RTM) for cargo. Simplistic as it may appear, it is nonetheless important to observe that high traffic and low yields can result in the same revenues as low traffic and high yields. However, since some variable costs are directly related to traffic, the short-term implication of the two combinations may differ substantially.

Prior to passage of the Airline Deregulation Act in 1978, airline fares were rigidly controlled by the Civil Aeronautics Board. Since passage of the Act, however, the CAB has relaxed its control of airline fares by expanding the zone of flexibility within which carriers may set fares with little risk of suspension.[2] Thus airline fares are being controlled more and more by the forces of competition rather than by the CAB. On January 1, 1983, the control of fares will be left entirely to competitive forces. This change has added a new dimension to estimating future yields.

Further confounding analysts since deregulation is the degree to which the airlines have responded to the new competitive environment by offering a wide variety of discount and promotional fares. As shown in figure 4-2, by 1980 well over half of U.S. domestic coach air travel was by reduced fare. In certain months of 1980, over two-thirds chose reduced fares. This is a substantially different pattern from the mid-1970s when over two-thirds of all U.S. domestic travel was by normal CAB-controlled fares.

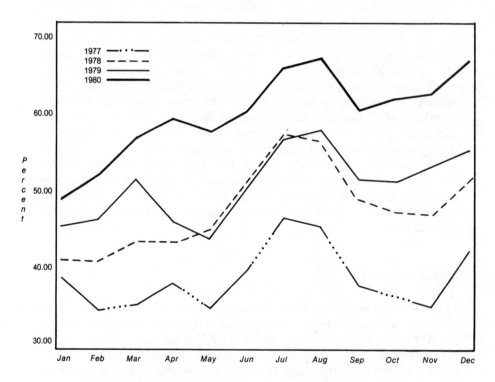

Source: Air Transport Association.

Figure 4-2. Reduced Fare RPMs as a Percentage of Total Coach—Forty-Eight States—Domestic Trunks

Not only have the market forces under deregulation caused significant changes affecting yield composition, but also unprecedented airline cost structure changes in recent years have caused major yield trend differences.

As shown in figure 4-3, since 1970 airline costs per ASM have declined in constant dollars, and airline yields in constant dollars have also declined—until 1980. The costs that an airline must incur to produce a seat-mile have, until the late 1970s, increased at a slower rate than the U.S. inflation rate. This was largely due to a steady flow of new, more productive technology, and by management decisions to increase seating densities, improve resource utilization, and make other changes. As a result of these improvements in productivity and higher load factors, the airlines have been able to increase fares at a slower rate than the cost of other goods and services. So yields in constant dollars have moved downward for the past two decades, as shown in figure 4-3.

Recently, however, airline costs (mainly fuel) have increased at unprecedented rates. The fuel cost increases are documented in chapter 5, and the cost increases for other goods and services required to operate an airline are discussed in chapter 1. The magnitude of these recent airline cost increases has been so much greater than the general U.S. inflation rate that constant dollar fares have been forced upward. But, as can be seen in figure 4-3, 1980 airline yields in constant dollars have only increased to the level between 1977 and 1978 despite the unprecedented increases in the airline operating costs.

Since fuel expense in 1980 is almost one-third of total airline operating expenses, and since increases in fuel prices can be expected to continue, it is

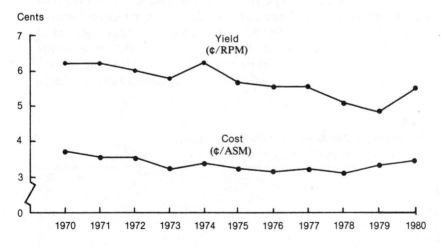

Figure 4-3. Constant Dollar Yield and Cost per ASM

unlikely that constant dollar yields will decline in the near future. Thus the airline forecaster today has to forecast with an assumption of much higher estimates of current dollar yield increases than has been the case in the past. Table 4-8 illustrates the recent trend in current dollar yields.

The factors discussed here have recently made the job of estimating future yields more difficult. At the same time, the consequences of errors in estimates have become greater. To airline management, a one percentage point difference in yield now means about $350 million in industry operating profit. To the airline analyst, an estimating error of one percentage point will produce a $350 million error in his or her forecast of industry operating profit.

In estimating future yield changes, a valuable concept is yield carry-over—the effect that changes in fares in one year have on the following year.

Fare changes since the Deregulation Act have been the product of two factors. First, airlines have been able to raise fares as the Standard Industry Fare Level (SIFL) has been adjusted upwards. Second, they have been able to raise fares to the limits of the fare flexibility zone, if the fares were not at the limit already. Recall that, in accordance with the Airline Deregulation Act, the CAB must adjust the SIFL at least semiannually by the percent change in airline unit operating costs. During 1980, CAB made SIFL adjustments effective on the first of the following months: January, March, May, and July.

As shown in table 4-9, the SIFL adjustment of 2.5 percent made effective March 1, 1980, was effective for the ten remaining months of 1980. On a year-over-year basis, the SIFL in the first two months of 1981 was 2.5 percent higher than it was in the first two months of 1980 as a direct result of the March 1980 adjustment. Since those two months represent one-sixth or 17 percent of a full year, 17 percent of the 2.5 percent SIFL increase of March 1, 1980, (or 0.43 percent) is carried over to 1981. In a similar fashion, the carry-over to any future year from other SIFL adjustments made in the previous year can be calculated. In the table we can see that in

Table 4-8
Airline Passenger Yields—U.S. Scheduled Airlines
(Percent Change from Previous Year)

1975	4.0
1976	5.1
1977	5.7
1978	(1.5)
1979	4.7
1980 Estimated	26.3

Source: CAB Form 41.

1981, for example, the yield carry-over due to SIFL changes was 3.76 percent.

Any fare increases not based on SIFL changes, but rather allowed by the zone of fare flexibility, will also be carried over into the next year in the same way. The total yield carry-over will be the sum of all changes in fares, based on SIFL changes or fare increases within the zone of flexibility, carried over to the following year.

The concept of yield carry-over tells us that, if fares are not increased or decreased during a year, and the mix of discount and full-fare traffic does not change, and the depth of discounts is not changed, average yields for the year will be higher than the previous year by the amount of yield carry-over.

Yield carry-over represents only a part of the yield increase in any year, and thus cannot be used alone to make yield estimates, but the yield carry-over derived from historical data does provide a point of departure for judging future yield estimates.

Since the SIFL is adjusted by the amount of change in unit operating costs and since, in a free-market environment, cost-based pricing is expected to prevail, it is not surprising that, except for periods of unusual conditions, overall airline yield changes have generally paralleled changes in the SIFL.

Beginning in 1983, however, all fare regulation by the CAB will end, and that will mark the end of the SIFL and its possible use as a guideline. If fares remain cost based, however, forecasts of cost inflation rates may provide a basis for judging yield forecasts.

Cargo yields have a history somewhat different from passenger yields. Following deregulation of cargo in 1977, carriers were no longer required to file cargo tariffs with the CAB, and a new era of competitive pricing was initiated. As table 4-10 shows, the rate of increase in cargo yields slowed in 1978 as price competition emerged. Rising costs soon overwhelmed the

Table 4-9
SIFL Increase Carry-Over for 1981

1980 SIFL Adjustments					
Effective Date	*Percent Adjustment*	*Number of Months in 1980*	*Number of Months in 1981*	*Percent of Year*	*1981 Carry-Over*
3/1/80	2.5	10	2	17	0.43%
5/1/80	5.4	8	4	33	1.78
7/1/80	3.1	6	6	50	1.55
					3.76%

Source: ATA.

Table 4-10
Current and Constant Dollar Cargo Yields—U.S. Scheduled Airlines

	Current Dollars	Constant 1970 Dollars
1970	20.67¢	20.67¢
1971	20.44	19.62
1972	20.84	19.35
1973	22.18	19.39
1974	24.96	19.65
1975	27.26	19.67
1976	29.00	19.80
1977	31.61	20.25
1978	33.50	19.30
1979	36.72	19.72
1980	41.40	19.51

Source: CAB Form 41 and Air Transport Association.
Note: Cargo yields are in cents per revenue ton mile.

moderating forces, however, and the rate of cargo yield accelerated. When adjusted for inflation (using Consumer Price Index as a measure of inflation) cargo yields are seen to have remained nearly constant from 1971-1976. A rise in 1977 was affected by deregulation, and real cargo yields did not return to early 1970 levels until 1980, as shown in table 4-10. As the air cargo industry stabilizes following deregulation, it is reasonable to expect that cargo yields will increasingly vary in approximate proportion to changes in unit costs.

Revenue Forecasting

Rather than merely multiplying passenger traffic and yield forecasts for a passenger revenue forecast and multiplying cargo traffic and yield forecasts for a cargo revenue forecast, it is useful to reexamine the relationship between yields and traffic. As earlier stated, no simple universal measure of price elasticity exists to aid in this examination.

Figure 4-4, 4-5, and 4-6 illustrate how traffic and yields have interacted between 1977 and 1980 to provide revenue growth from scheduled passenger service, scheduled cargo service, and charter service. On figure 4-4 it is clear that passenger revenues increased each year, but the greatest increase occurred in 1980 when the yield increase was the greatest, despite economic conditions that could be expected to reduce air travel.

Figure 4-5 displays a quite different pattern for cargo. In 1978, the year immediately following cargo deregulation, revenues, yields, and RTMs all

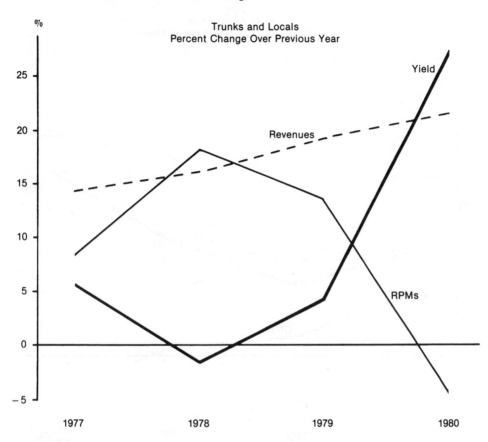

Source: CAB Form 41.

Figure 4-4. Traffic, Yield, and Revenue—Scheduled Passenger Services

grew at lower rates than in 1977. However, subsequent to 1978 cargo behaved more like the passenger market, with larger increases in yield in 1979 and 1980 contributing to a decline in RTMs, but an increased rate of growth in revenues.

Figure 4-6 displays the decline of charter travel as the scheduled carriers broadened and deepened their discount fare offerings, thus cutting deeply into the low-cost travel market of the charter carriers.

In all three of the figures we can see that the *components* of revenue changes can behave quite differently from revenue itself. In forecasting revenue, and in checking revenue forecasts, it is thus important to analyze its components separately.

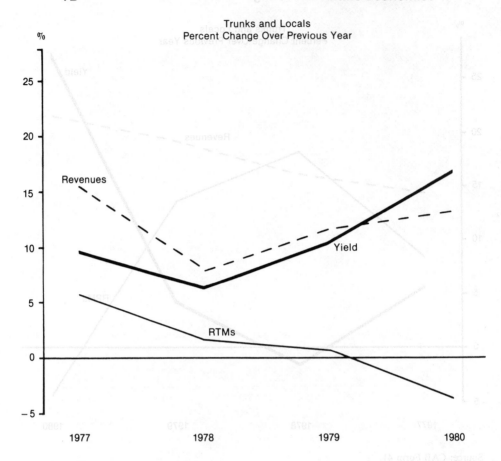

Source: CAB Form 41.
Figure 4-5. Traffic, Yield, and Revenue—Cargo

Operating Expense Analysis

As in the case of operating revenues, operating expense analysis is carried out by study of the components—in this case, capacity and unit costs.

Capacity Forecasting

Capacity is measured in the earnings equation by available seat-miles (ASMs) for passenger carriage, and by available ton-miles (ATMs) for cargo carriage. The two measures are sometimes combined either as equivalent ASMs or as equivalent ATMs.[3] As with the other major elements

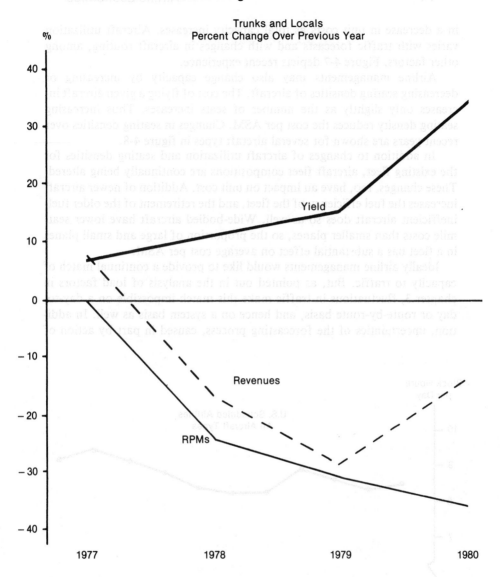

Trunks and Locals
Percent Change Over Previous Year

Figure 4-6. Traffic, Yield, and Revenue—Nonscheduled Passenger Services

of the earnings equation, the single term *capacity* is an oversimplification. Changes in capacity can be achieved with the same fleet of aircraft by different means, each having different unit cost implications. For example, if the utilization (hours-per-day per aircraft) of the fleet is increased, fixed costs of airline operations are spread over more production units, resulting

in a decrease in unit costs as total capacity increases. Aircraft utilization
varies with traffic forecasts and with changes in aircraft routing, among
other factors. Figure 4-7 depicts recent experience.

Airline managements may also change capacity by increasing or
decreasing seating densities of aircraft. The cost of flying a given aircraft increases only slightly as the number of seats increases. Thus increasing
seating density reduces the cost per ASM. Changes in seating densities over
recent years are shown for several aircraft types in figure 4-8.

In addition to changes of aircraft utilization and seating densities for
the existing fleet, aircraft fleet compositions are continually being altered.
These changes, too, have an impact on unit cost. Addition of newer aircraft
increases the fuel efficiency of the fleet, and the retirement of the older fuel-
inefficient aircraft does so as well. Wide-bodied aircraft have lower seat-
mile costs than smaller planes, so the proportion of large and small planes
in a fleet has a substantial effect on average cost per ASM.

Ideally airline managements would like to provide a continual match of
capacity to traffic. But, as pointed out in the analysis of load factors in
chapter 3, fluctuations in traffic make this match impossible on a day-to-
day or route-by-route basis, and hence on a system basis as well. In addition, uncertainties of the forecasting process, caused in part by action of

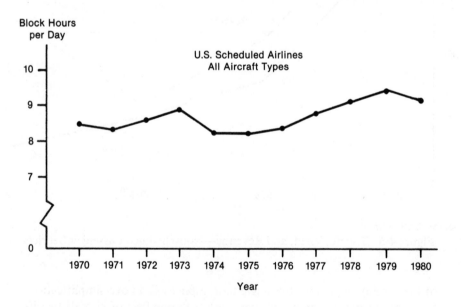

Source: CAB Form 41.

Figure 4-7. Aircraft Utilization—Block Hours per Day

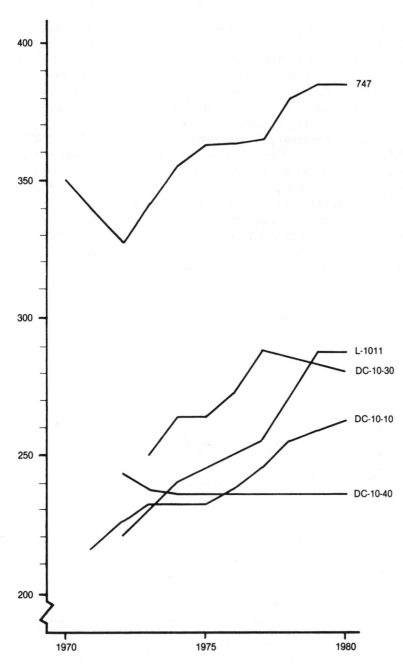

Source: CAB Form 41.
Figure 4-8. Average Seats per Aircraft

competitors, hamper attempts to approximate a match between traffic and capacity. In the longer run, other obstacles are encountered. Between the time an airline orders new aircraft models already in production and delivery of those aircraft, a minimum of eighteen months expires. For aircraft not in production, lead times for delivery can be five years or more. Lead times this long restrict management's ability to adjust capacity in the short term. The inability to match traffic and capacity is illustrated in figure 4-9, which shows fluctuations in passenger load factors for the period 1970 to 1980. Several other observations can be made from these data that provide additional insight for judging capacity estimates. Note the lag in adjusting capacity in the recessions of 1970-1971, 1974-1975, and 1979-1980.

At the onset of these recessions, traffic growth abated substantially, yet carriers did not respond with commensurate capacity adjustments until at least one quarter later. Similarly, during the recovery from the earlier recessions, a lag in increasing capacity commensurate with the increase in traffic is illustrated by sharply increasing load factors.

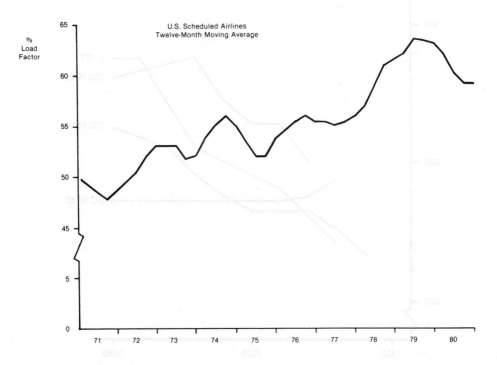

Source: CAB Form 41.

Figure 4-9. Passenger Load Factor—Scheduled Operations

Although recessions provide rather extreme examples, the same lag occurs on a more moderate scale as traffic growths fluctuate between recessions. Thus it is helpful to know how much capacity is on order by the industry at any point in time and when it is expected to be delivered. Such data, of course, will not reveal the level of capacity expected during a period of time in the future, since no information regarding retirement of aircraft is shown. Airlines often consider their aircraft retirement programs as confidential. Nor do these data show delivery dates for options for purchase of aircraft. Nonetheless, new capacity scheduled for delivery provides a departure point for judging future capacity estimates.

Other yardsticks for judging capacity estimates are provided by measurements of load factor, its relative, break-even load factor, and the relationship between the two. As explained in chapter 3, load factor is simply the percent of capacity that is being utilized, and is calculated by dividing RPMs by ASMs (RTMs by ATMs in the case of cargo). As discussed at length in chapter 3, there is some upper limit to average load factor above which service to the public will be adversely affected. Load factors that are too low, on the other hand, may indicate that airline resources are being underutilized, thus depressing operating profits. If the combination of estimated future traffic and estimated future capacity (as measured by load factor) deviates substantially from recent experience, the analyst must examine the reason for the anticipated swing and view the capacity estimate as suspect.

Unit Cost Forecasting

Because of the interrelationship between capacity and unit costs, some discussion of unit costs is necessary in this chapter. In addition, chapter 1 developed historical data on airline unit costs and the implication of some of the changing cost trends. This section will continue to discuss unit costs as they relate to development of airline short-term financial forecasts.

Unit costs are defined differently for different uses. For example, in the Airline Cost Index discussion of airline costs in chapter 1, the term unit costs refers to compensation per employee, cost per gallon of fuel, cost per 1,000 pounds of aircraft weight landed, and so forth. Since the volume of labor is employees, the volume of fuel gallons, and so on, those units are appropriate for tracking unit cost increases (inflation). The same unit cost changes are useful in arriving at estimates of cost changes in the broader aggregate cost categories used in short-term forecasting. However, a common denominator for unit costs is required to arrive at total operating expenses. ASMs have proved to be the best common denominator for this purpose.

Use of ASMs for unit cost measurement is not without its problems. For example, ASMs are not the proper units for cargo operations. Except for all-cargo carriers, it is impossible, using reported data, to separate those airline costs related to passenger operations from those related to cargo operations. Were it possible to separate costs of the two aspects of aircraft operations, it would be reasonable to use cost per ASM for the passenger portion of operating costs, and cost per ATM for the cargo portion. A solution to this problem is to convert freighter ATMs to equivalent ASMs for use in making unit operating cost estimates. Although not a perfect solution, the error is probably small, since the cargo portion of the airline industry is small in volume compared to passenger aircraft operations.

The factor used to convert freighter ATMs to equivalent ASMs is a composite of the ratios of seats-to-tons capacities of various freighter types. For example, CAB Form 41 data indicate that the average number of seats in a passenger B-747 is 385. The average capacity for a B-747 freighter is reported as 96 tons. The equivalent ASM ratio for the B-747 is 385/96 or 4 equivalent ASMs per ATM. A weighted composite ratio developed from the separate ratios for each of the freighter types is used for conversion of freighter ATMs to equivalent ASMs.

Another problem with using ASMs as a unit cost denomination is that ASMs are a measure of capacity, and some costs are related almost entirely to traffic levels. Costs such as fuel, aircraft maintenance, landing fees, and aircraft servicing are largely dependent on the level of aircraft operations or capacity. Changes in traffic volume have little effect on these costs. Therefore, we can properly call them capacity-related costs. Other costs such as ticketing, reservations, and other passenger and cargo sales and service activities are largely dependent upon traffic levels and are not affected by changes in capacity. These costs can properly be called noncapacity or traffic-related costs.

As long as changes in traffic and capacity are approximately parallel (in other words, load factor is fairly stable), there is little possibility for introduction of significant error in cost estimates by using costs per ASM as the unit cost basis. However, when large changes in load factor are foreseen, signaling anticipated differences in traffic and capacity changes, consideration must be given to the existence of traffic-related costs, or else the accuracy of the forecast will suffer. Although the operating expense summary schedule of the short-term model (depicted in appendix 4A) uses cost per ASM as a unit cost basis except for fuel, a separate schedule has been developed to help deal with traffic-related costs when the situation warrants (see table 4A-2 in appendix 4A). Note that traffic-related costs are normally about one-third of the total operating expenses. This is further indication that separate considerations for these costs is necessary when substantial load factor swings are anticipated. Further note that, during the time period shown, traffic was growing at a significantly different rate from capacity.

It is a useful aid to forecasting to examine historical long-term trends in traffic and capacity-related costs. Figure 4-10 illustrates the increases in these costs between 1975 and the third quarter of 1980. Note that in the period 1975 through 1978 traffic-related costs were increasing faster than capacity-related costs. Since 1978, however, capacity-related costs have increased at a much higher rate.

Operating Expense Forecasting

As in the case of revenue forecasting, the process of forecasting operating expense does not end with multiplication of capacity and unit costs. Means of evaluating the reasonableness of the forecast must be found. For this purpose, comparisons of actual load factors with break-even load factors can be helpful.

Break-even load factor, as the name implies, is that load factor which will produce zero profit or loss. A value of break-even load factor is applicable only to a specific period of time, since the value depends on the cost and yield structure of the period for which it is calculated.

In a free-market environment, competition forces prices down. Low yields with respect to cost result in high break-even load factors. In the past, when fares were more rigidly controlled by the CAB, the mechanisms used to determine ceiling fare levels were often not adequate to permit recovery of costs during periods of rapid inflation. That fares were held down relative to costs during these periods is exhibited in abnormally high break-even load factors. As shown in table 4-11, during the 1979-1980 period break-even load factors were at the 60-63 percent level. During much of this period, fuel prices were skyrocketing, fare flexibility was limited to 5 percent upward, and the base fare (SIFL) adjustment method initially adopted by the CAB proved inadequate to permit recovery of increased costs. As a result, industry profits eroded during this period, since the airlines were not able to achieve load factors sufficiently above the very high break-even values even in 1979—a year of relative economic prosperity in the U.S. economy. This illustrates the sensitivity of airline earnings to the spread between break-even and actual load factors. As shown in table 4-12, this sensitivity is steadily increasing, and it is estimated that one percentage point of spread now represents about $450 million in industry operating profit or loss.

For any set of assumptions made to produce an industry financial forecast, an estimate of the resulting break-even load factor can be computed. The actual load factor can also be computed. As a further check on the validity of assumptions, the analyst is compelled to reconcile wide swings in the spread between estimated actual and break-even load factors. Often, a reasonable first assumption to examine is capacity.

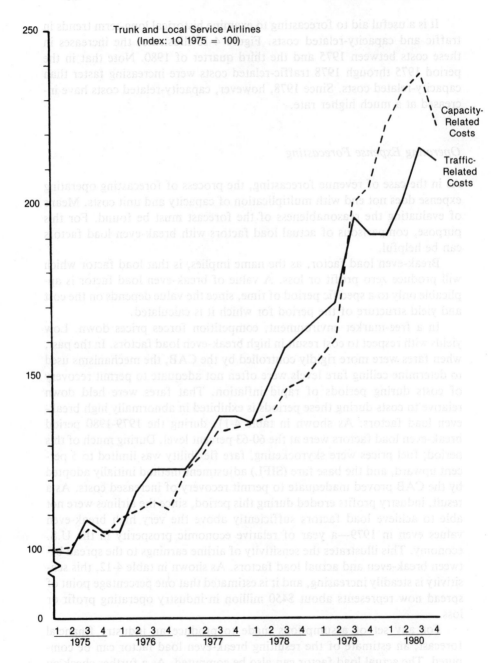

Figure 4-10. Capacity- and Traffic-Related Costs

Table 4-11

Actual and Break-Even Load Factors—Trunk and Local Service Airlines

	Load Factors	
	Actual	*Breakeven*
1978	62.1%	57.8%
1979	63.3	62.8
1980	59.2	59.6

Source: CAB Form 41 and Air Transport Association.

Operating Profit and Net Income

The forecast of operating profit results directly from the difference between forecasts of operating revenue and operating expenses.

The bottom line is not reached, however, with the operating profit forecast. To arrive at a forecast of net income, it is also necessary to forecast interest expense and income, gains or losses on disposal of assets, income taxes, adjustments to revenues and/or expenses from prior years as a result of legal or accounting rulings, and so forth. Table 4-13 shows the major categories of profit for the U.S. trunk and local service airlines in the years 1979 and 1980. One of those categories is nonoperating income expense. The separate components of this category are shown in table 4-14.

Forecasting by Individual Airlines

This chapter has discussed forecasting on an industrywide basis. A similar methodology would be used by individual airlines for their own profit

Table 4-12

Value of One Point in Load Factor to Income before Taxes—Trunk and Local Service Airlines

	Millions of Dollars
1975	$245
1976	270
1977	305
1978	310
1979	350
1980	415
1981 estimated	450

Source: Air Transport Association.

Table 4-13
Income Statement—Trunk and Local Service Airlines
(Thousands)

	Q1 1979	Q2 1979	Q3 1979	Q4 1979	Q1 1980	Q2 1980	Q3 1980	Q4 1980
Operating revenues	$5,570,046	$6,091,275	$7,076,848	$6,726,449	$7,021,523	$7,502,142	$8,240,728	$7,688,862
Operating expenses	5,590,305	5,824,053	6,947,821	6,957,455	7,345,343	7,658,260	8,031,823	7,683,636
Operating profit or loss	(20,259)	267,222	129,027	(231,006)	(323,820)	(156,118)	208,905	5,225
Nonoperating income or expense	12,129	(22,138)	196	35,773	(20,859)	(30,919)	(11,054)	120,370
Income before income taxes and special items	(8,130)	245,084	129,026	(195,233)	(344,679)	(187,037)	197,851	125,595
Income taxes for current period	(5,139)	(67,995)	5,789	(104,065)	(74,908)	(65,378)	38,979	14,819
Income before special items	(2,991)	313,079	123,237	(91,168)	(269,771)	(121,659)	158,872	110,776
Discontinued operations	0	0	0	0	0	0	0	(16,272)
Extraordinary items	0	0	0	(2,249)	0	0	99,254	23,704
Accounting changes	0	18,120	0	0	0	0	(197)	0
Net income	($ 2,991)	$ 331,199	$ 123,237	($ 93,417)	($ 269,771)	($ 121,659)	$ 257,929	$ 150,752

Source: CAB Form 41.
Note: Q1 = First quarter.

Table 4-14
Nonoperating Income or Expense—Trunk and Local Service Airlines
(Thousands)

	Q1 1979	Q2 1979	Q3 1979	Q4 1979	Q1 1980	Q2 1980	Q3 1980	Q4 1980
Interest income	$ 58,411	$ 51,552	$ 66,033	$ 66,536	$ 64,027	$ 59,539	$ 42,634	$ 58,328
Interest on long-term debt	(131,837)	(142,108)	(149,944)	(170,596)	(186,028)	(201,886)	(193,691)	(225,138)
Other interest expense	(6,045)	(8,921)	(6,697)	(4,322)	(10,231)	(14,798)	(11,263)	(21,091)
Capitalized interest	17,005	18,251	17,295	27,727	23,558	23,930	19,731	21,011
Amortization of debt discount, premium and expense	(1,665)	(1,586)	(1,803)	(2,677)	(2,455)	(2,867)	(3,967)	(4,561)
Foreign exchange gains and losses	(2,419)	(7,534)	(1,998)	(3,647)	2,312	(11,465)	(1,689)	(864)
Equity in income of investor-controlled companies	10,392	7,950	6,385	18,232	25,765	12,899	9,737	8,494
Income from nontransport ventures	10,049	10,970	11,778	10,065	9,643	7,457	14,489	11,790
Intercompany transaction adjustment-credit	10	8	2	0	0	0	0	0
Dividend income	543	549	157	733	56	73	5	1
Net unrealized gain or loss on marketable equity securities	0	0	0	0	(1,376)	188	(607)	1,795
Net realized gain or loss on marketable equity securities	(70)	(101)	(78)	19,624	(163)	1,009	169	(1,090)
Capital gains and losses—operating property	23,204	36,527	24,991	61,960	35,849	62,699	93,646	43,175
Capital gains and losses—other	12,891	5,870	37,571	4,224	9,453	23,895	15,142	251,183
Unapplied cash discount	5,896	4,768	5,463	5,368	6,482	7,697	6,475	6,495
Other miscellaneous nonoperating credits	19,871	2,604	1,207	14,609	9,888	6,266	4,231	10,748
Intercompany transaction adjustment	0	0	0	0	0	0	0	0
Other miscellaneous nonoperating debits	(4,108)	(1,619)	(10,353)	(12,072)	(7,640)	(6,101)	(6,096)	(39,905)
Total nonoperating income or expense	$ 12,129	($22,138)	$ 196	$ 35,773	($20,859)	($30,919)	($11,054)	$120,370

Source: CAB Form 41.
Note: Q1 = First quarter.

forecasts. As indicated earlier in this chapter, a principal purpose of a financial forecast is to provide management with a picture of future financial results early enough to permit a change of plans if those anticipated results are unsatisfactory. The operating profit forecast, then, provides a basis for planning; it allows management to reexamine operating plans and ask such questions as:

What effect on profits will there be if we curtail (or expand) capacity by x percent?

Should we introduce new fares—either higher or lower, selectively or across the board?

What new programs can be initiated to stimulate traffic?

Would an aggressive cargo sales campaign help us reduce break-even passenger load factors?

Should we inaugurate service in new markets?

A further use of the operating profit forecast is in preparing and checking short-term budgets to determine that operating expenses as budgeted are in agreement with accepted operating expenses as forecast.

For both individual airline forecasters and industry analysts, modern data processing equipment allows a forecaster to use a complex forecasting model such as the one described in appendix 4A to test the effect on the financial forecast of a large array of operating alternatives.

Notes

1. These include interest income and expense, capital gains and losses on sale of property and equipment, income taxes, accounting changes, and extraordinary items such as gains on exchanges of debentures.

2. The Airline Deregulation Act of 1978 provided for a Domestic Standard Industry Fare Level (SIFL) defined as the fare level in effect on July 1, 1977, to be adjusted not less than semiannually by the change in operating cost per available seat-mile. The Act further provided for use of prospective costs in the SIFL adjustment. An initial zone of flexibility of 5 percent above and 50 percent below the SIFL was established by the Act. In May 1980 the CAB expanded the downward zone to unlimited and the upward zone to unlimited for 0-200 mile markets, 50 percent in the 200-400 mile markets, and 30 percent in markets greater than 400 miles. Later in 1980 the upward zone was revised again, to 30 percent of SIFL + $15. In doing so the CAB stipulated that it would adjust the $15 upward or downward by the

percentage change of periodic SIFL adjustments. On January 1, 1981, the SIFL was adjusted downward by 3.7 percent. Thus the $15 was reduced to $14. In anticipation of substantial increases in fuel prices because of OPEC's actions in December 1980 and President Reagan's decontrol of domestic crude oil prices, the CAB temporarily increased the zone of flexibility to 35 percent of SIFL + $14, although several months later the board returned to the 30 percent level.

3. See chapter 1.

Appendix 4A:
Examples of ATA
Short-Term Forecasting
Model

This appendix contains examples of the short-term forecasting model used at ATA to assist in the development of short-term financial forecasts for the airline industry. The purpose of the model is: (1) to display historical data for airline revenue and expense elements in a fashion convenient for detecting trends, and (2) to provide for rapid calculation of financial results based on input of future assumptions. Items that are boxed in represent the assumptions which need to be made by the forecaster.

The model is a computerized system that computes the effect of assumptions and changes in assumptions. Revising a traffic growth assumption upward, for example, will change the assumption for revenue growth. The computerized model makes these changes automatically, thus allowing a check on assumptions for reasonableness by seeing their effect on all aspects of the forecast.

Revenue Detail Forecasts

As can be observed, the detail forecast shown in table 4A-1 is for major geographic regions. The example shown is for scheduled passenger operations. The model provides also for charter passenger operations and scheduled and charter cargo operations in a similar format. Note that each revenue forecast is the result of separate assumptions made for traffic growth and yield changes.

Capacity and Traffic Expense Summary

The format shown in table 4A-2 separates total operating expenses into those expenses related to the production of capacity and those related to the production of traffic.

Forecast Summaries

Examples of revenue, expense, and operating profit summary forecasts using the short-term model are shown in tables 4A-3 to 4A-5. This format is designed to facilitate forecasts for the current and following years. The example shown is for a forecast made during the fourth quarter of 1980. Note that the actual data for the first three quarters are drawn from the data base and displayed for reference. Assumptions for year-to-year changes of items enclosed in boxes may be made either for the remainder of the year (in this case the fourth quarter of 1980) or for the whole calendar year (1980). If inputs are made for the remainder of the year, the total year data will be calculated based on these inputs. Conversely, if calendar year inputs are made, values for the remainder of the year will be calculated. Once the analyst is satisfied with the current year forecast, inputs for the following year (in this case 1981) can be made and results tested.

Table 4A-1
Operating Revenue Forecast—Scheduled Passenger Services, Trunks and Locals

	Q4 1979	Q1 1980	Q2 1980	Q3 1980	Forecast 1980	Year 1980	Forecast 1981	Year 1981
Forty-eight state traffic								
RPMs (million)	43,361	43,242	43,961	46,280		173,997		165,819
Percent change	6.24	(0.736)	(4.54)	(9.17)	(5.40)		(4.70)	
¢/RPM	10.50	11.29	11.67	11.83		11.97		14.13
Percent change	18.05	31.17	31.31	30.81	29.50		18.00	
Revenue (millions of dollars)	4,552	4,882	5,131	5,475		20,830		23,424
Percent change	25.41	30.20	25.34	18.82	22.51		12.45	
Mainland-Hawaii traffic								
RPMs (million)	3,524	3,481	3,454	3,804		13,865		13,727
Percent change	0.603	(7.27)	2.24	(16.96)	(9.00)		(1.00)	
¢/RPM	5.11	5.92	6.08	6.06		6.14		7.19
Percent change	10.46	28.83	28.40	26.80	28.00		17.00	
Revenue (millions of dollars)	180	206	210	230		852		987
Percent change	11.13	19.46	31.27	5.30	16.48		15.83	
Other domestic traffic								
RPMs (million)	330	329	286	374		1,223		1,210
Percent change	(5.24)	1.67	(12.18)	(21.50)	(16.00)		(1.00)	
¢/RPM	6.32	5.06	7.50	7.63		6.31		6.94
Percent change	5.38	(13.92)	9.78	26.11	1.00		10.00	
Revenue (millions of dollars)	20.85	16.63	21.45	28.58		77.17		84.04
Percent change	(0.145)	(12.49)	(3.59)	(1.00)	(15.16)		8.90	

Foreign traffic						
RPMs (million)	12,126	11,586	13,577	16,393	52,994	51,934
Percent change	12.12	8.33	0.902	(1.63)	**0.100**	**(2.00)**
¢/RPM	8.27	8.56	8.60	9.12	9.00	10.44
Percent change	9.18	11.99	18.28	19.38	**17.00**	**16.00**
Revenue (millions of dollars)	1,002	992	1,168	1,495	4,768	5,421
Percent change	22.42	21.32	19.35	17.44	17.12	13.68
System traffic totals						
RPMs (million)	59,340	58,638	61,278	66,851	242,079	232,690
Percent change	6.96	0.519	(3.06)	(8.01)	(4.53)	(3.88)
¢/RPM	9.70	10.40	10.66	10.81	10.96	12.86
Percent change	16.19	27.46	28.21	28.23	26.89	17.32
Revenue (millions of dollars)	5,755	6,097	6,531	7,228	26,527	29,915
Percent change	24.27	28.12	24.28	17.96	21.15	12.77

Source: Airline Analytical Information Management System/CAB Form 41.

Table 4A-2
Operating Expense Forecast, by Capacity and Traffic Expense, Trunks and Locals

	Q4 1979	Q1 1980	Q2 1980	Q3 1980	Historical or 1980 Growth	1980 Forecast	1981 Growth	1981 Forecast
Total Capacity Expense								
ASM	105,020,777	104,505,633	105,061,148	109,407,600	1.3	415,934,611	(2.0)	407,615,919
Percent change	7.0	5.0	12.1	(2.6)				
ATM (freighter)	779,991	659,232	712,248	707,290	(5.0)	2,725,675	0.0	2,725,703
Percent change	(0.7)	(4.1)	11.8	(7.5)				
Total equivalent ASM	108,764,734	107,669,947	108,479,938	112,802,592	1.1	429,017,853	(1.9)	420,699,292
Percent change	6.7	4.7	12.1	(2.8)				
Labor expense	1,849,090	1,955,640	1,979,419	2,027,478	12.9	7,937,062	7.4	8,522,565
Percent change	15.8	14.0	20.3	11.4				
Labor expense/equivalent ASM	17.0	18.2	18.2	18.0	11.5	18.5	9.5	20.3
Percent change	8.5	8.9	7.3	14.6				
Fuel expense	1,955,434	2,196,450	2,321,566	2,443,569	45.6	8,997,078	14.7	10,322,473
Percent change	87.1	99.6	86.1	30.3				
Fuel expense/equivalent ASM	18.0	20.4	21.4	21.7	45.3	21.0	17.0	24.5
Percent change	75.3	90.6	66.1	34.0				
Other capacity expense	712,796	751,193	767,028	763,298	11.5	3,038,956	7.9	3,278,035
Percent change	8.6	16.7	15.7	8.0				
Other capacity expense/ equivalent ASM	6.6	7.0	7.1	6.8	10.0	7.1	10.0	7.8
Percent change	1.7	11.4	3.2	11.1				
Total capacity expense	4,517,320	4,903,283	5,068,013	5,234,345	25.3	19,973,096	10.8	22,123,072
Percent change	36.9	41.8	42.5	18.9				
Total capacity expense/ equivalent ASM	41.5	45.5	46.7	46.4	24.3	46.6	13.0	52.6
Percent change	28.3	35.4	27.2	22.3				

Total Traffic Expense

RPM	60,699,466	59,755,126	62,988,189	67,863,564	248,933,939	238,976,581
Percent change	5.7	(0.7)	(2.6)	(8.6)	(4.2)	(4.0)
RTM (freighter)	444,295	357,467	383,308	401,163	1,694,525	1,694,542
Percent change	(6.1)	(9.4)	(4.4)	(11.8)	0.0	0.0
Total equivalent RPM	62,832,082	61,470,968	64,828,067	69,789,146	257,067,658	247,110,382
Percent change	5.3	(1.0)	(2.7)	(8.7)	(4.1)	(3.9)
Labor expense	803,296	820,918	832,690	858,716	3,426,149	3,622,784
Percent change	12.4	9.1	8.1	6.6	9.4	5.7
Labor expense/equivalent RPM	12.8	13.4	12.8	12.3	13.3	14.7
Percent change	6.8	10.2	11.0	16.8	13.4	10.0
Other traffic expense	1,489,105	1,477,815	1,587,471	1,758,933	6,640,041	7,659,414
Percent change	19.3	17.7	17.4	12.3	17.3	15.4
Other traffic expense/ equivalent RPM	23.7	24.0	24.5	25.2	25.8	31.0
Percent change	13.3	18.9	20.7	23.1	22.0	20.0
Total traffic expense	2,292,401	2,298,733	2,420,161	2,617,649	10,066,190	11,282,199
Percent change	16.8	14.5	14.0	10.4	14.5	12.1
Total traffic expense/ equivalent RPM	36.5	37.4	37.3	37.5	39.2	45.7
Percent change	10.9	15.6	17.2	20.9	18.9	16.6

Transport-Related Expense

Total transportation related	147,733	143,327	170,085	179,828	662,985	742,543
Percent change	7.6	15.9	16.5	3.0	12.0	12.0

Total Operating Expense

Total operating expense	6,957,455	7,345,343	7,658,260	8,031,823	30,702,271	34,147,814
Percent change	28.9	31.4	31.5	15.6	21.3	11.2

Source: AAIMSΔII/CAB Form 41.
Note: Expenses per unit traffic or capacity are expressed in $/unit (000).

Table 4A-3
Operating Revenue Forecast for Trunks and Locals

	1979 Calendar Year	Last Four Quarter PCT Change	Year thru Q3 1980	1980 Remainder of Year	1980 Calendar Year	1981 Calendar Year
Scheduled passenger						
RPMs (millions)	253562.03		187518.83	55393.59	242912.43	233195.93
Percent change		−1.14	−3.45	−6.65	−4.20	−4.00
Cents/RPM	8.63		10.59	11.86	10.88	12.84
Percent change		24.70	27.41	22.38	26.00	18.00
$ revenue (millions)	21894.20		19856.11	6571.94	26428.06	29937.69
Percent change		23.28	23.01	14.24	20.71	13.28
Charter passenger						
RPMs (millions)	6285.76		3093.09	866.94	3960.03	2772.02
Percent change		−35.09	−37.21	−36.24	−37.00	−30.00
Cents/RPM	5.41		7.02	8.22	7.28	8.95
Percent change		30.98	34.12	35.45	34.50	23.00
$ revenue (millions)	340.21		217.05	71.23	288.28	248.21
Percent change		−14.98	−15.79	−13.63	−15.27	−13.90
Cargo revenue						
RTMs (millions)	5316.55		3803.69	1353.36	5157.05	5157.10
Percent change		−2.04	−2.80	−3.55	−3.00	0.0
Cents/RTM	39.86		45.49	47.59	46.04	52.95
Percent change		14.84	16.27	13.53	15.50	15.00
$ revenue (millions)	2119.44		1730.48	644.04	2374.52	2730.72
Percent change		12.50	13.01	9.49	12.03	15.00

Other revenues

$ total (millions)	1127.20	960.75	335.53	1296.28	1555.53
Percent change	21.90	18.97	4.97	15.00	20.00

Total operating revenue

$ total (millions)	25481.05	22764.39	7622.73	30387.12	34472.16
Percent change	21.76	21.49	13.01	19.25	13.44

Table 4A-4
Operating Expense Forecast for Trunks and Locals

	1979 Calendar Year	Last Four Quarter PCT Change	1980 Year thru Q3 1980	1980 Remainder of Year	1980 Calendar Year	1981 Calendar Year
Equivalent ASMs						
ASMs (millions)	410594.28		318974.38	96957.63	415932.01	407613.37
Percent change		5.02	4.39	-7.68	1.30	-2.00
Freighter ATMs (millions)	2869.03		2078.80	646.78	2725.58	2725.60
Percent change		-0.55	0.49	-17.08	-5.00	0.0
Equivalent ASMs (millions)	424365.62		328952.61	100062.17	429014.78	420696.27
Percent change		4.84	4.23	-8.00	1.10	-1.94
Labor expense						
Cents per equivalent ASM	2.30		2.47	2.72	2.53	2.77
Percent change		7.91	8.07	16.44	10.00	9.50
Total labor (millions)	9749.14		8114.94	2726.60	10841.54	11641.30
Percent change		13.13	12.65	7.13	11.21	7.38
Fuel expense						
Cents per gallon	57.79		88.32	91.30	89.00	110.36
Percent change		71.12	57.93	24.28	54.00	24.00
Equivalent ASMs per gallon	39.70		41.74	43.24	42.08	44.60
Percent change		5.99	6.17	5.83	6.00	6.00
Cents per equivalent ASM	1.46		2.12	2.11	2.12	2.47
Percent change		61.46	58.17	17.44	45.28	16.98
Total fuel expense (millions)	6178.21		6961.59	2112.64	9074.23	10409.31
Percent change		69.27	64.86	8.04	46.87	14.71
Total gallons (millions)	10690.49		7881.87	2313.98	10195.86	9432.23
Percent change		-1.08	-1.83	-13.07	-4.63	-7.49

Other expense

Cents per equivalent ASM	2.07	2.27	2.58	2.34	2.65
Percent change	9.77	10.34	21.81	13.00	13.00
Total other expense (millions)	8795.13	7465.66	2581.72	10047.38	11133.40
Percent change	15.08	15.01	12.06	14.24	10.81

Transport related

Total transport related (millions)	609.39	493.24	170.99	664.23	743.94
Percent change	13.21	11.04	3.52	9.00	12.00

Total operating expenses

Total operating expenses (millions)	25331.87	23035.43	7591.96	30627.38	33927.95
Percent change	28.27	25.45	8.93	20.90	10.78

Table 4A-5
Operating Profit Forecast for Trunks and Locals

	1979 Calendar Year	Last Four Quarter Change	Year thru Q3 1980	1980 Remainder of Year	Calendar Year	1981 Calendar Year
Operating profit (millions)	149.18		−271.03	30.77	−240.26	544.21
Dollar change		−970.13	−647.02	255.08	−389.44	784.47

**Part II
Recent Developments in the
Airline Industry and the
Outlook for the Future**

5

The Airline Fuel Crisis of the 1970s

Kathleen O. Argiropoulos

7230
6150
US

The economic importance of jet fuel to the airline industry has increased tremendously in the past decade, marked by its change from an inexpensive and readily available commodity to a high-priced one whose availability is uncertain, depending to a great extent on unpredictable international economic and political conditions. This chapter describes the nature of the jet fuel crisis and outlines the changes in the airline industry it has caused and will cause in the future.

What Is Jet Fuel?

Kerosene-based jet fuel (kerojet), along with naphtha-based jet fuel, diesel fuel, home heating oil, and kerosene, is a middle distillate product. During the refining process, crude oil is converted into various petroleum products, and middle distillates, as the name implies, include those products whose boiling range is in the middle of the product spectrum—above motor gasoline and below residual fuel oil. Middle distillates account for approximately 22 percent of refinery yield. Only about 4.5 percent, however, is processed and sold as kerosene-based jet fuel, although from a molecular point of view all the distillates are similar, and approximately 10 percent of each barrel is capable of being converted into kerojet.

Kerojet has a kerosene base that is produced by simple distillation. Several additional processes are required to produce aviation-quality jet fuel according to applicable specifications.

The overwhelming majority of kerojet, 86 percent, is used by the commerical airlines. General aviation and the military each accounts for about 5.5 percent. The remaining 3 percent is used by aircraft manufacturers and electric utilities, the latter turning to kerojet when it is more abundant and/or less expensive than alternative fuels. The similarity among middle distillates makes conversion quite simple; in fact, it is possible to interchange certain distillates—for example, jet fuel can be sold and used as heating oil.

In 1979 supplies of kerosene-based jet fuel accounted for close to 5 percent of the U.S. petroleum supply, with the bulk of kerojet supplies, 93 percent, coming from domestic refiners, although not necessarily from domestic crude oil sources.

99

Figures 5-1 to 5-4 depict the importance of airline fuel in the U.S. transportation picture.

The Recent History: 1973-1980

For many years, jet fuel prices were stable and low. Between 1967 and 1972, fuel prices rose at an annual rate of only 2.6 percent. Prices rose 8.5 percent between 1972 and 1973, to a 1973 average of 12.8 cents a gallon. The 1973 oil embargo, however, marked the real beginning of the fuel problem. Between 1973 and 1974, the average price rose from 12.8 cents to 24.2 cents per gallon, an increase of nearly 90 percent in a single year. The rise in prices continued throughout the decade, with jet fuel costs increasing approximately 600 percent between 1973 and 1980. That price increases were not uniform from year to year, but occurred in sporadic, spectacular fashion, led to serious problems within the industry.

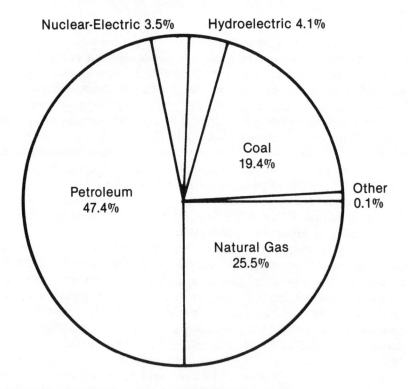

Source: FAA, *Aviation Energy Conservation Policy*, January 1981.
Note: 1979 percentages.
Figure 5-1. Total U.S. Energy Consumption, by Type of Energy

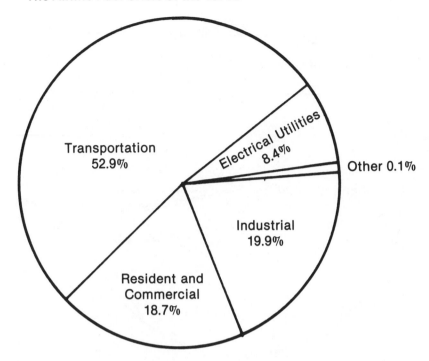

Source: FAA, *Aviation Energy Conservation Policy*, January 1981.
Note: 1979 estimated data by percent.
Figure 5-2. Use of Petroleum Products, by Major Sectors of the Economy

The discrepancy between domestic and international prices in table 5-1 reflects the U.S. regulatory structure existing during the 1970s, which maintained average domestic crude oil and refined petroleum product prices at levels below the world price. The existence of such controls had a significant effect on the price and availability of crude and petroleum products.

On April 5, 1979, President Carter introduced a program of phased decontrol of crude oil prices that was to be completed by September 30, 1981. As a result of this program, by mid-1980 about 70 percent of the crude oil used to make jet fuel in U.S. refineries was free from direct government price controls. By January 1, 1981, controls applied to only about 15 percent of the crude oil used to make jet fuel in the United States. Nevertheless, over the years crude oil price controls did mitigate the effects of the price increases by Organization of Petroleum Exporting Countries (OPEC) since domestic suppliers were required to pass through the average cost of the mix between controlled and uncontrolled crude oil in sales to their customers.

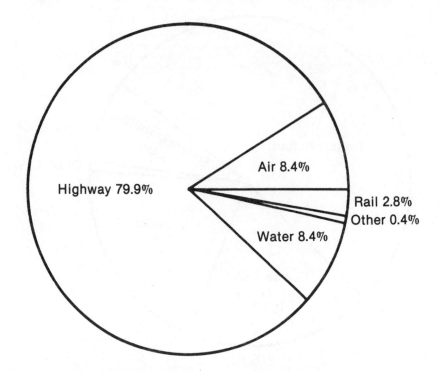

Source: FAA, *Aviation Energy Conservation Policy*, January 1981.
Note: 1980 estimated data by percent.
Figure 5-3. Transportation Petroleum Consumption, by Mode

On January 28, 1981, however, President Reagan removed all price controls on crude oil, thereby allowing the price to move toward the level of imported crude—at the time ranging between $37 and $38/barrel.[1]

As noted previously, kerosene-based jet fuel was also subject to federal price and allocation controls. These controls were removed in late February 1979.[2]

Subsequent to the removal of price and allocation controls from jet fuel, the major jet fuel suppliers began in 1979 (the year of the Iranian revolution) to allocate fuel because of reduced supplies. In addition to impeding the operation of normal schedules, the fuel allocations tempered the vigorous expansion of routes that was occurring in the wake of the Airline Deregulation Act of 1978.[3] Moreover, airlines that did expand routes were forced at times during 1979 into the spot market for fuel, thus exacerbating the already serious problem of skyrocketing prices. These refiner-imposed allocations continued until the first quarter of 1980. Even after allocations per se disappeared, however, new contracts offered by major suppliers in

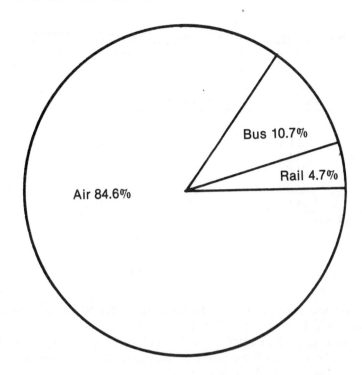

Source: FAA, *Aviation Energy Conservation Policy*, January 1981.
Note: 1979 passenger-miles.
Figure 5-4. Distribution of Intercity Passenger Travel, by Common Carrier

late 1979 and early 1980 were for volumes tied to historic quantities and did not generally provide for growth.

An important element in fuel availability at this time was the design of the jet fuel distribution system. First and most important, the distribution system was designed during an era when oil was plentiful. Storage facilities for kerojet were minimal, so disruptions in supply had a severe impact on availability of fuel at airports. A second problem was that the fuel distribution facilities were principally owned by private, nonairline corporations, except at the airports, where they were generally owned by public airport authorities and financed indirectly by the airlines through landing fees and rental charges. Even at the airports, actual delivery of fuel into the aircraft was often handled by service companies under contract with the airlines. In sum the airlines were not vertically integrated to ensure continuous fuel supply. It is this area that poses the most significant energy challenge to the air carriers in the 1980s.

Table 5-1
Average Price per Gallon of Airline Fuel—U.S. Scheduled Airlines

Year	Domestic	International	Total	Percent Increase over Prior Year
1973	12.6¢	13.6¢	12.8¢	8.5%
1974	21.8	33.6	24.2	89.0
1975	27.5	35.8	29.1	20.2
1976	30.5	36.7	31.6	8.6
1977	35.3	40.1	36.3	14.9
1978	38.6	42.5	39.2	8.0
1979	56.4	63.4	57.8	47.4
1980	86.5	101.7	89.2	54.3

Source: CAB data.

The Impact of Fuel Price Increases on the Industry

As we have seen, the price of jet fuel shot up about 600 percent between 1973 and 1980. This had an extraordinary impact on airline expenses. The airlines' total fuel bill in 1980 was $10.1 billion, compared with only $1.4 billion in 1973. On a daily basis, the airlines spent $27.6 million for fuel in 1980, compared with $3.7 million in 1973.

Some of the increased outlays for fuel were because of increased fuel purchases for expanded service (76 billion additional revenue passenger-miles were flown in 1980 compared with 1973). Nevertheless, price increases alone accounted for a considerable portion of the jump in annual fuel costs between 1973 and 1980. At the 11 billion gallons per year consumption level of 1980, a fuel price increase of 1 cent per gallon translates into an industry cost increase of about $110 million a year.

One important implication of the rise in fuel prices and the related jump in airline costs has been the need for increases in airline ticket prices. In real terms, airline fares have fallen consistently over the past twenty-five years (see figure 1-1 in chapter 1).

However, the large increases in fuel costs in recent years have strained the ability of the airlines to offer fares reflecting decreases in real terms. In 1980, for the first time, fares increased in real terms. Should this continue, it will have a profound effect on the airline industry's marketing environment. For many years the airlines have enjoyed significant yearly traffic growth, in part because of declining real fares. If real fares rise in the future, the airlines will face a difficult challenge in maintaining historical traffic growth trends. This may loom in the long run as one of the most serious effects of the fuel crisis.

An equally important effect of the rise in fuel prices has been a sharp change in the breakdown of airline costs. In 1969 the airlines spent a total of about $1 billion on fuel; by 1980 this had increased 900 percent to over $10 billion. In the same period all other airline operating costs grew only 221 percent. The result is a markedly greater role for fuel costs in total airline costs, with fuel costs rising from 14 percent of total cash expenses (including interest) in 1969, to 31 percent of total expenses in 1980.

The corollary to this development is a new relationship between fixed and variable costs. Of course, these categories are somewhat imprecise, as all costs are variable in the long run. If one looks just at the cost category flying operations as embodying variable costs, however, it is possible to see how the economics of the airlines have changed.[4] In 1969 flying operations represented 29 percent of total airline cost; by 1980, that percentage had risen to 41.5 percent. The implication is that the traditional view of the airlines as a high fixed cost industry will have to be revised, especially by airline managements themselves.

Variation in Fuel Prices among Carriers and Regulatory Limitations

A significant cost-recovery problem arose with respect to fuel expenditures during the era (pre-1979) of strict airline fare and rate regulation by the Civil Aeronautics Board (CAB). Fuel prices paid by individual carriers often varied from the industry average, as shown in figure 5-5, but the CAB established industry fares and rates on the basis of average costs.

Variations in fuel costs arose for several reasons. Rapidly expanding carriers facing fuel availability problems ventured into the spot market and found high prices. Suppliers, of course, charged different prices, and, since major suppliers were unwilling to accept new customers during shortage periods, airlines with high-cost suppliers could not readily switch to low-cost suppliers. Finally, fuel prices varied from city to city, so airlines with certain route systems faced higher prices than others.

As a consequence of these unstable supply conditions and regulatory prohibitions, airlines paying higher-than-average fuel prices were restricted from setting passenger fares above the CAB's standard. Those airlines whose costs were above the industry average were thus forced to maintain fares based on costs considerably lower than their own. On those routes where all carriers faced high fuel costs, no carrier could charge prices high enough to reflect its higher-than-industry-average costs. Moreover, adjustment of the standard fare always proceeded more slowly than the increase in fuel prices, so all carriers faced a cost-price squeeze caused by regulatory lag. The volatility and variability of fuel costs among carriers thus seriously

Airline Economics

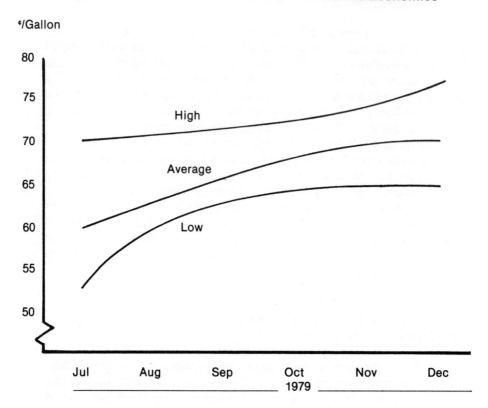

Source: CAB Form 41.

Figure 5-5. Range of Fuel Prices

strained the CAB's system of setting industry fares on an average cost basis. This situation was ameliorated somewhat by a CAB order in 1980 that allowed more responsive upward-fare flexibility by the airlines. Nevertheless, fuel price variability will continue to be a problem as long as the air carriers are subject to government fare and rate restrictions.

Industry Changes in Response to the Fuel Crisis

Confronted with rising fuel costs, the airlines have strived to improve fuel efficiency. During recent years, the airlines have become increasingly more efficient in their use of petroleum resources through operational improvements and the use of more fuel-efficient aircraft. Between 1973 and 1979 the number of airline passengers transported yearly increased about 56 percent to over 300 million in 1979, while airline fuel consumption increased only about 5 percent.

There are two ways to measure the fuel efficiency of passenger aircraft: by available seat-miles per gallon (ASMs/gallon) and by revenue passenger-miles per gallon (RPMs/gallon).[5] ASMs/gallon is a more precise measure, since it is not influenced by fluctuations in traffic, as is the case in RPMs/gallon measurements. ASMs/gallon is influenced, however, by the number of seats in the aircraft. The airlines have taken a number of steps to increase ASMs/gallon since fuel prices have risen, including:

1. Increased seating density and use of larger aircraft. The number of seats per aircraft has risen about 21 percent between 1973 and 1980.
2. Reducing cruise speed. A few miles-per-hour reduction in speed extends a flight only a few minutes, but results in significant fuel savings. For example, reducing the speed of a jet from 520 to 500 miles per hour on a 500 mile flight reduces fuel consumption by 7 percent.
3. Expanding use of flight simulators. This eliminates thousands of training flights per year.
4. Increasing the use of computerized flight planning. This permits selection of altitudes that results in the consumption of the minimum amount of fuel.
5. Developing sophisticated monitoring systems to identify aircraft that may be using excess fuel.
6. Shutting down one or more engines during taxiing before takeoff and after landing.
7. Reducing aircraft weight. Airlines have reduced the amount of paint on their aircraft (several hundred pounds per plane), lightened carpets and furnishings, and so on.
8. Reducing "tankering," the practice of carrying more fuel on board than is necessary for a segment to avoid refueling (with attendant ground costs) before flying the second segment of a flight.
9. Increasing the use of more fuel-efficient two- and three-engine aircraft (where applicable) instead of four-engine planes. The greater fuel efficiency of these jets is illustrated in figure 5-6.

The Federal Aviation Administration (FAA) has also taken steps to promote reduced fuel consumption. The FAA has authority over the air traffic control system, which controls airport arrivals and departures, cruise altitudes, and other variables important to airline fuel efficiency.

One major factor in airline fuel consumption is delay in aircraft departure/arrival at airports, and the FAA has instituted measures to reduce unnecessary delays. A related FAA measure is a gate-hold program. An airplane preparing for departure has its power supplied by an auxiliary power unit (APU) instead of by its own engines. APUs burn less fuel than jet engines. By holding planes at the gate (where they are powered by APUs)

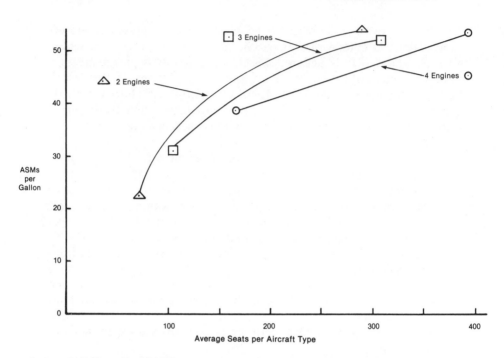

Source: CAB Form 41 and ATA.

Figure 5-6. Fuel Consumption, by Aircraft Size and Number of Engines

until they have clear access to a runway, the FAA seeks to reduce long lines of aircraft waiting for takeoff and thereby to conserve significant quantities of fuel.

The result of airline-initiated and FAA-initiated fuel conservation measures has been an increase in ASMs/gallon of about 27 percent between 1973 and 1980, as shown in figure 5-7.

RPMs/gallon is another measure of fuel efficiency. Its chief drawback is its sensitivity to airline load factors (RPMs/ASMs). If load factors increase, then RPMs/gallon increase as well. Load factors have risen in response to, among other factors, fuel price increases—that is, such increases have forced curtailment of marginal flights, thereby raising overall load factors. Figure 5-8 depicts how RPMs/gallon have increased since 1973, notwithstanding the slight dip in 1980 as the recession cut into traffic and hence load factors. Figure 5-9 sums up the effects of rising fuel price and increased fuel efficiency by depicting cost per gallon, and cost per ASM and RPM.

Fuel Availability

In addition to conserving fuel, the airlines have moved to take more control over their fuel supplies, both to ensure future availability and to hold the

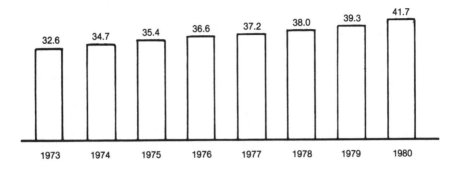

Source: CAB Form 41.
Figure 5-7 Available Seat-Miles per Gallon

line on price increases. Some of these efforts have been on an individual carrier basis, although many involve consortiums of airlines working together. In September 1979, for example, the CAB approved formation of a joint venture called the Airline Fuel Corporation (AFCO), whose purposes include common ownership of storage and distribution facilities.[6] In addition, in at least fifteen cities various carriers have joined together to secure storage facilities on or near airports and/or to finance construction of pipelines that supply them or to secure optimal dedication of existing pipelines. This should make the airlines much more independent should fuel availability problems develop in the future.

A second approach taken by many airlines has been increasing the number of refiners from whom they buy fuel. This involves cultivating many independent refiners which in the past were not involved in the jet fuel business. Buying fuel from many different suppliers decreases the possibility that problems with a major supplier will critically affect an airline's operations.

The final move is the most direct of all: actual vertical integration. At least two airlines have formed wholly owned subsidiaries devoted to energy exploration. If these ventures succeed, they may provide in-house supplies of fuel that will help keep costs down as well as ensure that the airlines will have the fuel they need to operate.

Fuel supplies are likely to remain somewhat precarious for some time to come, although recent technological developments offer the possibility that new sources of refiner-grade crude may be found. The high cost of fuel has made more elaborate oil recovery cost effective, so some wells previously considered depleted may again become operational. Production of synthetic fuels may also become economically justifiable.

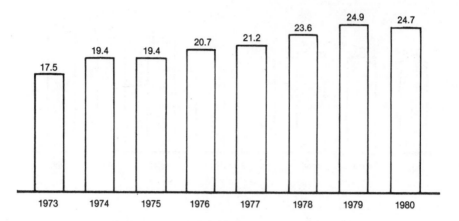

Source: CAB Form 41.

Figure 5-8. Revenue Passenger-Miles per Gallon

Major areas of technological interest are liquid hydrogen from water and/or coal, liquid methane from coal, and jet fuel from shale oil. However, an immediate replacement for Jet-A (the standard fuel for non-military jet aircraft) on a commercial scale is not available, nor can it be expected in large quantities for a number of years.

The technology that appears most promising today as a source of jet fuel is that of coal liquification and shale oil production. Pilot plants for the liquification of coal are currently in operation and under construction, and the characteristics of coal liquids are well known. Since these liquids are low in hydrogen content, additional hydrogen must be added in the refining process to produce a suitable jet fuel.

The technology for the extraction of oil from shale is currently well developed and produces a shale oil that is an excellent refinery feed stock for the production of jet fuel. The major problems to be overcome are primarily environmental and economic.

Conclusion

The jet fuel crisis of the 1970s was a watershed for the airline industry. Coinciding as it did with the deregulation of domestic aviation, the sudden problem of skyrocketing fuel prices and uncertain availability transformed the industry. Three major effects of the fuel crisis have already developed

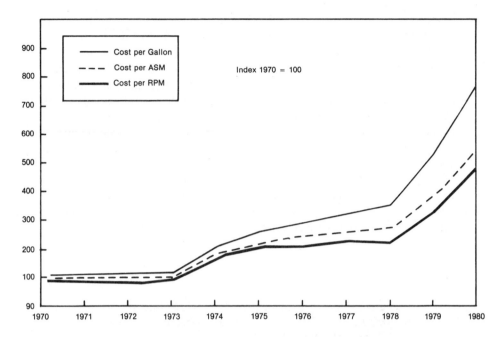

Source: Lehman Brothers, Kuhn, Loeb (Air Transport Association data).
Figure 5-9. Trend in Fuel Indexes, 1970-1980

and will likely continue through the 1980s, particularly if fuel prices continue to rise dramatically.

First, fares have risen sharply, due primarily to the cost of fuel. In 1980 for the first time in decades the price of air transportation rose faster than the Consumer Price Index. Should these fare increases continue, they would undoubtedly have an effect on traffic growth.

Second, the high cost of fuel has made many older aircraft, particularly four-engine planes, uneconomical to operate. Although these aircraft are by no means too old to fly, they were designed for an era of inexpensive fuel and are much too expensive to operate profitably today. Moreover, many airplanes that can be maintained economically in fleets nevertheless require expensive engine retrofitting and other improvements to be cost effective. Thus the increases in fuel costs have created a sudden and unexpected need for large capital investment in fuel-efficient aircraft, and have led some airlines into difficult financial positions as they are forced to operate uneconomical aircraft while awaiting delivery of the new, more modern jets that should enter the fleet in the mid-1980s.

Third, the increasing cost of fuel has changed the basic economics of the industry and forced airline managements to reconsider traditional operating strategies. In the past, fuel and other direct operating costs have been relatively low, while depreciation, interest on long-term debt, and other fixed costs, have been relatively high. This meant that the load factors necessary to cover cash costs were fairly low, even while the fully allocated break-even cost was high. In this context of low marginal costs and high fixed costs it was economically rational to operate aircraft as intensively as possible, because as long as a flight could cover its low cash operating expense, it could generate some revenue to apply toward depreciation and interest expense. Thus high aircraft utilization was an unquestioned part of good airline management.

Now that fuel is so expensive, cash operating expenses have increased dramatically. Load factors high enough to cover marginal costs are now more difficult to achieve—and flights must be carefully scheduled to avoid falling below break-even levels even for cash costs alone.

Notes

1. Executive Order 12287, 46 *Fed. Reg.* 9909 (January 30, 1981).
2. 44 *Fed. Reg.* 7070 (Feb. 5, 1979; for effectiveness, Feb. 26, 1979).
3. Pub. L 95-504, Oct. 24, 1978.
4. Flying operations include fuel, flight crew salaries, direct maintenance, depreciation, and insurance. Other expenses required to run an airline, such as aircraft handling and servicing, traffic servicing (including ticketing), advertising and promotion, and general management, are *not* included.
5. For freighter aircraft the relevant measures are available ton-miles per gallon (ATMs/gallon) and revenue ton-miles per gallon (RTMs/gallon). Increases in these have paralleled increases in ASMs/gallon and RPMs/gallon.
6. CAB Order 79-9-120, dated September 20, 1979.

6

The Challenge of Capital Acquisition in the 1980s

6150
5220
US

Lee R. Howard,
Carl D. Hart, and
Raymond T. Glembocki

Long-term planning for capital needs is a necessity in most businesses, but few industries face more needs and uncertainties for long-term planning than the airlines. The continued market growth that is expected over the next decade will require increases in the size of airline fleets. At the same time, much of the present fleet requires modernization and will need to be replaced within the next ten years. Compounding the problem is the explosive rise in fuel prices that has rendered even some relatively new aircraft uneconomical and hastened their replacement by aircraft incorporating the latest fuel-saving technology.

There is typically a long lead time between ordering and the delivery of aircraft. The airlines must order planes today that are still on the drawing board if they are to have fleets sufficiently large and sufficiently economical to be successful in the 1980s. To do so, they must do a significant amount of long-term capital planning.

The great importance of long-range capital planning derives from the cost structure of the industry. Since the airlines have higher fixed costs than most industries, capital planning is crucial to profitability. It is difficult to adjust to unanticipated drops in demand because in the short to medium run the capital stock is fixed, and the cost of that capital is a large proportion of total costs. In periods of overcapacity, then, the airlines cannot easily reduce costs to compensate for falling demand, and losses are likely to occur.

Long-term planning is not insulated from short-term considerations. As the operating climate changes, so will the long-term forecast. In 1976 the Air Transport Association (ATA) carried out a study of airline capital requirements and concluded that a total investment of $60 billion would be needed for the 1980s. By 1979 traffic had grown faster than expected and aircraft prices had rocketed to new levels, suggesting that the 1976 report needed to be revised.

The ATA undertook a new study in 1979 that determined airline capital requirements through the 1980s to be about $90 billion in current dollars, including $83 billion for passenger aircraft and related ground property and equipment, and $7 billion for freighter aircraft. To put these figures in perspective, consider that the price paid for all airline flight equipment and related ground equipment in use today was only about $27 billion. Thus the new capital investment necessary before 1990 is equivalent to reproducing the current fleet three times over.

This chapter addresses two factors. First, it looks into the method employed in forecasting capital needs to give the reader a sense of the considerations involved in long-term capital planning. Second, the specific conclusions of the 1979 ATA capital requirements study are presented, and the ramifications for the industry are analyzed.

Determining Capital Requirements

Two primary factors determine the demand for capital investment in the airline industry: traffic growth and aircraft replacement. All else being equal, generally when traffic grows capacity grows as well, which means additional aircraft must be purchased. Aircraft must also be purchased to replace those which are old and uneconomical to operate.[1] In addition, many airplanes are now facing retirement before the end of their normal operating life because they are uneconomical to operate with expensive fuel (like old automobiles, old planes were not designed with fuel economy in mind), or because federal noise restrictions will disallow their use after 1985.

Traffic growth and the need to replace aircraft are the primary factors influencing capital investment, but other considerations are important as well. In particular, passenger load factors, aircraft utilization rates, and average seating densities affect capital requirements. An increase in average passenger load factors, hours of aircraft utilization per day, or average seating density would accommodate some traffic growth without additional aircraft. However, these methods of handling new traffic without new aircraft are limited.

Load factors can rise only so far before service to passengers is seriously disrupted by the lack of available seats.[2] The only way to maintain high load factors while avoiding such shortages of available seats is to match closely capacity to accommodate hourly, weekly, and seasonal variation in demand.

Generally when traffic grows new aircraft must be purchased. However, estimating the number of new aircraft to be purchased depends on assumptions regarding load factors, aircraft utilization, and seating density. Finally, and most important, traffic growth itself must be forecast, and this is difficult.

To determine airline capital requirements in the 1980s, the following assumptions were used in the ATA study conducted in 1979.

Passenger Needs

Annual Passenger Traffic Growth Rate of 7 Percent. In the three years 1976 through 1978 annual passenger traffic growth averaged 11 percent. During the first six months of 1979, this high growth rate continued, with the average annual growth rate being 15.6 percent. Although traffic softened somewhat in the second half of the year, experience suggests that downturns in airline traffic are short, so the forecast relied less on current data and more on the growth rate for several years prior to the study.

Passenger Load Factor of 63 Percent. Prior to 1974 the annual load factor generally fluctuated between 50 and 55 percent. In 1978, for the first time in the ten-year period, the annual load factor exceedced 60 percent, finally reaching 61 percent for the year. While the 63 percent long-term factor assumed in the study is higher than has been attained in a single year throughout the past ten-year period, continued public acceptance of the new and varied off-peak discount fares should produce future load factors above 60 percent.

Aircraft Utilization Rate of 9.5 Hours per Day. Aircraft utilization increased from 8.3 hours per day in 1975 to 9 hours in 1978 in part because of better scheduling to meet rising demand and increased cost pressures. The Deregulation Act of 1978 permits carriers to more easily acquire new routes that complement their existing systems and help maintain a high rate of utilization.

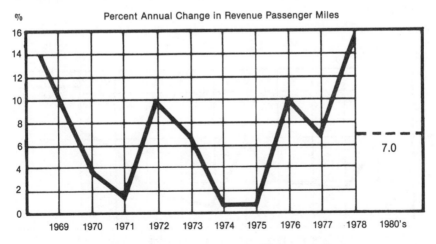

Figure 6-1. Passenger Traffic Growth Rate

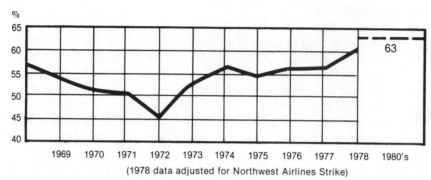

(1978 data adjusted for Northwest Airlines Strike)

Figure 6-2. Passenger Load Factor

Increase in Average Seating Density of 2 Percent. Airlines have continually made cabin configuration changes in recent years to achieve higher seating density. Many wide-bodied aircraft now provide ten abreast seating in 747s instead of nine, and nine abreast instead of eight in DC-10s and L-1011s. Airlines are approaching maximum seating density; nevertheless, allowance was made for a moderate 2 percent increase from 1979 through 1989.

Cargo Needs

Annual Cargo Traffic Growth Rate (Freighter Aircraft) of 9 Percent. Although averaging only 5.8 percent during the three years 1976-1978, cargo traffic growth is accelerating rapidly, especially with the impetus of deregulation.[3]

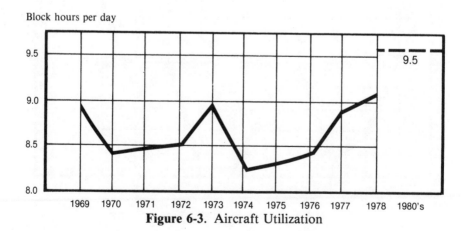

Figure 6-3. Aircraft Utilization

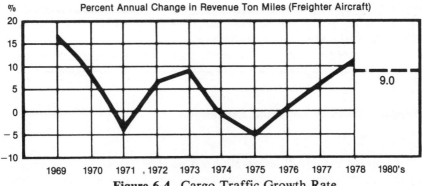

Figure 6-4. Cargo Traffic Growth Rate

Cargo Load Factor for Freighter Aircraft of 65 Percent. Load factors for cargo aircraft have risen steadily over the past decade, reaching a high of nearly 63 percent in 1978.

With these assumptions it is possible to estimate the needed number of available seat miles (ASMs, or total available seats times the miles flown) for passenger aircraft, and the needed number of available ton-miles (ATMs, or total available tons of capacity times the miles flown) for freighter aircraft. Obviously, some of these future ASM and ATM requirements will be met by aircraft already in the fleet, although eventually these will have to be retired.

Thus another assumption is necessary—average aircraft service life. The study assumed an average service life of 18 years, which is significantly longer than historical data reflect. Once data were completed on an inven-

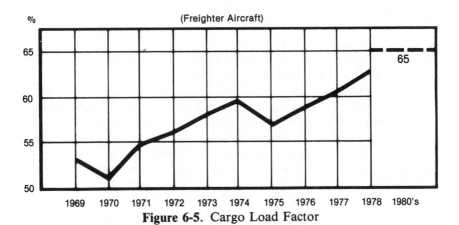

Figure 6-5. Cargo Load Factor

tory of the current fleet and estimates for the retirement date of aircraft in the fleet, it was possible to develop future ASM and ATM needs to replace retiring aircraft and to handle traffic growth.

A computer program was designed to integrate these assumptions and calculate capital requirements. The results are shown in Appendix 6A.

Possible Constraints on Airline Expansion

When considering growth assumptions, it must be recognized that several factors could potentially restrict the growth of the airline industry in the 1980s. These factors, which involve the prospect of handling about 200 million more passengers in 1990 than 1979, include airport capacity to accommodate these additional passengers and the availability and price of fuel to move the aircraft carrying them. While a clearer understanding of these factors would require a detailed examination, certain basic observations can be made.

Given the average size of aircraft today, handling the needs of 1990 would require over 1,000 additional aircraft in the fleet. However, because of the increasing average size of aircraft, it was estimated that aircraft will have as many as 40 percent more seats by 1990. Since the new aircraft will be larger, the number of aircraft in 1990 may not be substantially greater than the number in the present fleet. Nevertheless, passenger growth will require nearly double the terminal capacity now available, even if the number of aircraft does not increase.

The rising cost and short supply of fuel has adversely affected the airline industry, as it has many other industries. Through the utilization of new aircraft, greater fuel economy, and higher load factors, the airlines have increased overall fuel efficiency. Yet the availability and the cost of fuel remain serious problems that confront the industry and could conceivably restrict future airline growth.

From a forecasting perspective, an important technical issue is the sensitivity of the forecast to changes in the assumptions on which it is based. If traffic growth were to be constrained, or utilization rates to fall, what would be the result? It is clear that changes in the values of these assumptions would alter the final figure for capital requirements. Figure 6-6 shows that such variations do not change the need for unprecedented capital in the 1980s. Overall, variations in the assumptions provide a range of investment from $70 billion to $113 billion—four to seven times the expenditure level of the 1970s.

For Alternate Assumptions
1979-1989

ASSUMPTIONS	BASE STUDY	ALTERNATE ASSUMPTIONS									
ANNUAL GROWTH RATE PASSENGER RPMS CARGO RTMS	7% 9%	5% 7%	9% 11%								
LOAD FACTOR PASSENGER A/C CARGO A/C	63% 65%			61% 63%	65% 67%						
AIRCRAFT SERVICE LIFE PASSENGER CARGO	18 YR 18 YR					16 YR 16 YR	20 YR 20 YR				
INFLATION RATE PASSENGER A/C CARGO A/C	7% 7%							6% 6%	8% 8%		
UTILIZATION PASSENGER A/C CARGO A/C	9.5 HR/DAY									9 HR/ DAY	10 HR/ DAY
SEATING DENSITY PASSENGER A/C	+2%									+2%	+2%
CAPITAL REQUIREMENTS (BILLIONS)	$90	$70	$113	$93	$87	$96	$82	$83	$96	$95	$83

Figure 6-6. Summary of Capital Requirements

The Effect of Large Capital Needs on the Airlines

We can now turn to an analysis of the implications of the capital requirements the airlines face, looking at an approximate mid-point of the
$70 to $113 billion range, or $90 billion. Ninety billion dollars is a con-
siderable amount of money—particularly for an industry whose total
capitalization (net book value) in 1979 was only $16.4 billion.

The amount of capital to be invested by the airline industry in the 1980s
is not comparable to any previous period. Figure 6-7 illustrates prior capital
expenditures grouped in five-year periods and compares those with the
capital requirements in the 1980s. In the five-year period 1960-1964, when
jet aircraft were replacing piston aircraft, total capital expenditures
amounted to $3 billion. Capital additions rose to $7 billion during 1965
through 1969, and to $9 billion during 1975 through 1979, including the $3

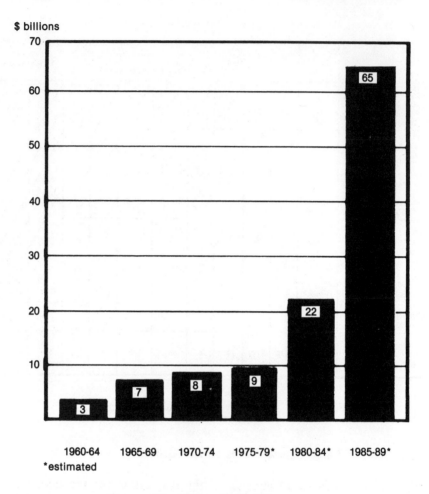

$ billions

Figure 6-7. Airline Capital Investment

billion for aircraft on order for 1979. In the five years 1980-1984, investment of $22 billion—double the amount spent during the previous five
years—will be needed. However, the last five years of the decade, 1985
through 1989, will be marked by a $65 billion airline capital investment. In
that period alone, the airline capital investment will substantially exceed the
total requirement over the previous twenty-five years.

In this study, as noted, an aircraft's useful life was assumed to be eighteen years. Under this assumption, it is striking to note that in the 1980-1984
period the requirement to meet new traffic growth predominates. However,
during the interval 1985 through 1989, the replacement factor plays a more
prominent role. This shift reflects the need to replace the large numbers of
jet aircraft purchased eighteen years earlier, 1967 through 1971. Of a total

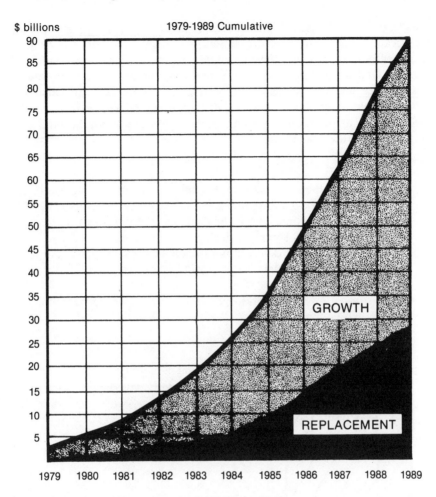

Figure 6-8. Airline Capital Requirements

capital requirement of $90 billion, figure 6-8 reveals that over $29 billion is for the replacement of aircraft as they reach the end of their service lives.

Meeting Future Capital Requirements

The early years of prosperous jet operations, beginning in the early 1960s, provided sufficient internal cash flow to finance the continuing replacement of piston aircraft as well as substantial industry expansion. During this period airlines were able to acquire additional long-term debt and equity capital at relatively reasonable terms.

Beginning in 1967, however, total capital investment needs began to ex-

ceed internally generated funds. By 1970, this disparity had grown
significantly and, until recently, capital investment needs since 1970 have
consistently exceeded the industry's internally generated funds. Much of
this shortfall was temporarily overcome through special long-term financing and leasing arrangements. To examine various ways in which the
airlines might meet the estimated $90 billion capital requirement in the
1980s, several assumptions were made in the 1979 study about the industry's
financial structure, including:

1. The airlines will pay 25 percent of their net income in stockholders'
    dividends. Figure 6-9 shows that U.S. industry paid an average of 44.7
    percent of net income in dividends from 1969 through 1978. The
    airlines paid only 26.8 percent during the same period.
2. The level of long-term debt will not rise much above 50 percent of total
    capital—a one-to-one debt/equity ratio. At March 31, 1981 this ratio
    was 1.44.
3. The historical levels of working capital, with respect to operating ex-
    penses, will be maintained.

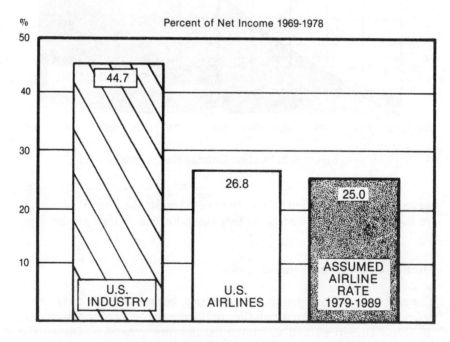

Figure 6-9. Dividend Rates

4. Debt will have average loan periods of eleven years at an interest rate of 10 percent per year. For the twelve months ending March 1981 the average interest rate was 10.7 percent.

Based on these assumptions, the industry will need to achieve return on investment estimated to be between 13 and 15 percent.[4] Figures 6-10 and 6-11 illustrate projections of required net income and the resulting debt/equity ratios through 1989 based on a 13 and 15 percent ROI. Figure 6-10 shows that ROIs in this range would generate steadily rising net incomes ranging between $5.8 billion and $7.8 billion by 1989.

Figure 6-11 shows that in 1970 long-term debt represented more than 75 percent of capital. However, this ratio has declined steadily during the past

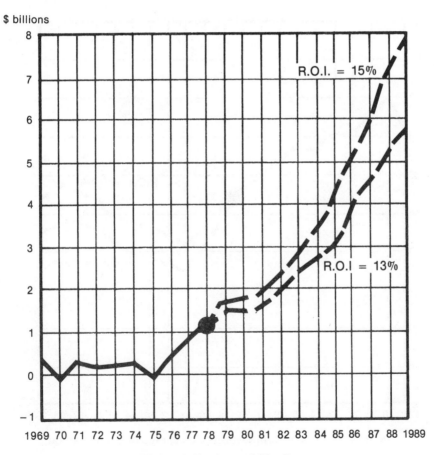

Figure 6-10. Annual Net Income

decade, indicating that the industry has taken advantage of higher earnings to restructure more favorable balance sheets. A 13 to 15 percent ROI would provide continued improvement in the debt/equity ratio during the early years of the 1980s, and produce debt to total capital levels near 50 percent in the later years of the decade. Figure 6-12 depicts airline ROIs since 1969. Notice that the airline industry average ROI was 3.8 percent until 1975, 8 percent in 1976, 10.9 percent in 1977, and 13 percent in 1978. Finally, it dropped again to 7 percent in 1979. Thus the average airline ROI has reached the estimated necessary minimum only once in the past eleven years.

Does this suggest that the 13 to 15 percent ROI predicted in the study is unrealistic? That may be the case. If the airlines cannot get a return suffi-

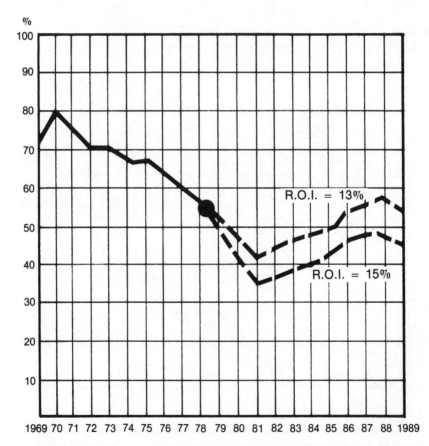

Figure 6-11. Long-Term Debt as Percentage of Total Capital*

*Long Term Debt + Stockholders Equity

cient to justify the investment, they will not be able to invest. The result could be one of several options. Perhaps aircraft would not be purchased to handle future growth, which would result in much higher load factors (that is, crowded airplanes) and attendant seat shortages. Alternatively, airlines might be forced to keep uneconomical planes in the fleet longer, further driving down ROIs and further reducing the potential for obtaining capital equipment. Still a third option would be contraction of the size of the present scheduled system.

The total value of the financial requirement that the 1979 ATA study projected was $122 billion, including the $90 billion for capital equipment, plus funds for debt maintenance, stockholders' dividends, and additions to working capital. This $122 billion requirement would be financed by net in-

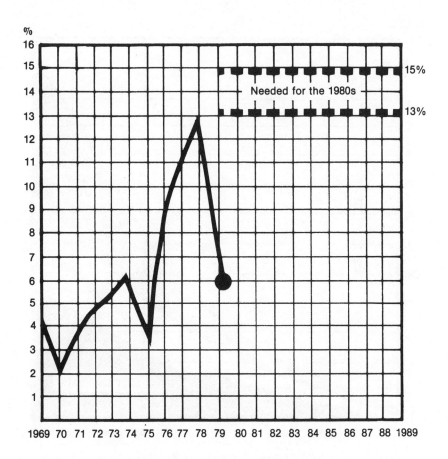

Figure 6-12. Corporate Return on Investment

come of $45 billion (15 percent ROI), depreciation of $34 billion, and new debt of $43 billion. Figures 6-13 and 6-14 show graphically the sources and applications of the $122 billion. Although the possibility exists, the study did not assume that airlines would enter the equity markets for financing.

Conclusion

Through the decade of the 1980s the airline industry will have to invest enormous sums to provide airline service at today's standards. This chapter has outlined the various factors that affect the level of capital investment in the industry, and has used the 1979 ATA study as an example of airline capital forecasting.

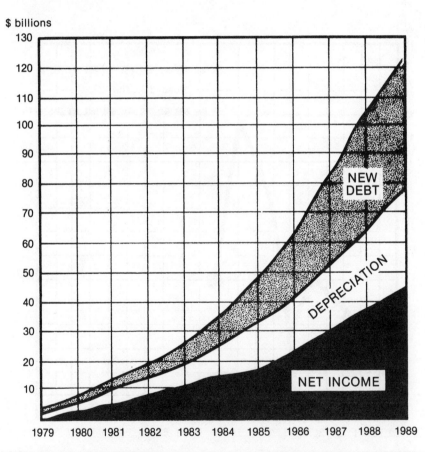

Figure 6-13. Sources of Funds, 15 Percent Corporate ROI, Cumulative, 1979-1989

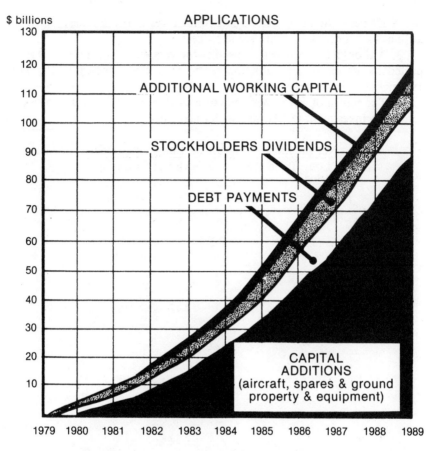

$ billions

APPLICATIONS

ADDITIONAL WORKING CAPITAL

STOCKHOLDERS DIVIDENDS

DEBT PAYMENTS

CAPITAL
ADDITIONS
(aircraft, spares & ground
property & equipment)

1979 1980 1981 1982 1983 1984 1985 1986 1987 1988 1989

Figure 6-14. Application of Funds, Cumulative, 1979-1989

Except for 1978, the ROI needed to support future investment levels is higher than has been reached since the mid-1960s.

Notes

1. In theory, airplanes can fly indefinitely, but, like automobiles, there comes a point where maintenance becomes too expensive to justify continued use.

2. The problem of unaccommodated demand at high average load factors is treated in chapter 3. There is one way to raise load factors without sacrificing aircraft utilization rates or service convenience: channeling traf-

fic to off-peak flights by offering discount fares at those times, which the airlines have been doing with some success.

3. Although cargo growth slowed at the very end of the decade, it is expected to rebound again with the recovery of the economy in the early 1980s.

4. The return on investment measure used in this study is the corporate return on investment (ROI), and is defined as:

$$\frac{\text{Net Income} + \text{Interest on Long Term Debt}}{\text{Long Term Debt} + \text{Stockholder's Equity}}$$

Appendix 6A:
Capital and Financing
Requirements
Data and Description

Capital Requirements Data and Description

An example computer print-out of results of the capital requirements analysis used in this study follows in tables 6A-1 to 6A-3, preceded by a complete description of each of the columns.

The example incorporates the following basic assumptions:

Traffic growth:
Passenger RPMs	7 percent
Cargo RTMs	9 percent

Load factor:
Passenger	63 percent
Cargo	65 percent

Aircraft service life	18 years
Aircraft annual inflation rate	7 percent
Aircraft utilization	9.5 block hours per day
Aircraft seating density	2 percent over 1978 seating

Similar analyses were made for other sets of assumptions described in the report.

Total Aircraft Capital Requirement Forecast (Table 6A-1)

Column Heading	Description
Year	Year of forecast
Annual Capital Requirements	
Aircraft	Annual cost of new passenger and freighter aircraft and spare engines in millions of current dollars.
Ground Property and Equipment	Annual cost of new ground property and equipment and spare parts associated with

129

new aircraft acquisitions amounting to 20 percent of new aircraft cost.

Total   Total annual capital requirements. Sum of A/C and GP&E.

Cumulative Capital Requirements

Replace   Cumulative capital requirements for equipment replacement (aircraft, spare engines, ground property and equipment and spare parts) for aircraft phased out after eighteen-year service life.

Growth   Cumulative capital requirements for new equipment to meet growth needs.

Total   Total cumulative capital requirements. Sum of columns Replace and Growth.

Passenger (Freighter) Aircraft Capital Requirements Capacity (Tables 6A-2 and 6A-3)

Year   Year of forecast

RPMs (RTMs)   Annual system revenue passenger-miles (revenue ton-miles) of U.S. scheduled airlines at forecast growth rate.

Load Factor   Passenger (cargo) load factor

ASMs (ATMs) Required   Fleet capacity required to accommodate traffic at forecast load factor; RPMs (RTMs) divided by Load Factor.

Current Fleet ASMs (ATMs)   Capacity of fleet after phase-out of aircraft in existing fleet at specified service life (eighteen years) with no change in current or future aircraft utilization or seating.

Additional ASMs (ATMs) Required

Replace   Additional capacity required to replace phased-out aircraft. Previous year minus current year Current Fleet ASMs (ATMs).

Growth   Additional capacity required for traffic growth. ASMs (ATMs) Required minus Current Fleet ASMs (ATMs) minus Replace.

Total

Total additional capacity required for both growth and replacement. ASMs (ATMs) Required minus Current Fleet ASMs (ATMs).

Utilization and Seat Adjustment Adjusted Current Fleet

ASMs (ATMs)

Current fleet capacity adjusted to reflect utilization and seating density changes; Current Fleet ASMs (ATMs) times percent change in utilization and seating density.

ASM (ATM) Gain

Annual gain in capacity from utilization and seating density changes. Current Fleet ASMs (ATMs) minus Adjusted Current Fleet ASMs (ATMs).

Adjusted Additional ASMs (ATMs) Required

Replace

Additional capacity required to replace phased-out aircraft adjusted for utilization and seating density changes. Replace divided by Total Additional ASMs (ATMs) Required times Adjusted Additional ASMs (ATMs) Required—Total.

Growth

Additional capacity required for traffic growth adjusted for utilization and seating density changes. ASMs (ATMs) Required minus Adjusted Current Fleet ASMs (ATMs) minus Adjusted Additional ASMs (ATMs) Required—Replace.

Total

Total additional capacity required for both growth and replacement adjusted for utilization and seating density changes. ASMs (ATMs) Required minus Adjusted Current Fleet ASMs (ATMs).

Annual Additional ASMs (ATMs) Required

Annual change in Adjusted Additional ASMs (ATMs) Required—Total

Aircraft Cost per ASM (ATM)

Cost per ASM (ATM) of equipment purchased in 1978 at assumed inflation rate.

Note: The remaining columns are computed as decribed above in *Total Aircraft Capital Requirement Forecast.*

Financing Requirements Data and Description

Computer print-outs of analyses to determine financing requirements, debt structure and flow of funds resulting from two levels of profitability— 13 percent and 15 percent ROI are reproduced in tables 6A-4 to 6A-11, preceded by complete descriptions of the column headings.

The examples shown are based on the following assumptions:

Loan period	11 years
Interest rate	10 percent
Divident rate	25 percent of Net Income
Working capital	1978 level increased at 12 percent per year

Debt Summary (Tables 6A-4 and 6A-8)

Column Name	Description
Year	Year of forecast
Annual:	
New Debt	Capital Additions less Net Internal Funds up to the maximum Debt/Equity Ratio assumption; additional requirements are provided by New Equity.
Amortization of New Debt	Annual amount of amortization of debt shown in the New Debt column. Amortization is made over the assumed loan period.
Amortization of Old Debt	Annual amount of amortization of debt outstanding in base year (1978). Amortization is made over the assumed loan period.
Outstanding Debt Balance	Previous year's Outstanding Debt Balance plus New Debt minus Amortization of New Debt and Amortization of Old Debt.
Interest	Annual interest at the assumed interest rate as applied to previous year's Outstanding Debt Balance.
Cumulative:	Cumulative values for New Debt, Amortization of New Debt, Amortization of Old Debt and Interest.

Debt and Equity (Tables 6A-5 and 6A-9)

Column Name	Description
Year	Year of forecast
Debt: Debt Payment	Sum of Amortization of New Debt and Amortization of Old Debt.
New Debt	Previously described.
Debt Outstanding	Same as Outstanding Debt Balance (previously described).
Equity: Net Income	Earnings after taxes.
Dividends	Return to stockholders at an assumed rate.
New Equity	Sale of stock.
Stockholder Equity	Previous year's Stockholder Equity plus Net Income and New Equity, less Dividends.
Debt and Equity	Sum of Debt Outstanding and Stockholder Equity.
Debt Ratio	Debt Outstanding divided by Debt Outstanding plus Stockholder Equity.

Capital Requirements and Funds (Tables 6A-6 and 6A-10)

Column Name	Description
Year	Year of forecast

Annual:
  Net Available
    Internal Funds
  Capital Additions
	Net Income plus Depreciation less Debt Payment and Dividends.
	Annual cost of aircraft, spare engines, spare parts, and associated ground property and equipment.

Cumulative:	Cumulative values for Net Available Internal Funds and Capital Additions.
Financing:	Sources of funds used to provide for capital additions.

Working Capital (Tables 6A-7 and 6A-11)

Column Name	Description
Year	Year of forecast
Annual:	
Sources:	
Net Income	Previously described.
Depreciation	Annual straight-line depreciation for assumed depreciation period.
New Debt	Previously described.
New Equity	Previously described.
Applications:	
Capital Additions	Previously described.
Debt Payment	Previously described.
Dividends	Previously described.
Change in Working Capital	Sources less Application.
Working Capital	Previous year's Working Capital plus Change in Working Capital. Working Capital for base year 1978 is Current Assets less Current Liabilities with Current Maturities of Long-Term Debt and Current Obligations Under Capital Leases excluded from Current Liabilities.
Cumulative:	Cumulative values for items listed here, except Working Capital is cumulative Change in Working Capital.

Table 6A-1
Total Aircraft Capital Requirements Forecast
(Data in Millions)

Year	Annual Capital Requirements			Cumulative Capital Requirements		
	Aircraft	Ground Property and Equipment	Total	Replace	Growth	Total
1978						
1979	2,489	498	2,987	32	2,955	2,987
1980	1,688	338	2,026	379	4,633	5,013
1981	1,805	361	2,166	567	6,611	7,178
1982	4,369	874	5,243	1,814	10,607	12,421
1983	4,779	956	5,735	3,086	15,070	18,156
1984	5,688	1,138	6,826	4,789	20,193	24,982
1985	7,528	1,506	9,033	7,752	26,263	34,015
1986	10,981	2,196	13,177	13,548	33,644	47,192
1987	10,906	2,181	13,087	18,697	41,583	60,280
1988	12,998	2,600	15,598	25,154	50,724	75,878
1989	11,371	2,274	13,646	29,108	60,415	89,523

Table 6A-2
Passenger Aircraft Capital Requirements
(Data in Millions)

Capacity

					Additional ASMs Required			Adjusted Current Fleet		Adjusted Additional ASMs Required			Cumulative Capital Requirements		
Year	RPMs	Load Factor	ASMs Required	Current Fleet ASMs	Replace	Growth	Total	ASMs	ASM Gain	Replace	Growth	Total	Replace	Growth	Total
1978	236,865	62.0%	382,040	382,922				382,922							
1979	260,551	62.3	418,221	382,522	400	35,299	35,699	386,347	3,825	357	31,516	31,873	32	2,792	2,824
1980	278,790	63.0	442,524	377,632	5,290	59,602	64,892	390,849	13,217	4,213	47,462	51,675	379	4,274	4,654
1981	298,305	63.0	473,501	376,354	6,568	90,579	97,147	403,075	26,721	4,761	65,664	70,426	435	6,003	6,439
1982	319,187	63.0	506,646	366,105	16,817	123,724	140,541	392,098	25,993	13,707	100,841	114,547	1,308	9,624	10,932
1983	341,530	63.0	542,111	354,362	28,560	159,189	187,749	379,522	25,160	24,733	137,856	162,589	2,459	13,709	16,168
1984	365,437	63.0	580,059	339,837	43,085	197,137	240,222	363,965	24,128	38,757	177,336	216,093	4,019	18,388	22,407
1985	391,018	63.0	620,663	315,552	67,370	237,741	305,111	337,956	22,404	62,423	220,284	282,707	6,783	23,936	30,719
1986	418,389	63.0	664,109	269,959	112,963	281,187	394,150	289,126	19,167	107,470	267,513	374,983	12,335	30,703	43,038
1987	447,676	63.0	710,597	232,608	150,314	327,675	477,989	249,123	16,515	145,120	316,353	461,474	17,420	37,974	55,393
1988	479,013	63.0	760,339	189,533	193,389	377,417	570,806	202,990	13,457	188,830	368,519	557,349	23,732	46,316	70,048
1989	512,544	63.0	813,562	169,726	213,196	430,640	643,836	181,777	12,051	209,206	422,580	631,786	27,227	54,996	82,222

Capital

	Annual Additional ASMs Required	Aircraft Cost Per ASM	Annual Capital Requirements		
Year			Aircraft	Ground Property and Equipment	Total
1978		0.0697¢			
1979	31,873	0.0738	2,353	471	2,824
1980	19,801	0.0770	1,525	305	1,830
1981	18,751	0.0793	1,487	297	1,785
1982	44,122	0.0849	3,745	749	4,494
1983	48,042	0.0908	4,363	873	5,236
1984	53,504	0.0972	5,199	1,040	6,239
1985	66,613	0.1040	6,926	1,385	8,311
1986	92,276	0.1113	10,266	2,053	12,319
1987	86,491	0.1190	10,296	2,059	12,355
1988	95,875	0.1274	12,212	2,442	14,655
1989	74,437	0.1363	10,145	2,029	12,174

Table 6A-3
Freighter Aircraft Capital Requirements
(Data in Millions)

Capacity

					Additional ATMs Required			Utilization Adjustment Adjusted Current Fleet		Adjusted Additional ATMs Required		
Year	RTMs	Load Factor	ATMs Required	Current Fleet ATMs	Replace	Growth	Total	ATMs	ATM Gain	Replace	Growth	Total
1978	3,909	65.0%	6,014	6,117				6,117				
1979	4,261	65.0	6,555	6,117		438	438	6,148	31		408	408
1980	4,644	65.0	7,145	6,117		1,028	1,028	6,270	153		875	875
1981	5,062	65.0	7,788	5,754	363	1,671	2,034	6,042	288	312	1,435	1,746
1982	5,518	65.0	8,489	4,896	1,221	2,372	3,593	5,141	245	1,138	2,210	3,348
1983	6,014	65.0	9,253	4,673	1,444	3,136	4,580	4,907	234	1,370	2,976	4,346
1984	6,556	65.0	10,086	4,422	1,695	3,969	5,664	4,643	221	1,629	3,814	5,443
1985	7,146	65.0	10,994	4,086	2,031	4,877	6,908	4,290	204	1,971	4,732	6,703
1986	7,789	65.0	11,983	3,696	2,421	5,866	8,287	3,811	185	2,367	5,735	8,102
1987	8,490	65.0	13,061	3,660	2,457	6,944	9,401	3,843	183	2,409	6,809	9,218
1988	9,254	65.0	14,237	3,499	2,618	8,120	10,738	3,674	175	2,575	7,988	10,563
1989	10,087	65.0	15,518	2,853	3,264	9,401	12,665	2,996	143	3,227	9,295	12,523

Capital

			Annual Capital Requirements			Cumulative Capital Requirements		
Year	Annual Additional ATMs Required	Aircraft Cost Per ATM	Aircraft	Ground Property and Equipment	Total	Replace	Growth	Total
1978		0.3129¢						
1979	408	0.3331	136	27	163		163	163
1980	468	0.3493	163	33	196		359	359
1981	871	0.3642	317	63	381	132	608	740
1982	1,602	0.3896	624	125	749	506	983	1,489
1983	998	0.4169	416	83	499	627	1,361	1,988
1984	1,096	0.4461	489	98	587	771	1,804	2,575
1985	1,261	0.4773	602	120	722	969	2,328	3,297
1986	1,399	0.5107	714	143	857	1,214	2,941	4,154
1987	1,116	0.5465	610	122	732	1,277	3,609	4,886
1988	1,345	0.5847	786	157	943	1,421	4,408	5,830
1989	1,960	0.6257	1,226	245	1,471	1,882	5,420	7,301

Table 6A-4
Debt Summary 13 Percent ROI
(Thousands of Dollars)

	Annual					Cumulative			
Year	New Debt	Amortization of New Debt	Amortization of Old Debt	Outstanding Debt Balance	Interest	New Debt	Amortization of New Debt	Amortization of Old Debt	Interest
1979	$ 1,012,118	$ 0	$687,618	$ 7,888,295	$ 605,104	$ 1,012,118	$ 0	$ 687,618	$ 605,104
1980	150,621	92,011	687,618	7,259,287	709,947	1,162,738	92,011	1,375,235	1,315,050
1981	336,714	105,703	687,618	6,802,690	725,929	1,499,453	197,714	2,062,853	2,040,979
1982	2,958,713	136,314	687,618	8,937,461	680,268	4,458,165	334,028	2,750,471	2,721,247
1983	3,229,632	405,288	687,618	11,074,188	893,746	7,687,797	739,316	3,438,089	3,614,993
1984	4,028,201	698,891	687,618	13,715,880	1,107,419	11,715,998	1,438,206	4,125,706	4,722,412
1985	5,753,443	1,065,091	687,618	17,716,615	1,371,588	17,469,441	2,503,297	4,813,324	6,094,000
1986	8,937,024	1,588,131	687,618	24,377,890	1,771,661	26,406,465	4,091,428	5,500,942	7,865,661
1987	8,551,131	2,400,588	687,618	29,840,815	2,437,789	34,957,596	6,492,016	6,188,560	10,303,450
1988	10,291,606	3,177,963	687,618	36,266,841	2,984,082	45,249,202	9,669,979	6,876,177	13,287,532
1989	8,224,305	4,113,564	687,618	39,689,964	3,626,684	53,473,507	13,783,543	7,563,795	16,914,216

Table 6A-5
Debt and Equity 13 Percent ROI
(Thousands of Dollars)

	Debt					Equity			
Year	Debt Payment	New Debt	Debt Outstanding	Net Income	Dividends	New Equity	Stockholder Equity	Debt and Equity	Debt Ratio
1979	$ 687,618	$ 1,012,118	$ 7,888,295	$1,455,474	$ 363,869	0	$ 7,962,306	$15,850,601	49.8
1980	779,628	150,621	7,259,287	1,405,940	351,485	0	9,016,761	16,276,048	44.6
1981	793,321	336,714	6,802,680	1,474,347	368,587	0	10,122,521	16,925,201	40.2
1982	823,932	2,958,713	8,937,461	1,991,723	497,931	0	11,616,313	20,553,775	43.5
1983	1,092,905	3,229,632	11,074,188	2,278,137	569,534	0	13,324,916	24,399,104	45.4
1984	1,386,508	4,028,201	13,715,880	2,668,016	667,004	0	15,325,929	29,041,809	47.2
1985	1,752,708	5,753,443	17,716,615	3,239,826	809,956	0	17,755,798	35,472,412	49.9
1986	2,275,749	8,937,024	24,377,890	4,106,059	1,026,515	0	20,835,342	45,213,231	53.9
1987	3,088,205	8,551,131	29,840,815	4,598,461	1,149,615	0	24,284,188	54,125,003	55.1
1988	3,865,581	10,291,606	36,266,841	5,415,570	1,353,893	0	28,345,865	64,612,706	56.1
1989	4,801,182	8,224,305	39,689,964	5,781,688	1,445,422	0	32,682,132	72,372,096	54.8

Table 6A-6
Capital Requirements and Funds 13 Percent ROI
(Thousands of Dollars)

Year	Annual Net Available Internal Funds	Annual Capital Additions	Cumulative Net Available Internal Funds	Cumulative Capital Additions	Financing
1979	$1,974,682	$ 2,986,800	$ 1,974,682	$ 2,986,800	Some external, all debt
1980	1,874,979	2,025,600	3,849,662	5,012,400	Some external, all debt
1981	1,829,286	2,166,000	5,678,947	7,178,400	Some external, all debt
1982	2,284,087	5,242,800	7,963,035	12,421,200	Some external, all debt
1983	2,505,168	5,734,800	10,468,203	18,156,000	Some external, all debt
1984	2,797,399	6,825,600	13,265,602	24,981,600	Some external, all debt
1985	3,280,157	9,033,600	16,545,759	34,015,200	Some external, all debt
1986	4,240,176	13,177,200	20,785,935	47,192,400	Some external, all debt
1987	4,536,069	13,087,200	25,322,004	60,279,600	Some external, all debt
1988	5,305,994	15,597,600	30,627,998	75,877,200	Some external, all debt
1989	5,420,895	13,645,200	36,048,893	89,522,400	Some external, all debt

Table 6A-7
Working Capital 13 Percent ROI
(Thousands of Dollars)

Annual

Year	Sources				Applications			Change in Working Capital	Working Capital
	Net Income	*Depreciation*	*New Debt*	*New Equity*	*Capital Additions*	*Debt Payment*	*Dividends*		
1979	$1,455,474	$1,682,585	$1,012,118	0	$2,986,800	$687,618	$363,869	$111,890	$1,044,310
1980	1,405,940	1,725,470	150,621	0	2,025,600	779,628	351,485	125,317	1,169,628
1981	1,474,347	1,657,202	336,714	0	2,166,000	793,321	368,587	140,355	1,309,983
1982	1,991,723	1,771,425	2,958,713	0	5,242,800	823,932	497,931	157,198	1,467,181
1983	2,278,137	2,065,532	3,229,632	0	5,734,800	1,092,905	569,534	176,062	1,643,243
1984	2,668,016	2,380,084	4,028,201	0	6,825,600	1,386,508	667,004	197,189	1,840,432
1985	3,239,826	2,823,848	5,753,443	0	9,033,600	1,752,708	809,956	220,852	2,061,284
1986	4,106,059	3,683,735	8,937,024	0	13,177,200	2,275,749	1,026,515	247,354	2,308,638
1987	4,598,461	4,452,465	8,551,131	0	13,087,200	3,088,205	1,149,615	277,037	2,585,674
1988	5,415,570	5,420,178	10,291,606	0	15,597,600	3,865,581	1,353,893	310,281	2,895,955
1989	5,781,688	6,233,325	8,224,305	0	13,645,200	4,801,182	1,445,422	347,515	3,243,470

Cumulative

Year	Sources				Applications			Working Capital
	Net Income	*Depreciation*	*New Debt*	*New Equity*	*Capital Additions*	*Debt Payment*	*Dividends*	
1979	$1,455,474	$1,682,585	$1,012,118	0	$2,986,800	$687,618	$363,869	$111,890
1980	2,861,414	3,408,055	1,162,738	0	5,012,400	1,467,246	715,354	237,208
1981	4,335,762	5,065,257	1,499,453	0	7,178,400	2,260,567	1,083,940	377,563
1982	6,327,484	6,836,681	4,458,165	0	12,421,200	3,084,499	1,581,871	534,761
1983	8,605,622	8,902,214	7,687,797	0	18,156,000	4,177,404	2,151,405	710,823
1984	11,273,638	11,282,298	11,715,998	0	24,981,600	5,563,913	2,818,410	908,012
1985	14,513,464	14,106,146	17,469,441	0	34,015,200	7,316,621	3,628,366	1,128,864
1986	18,619,522	17,789,881	26,406,465	0	47,192,400	9,592,370	4,654,881	1,376,218

1987	23,217,984	22,242,346	0	34,957,596	60,279,600	12,680,575	5,804,496	1,653,254
1988	28,633,554	27,662,524	0	45,249,202	75,877,200	16,546,156	7,158,388	1,963,535
1989	34,415,242	33,895,849	0	53,473,507	89,522,400	21,347,338	8,603,811	2,311,050

Minimum working capital in base year 1978 = $932,420
Increased at 12 percent per year
Dividends at 25 percent of net income

Table 6A-8
Debt Summary 15 Percent ROI
(Thousands of Dollars)

	Annual					Cumulative			
Year	New Debt	Amortization of New Debt	Amortization of Old Debt	Outstanding Debt Balance	Interest	New Debt	Amortization of New Debt	Amortization of Old Debt	Interest
1979	$ 774,359	$ 0	$687,618	$ 7,650,536	$ 605,104	$ 774,359	$ 0	$ 687,618	$ 605,104
1980	0	201,579	687,618	6,761,339	688,548	774,359	201,579	1,375,235	1,293,652
1981	10,183	70,396	687,618	6,013,508	676,134	784,541	271,976	2,062,853	1,969,786
1982	2,526,226	71,322	687,618	7,780,794	601,351	3,310,768	343,297	2,750,471	2,571,136
1983	2,672,586	300,979	687,618	9,464,784	778,079	5,983,354	644,276	3,438,089	3,349,216
1984	3,316,919	543,941	687,618	11,550,144	946,478	9,300,273	1,188,218	4,125,706	4,295,694
1985	4,839,315	845,479	687,618	14,856,362	1,155,014	14,139,588	2,033,697	4,813,324	5,450,709
1986	7,741,592	1,285,417	687,618	20,624,920	1,485,636	21,881,180	3,319,114	5,500,942	6,936,345
1987	7,046,394	1,989,198	687,618	24,994,497	2,062,492	28,927,574	5,308,312	6,188,560	8,988,837
1988	8,410,758	2,629,779	687,618	30,087,858	2,499,450	37,338,332	7,938,092	6,876,177	11,498,287
1989	5,956,130	3,394,394	687,618	31,961,977	3,008,786	43,294,462	11,332,486	7,563,795	14,507,072

Table 6A-9
Debt and Equity 15 Percent ROI
(Thousands of Dollars)

Year	Debt Payment	New Debt	Debt Outstanding	Net Income	Dividends	New Equity	Stockholder Equity	Debt and Equity	Debt Ratio
1979	$ 687,618	$ 774,359	$ 7,650,636	$1,772,486	$ 443,122	0	$ 8,200,065	15,850,601	48.3
1980	889,197	0	6,761,339	1,752,859	438,215	0	9,514,709	16,276,048	41.5
1981	758,014	10,183	6,013,508	1,862,646	465,662	0	10,911,694	16,925,201	35.5
1982	758,940	2,526,226	7,780,794	2,481,715	620,429	0	12,772,980	20,553,775	37.9
1983	988,597	2,672,586	9,464,784	2,881,786	720,447	0	14,934,320	24,399,104	38.8
1984	1,231,559	3,316,919	11,550,144	3,409,793	852,448	0	17,491,665	29,041,809	39.8
1985	1,533,097	4,839,315	14,856,362	4,165,847	1,041,462	0	20,616,050	35,472,412	41.9
1986	1,973,035	7,741,592	20,624,920	5,296,348	1,324,087	0	24,588,312	45,213,231	45.6
1987	2,676,816	7,046,394	24,994,497	6,056,258	1,514,065	0	29,130,506	54,125,003	46.2
1988	3,317,397	8,410,758	30,087,858	7,192,456	1,798,114	0	34,524,848	64,612,706	46.6
1989	4,082,012	5,956,130	31,961,977	7,847,029	1,961,757	0	40,410,119	72,372,096	44.2

Table 6A-10
Capital Requirements and Funds 15 Percent ROI
(Thousands of Dollars)

Year	Annual Net Available Internal Funds	Annual Capital Additions	Cumulative Net Available Internal Funds	Cumulative Capital Additions	Financing
1979	$2,212,441	$ 2,986,800	$ 2,212,441	$ 2,986,800	Some external, all debt
1980	2,025,600	2,025,600	4,238,041	5,012,400	Internal funds, reduce old debt
1981	2,155,817	2,166,000	6,393,859	7,178,400	Some external, all debt
1982	2,716,574	5,242,800	9,110,432	12,421,200	Some external, all debt
1983	3,062,214	5,734,800	12,172,646	18,156,000	Some external, all debt
1984	3,508,681	6,825,600	15,681,327	24,981,600	Some external, all debt
1985	4,194,285	9,033,600	19,875,612	34,015,200	Some external, all debt
1986	5,435,608	13,177,200	25,311,220	47,192,400	Some external, all debt
1987	6,040,806	13,087,200	31,352,026	60,279,600	Some external, all debt
1988	7,186,842	15,597,600	38,538,868	75,877,200	Some external, all debt
1989	7,689,070	13,645,200	46,227,938	89,522,400	Some external, all debt

Table 6A-11
Working Capital 15 Percent ROI
(Thousands of Dollars)

Annual

Year	Sources				Applications			Change in Working Capital	Working Capital
	Net Income	Depreciation	New Debt	New Equity	Capital Additions	Debt Payment	Dividends		
1979	$1,772,486	$1,682,585	$774,359	0	$2,986,800	$687,618	$443,122	111,890	$1,044,310
1980	1,752,859	1,725,470	0	0	2,025,600	889,197	438,215	125,317	1,169,628
1981	1,862,646	1,657,202	10,183	0	2,166,000	758,014	465,662	140,355	1,309,983
1982	2,481,715	1,771,425	2,526,226	0	5,242,800	758,940	620,429	157,198	1,467,181
1983	2,881,786	2,065,532	2,672,586	0	5,734,800	988,597	720,447	176,062	1,643,243
1984	3,409,793	2,380,084	3,316,919	0	6,825,600	1,231,559	852,448	197,189	1,840,432
1985	4,165,847	2,823,848	4,839,315	0	9,033,600	1,533,097	1,041,462	220,852	2,061,284
1986	5,296,348	3,683,735	7,741,592	0	13,177,200	1,973,035	1,324,087	247,354	2,308,638
1987	6,056,258	4,452,465	7,046,394	0	13,087,200	2,676,816	1,514,065	277,037	2,585,674
1988	7,192,456	5,420,178	8,410,758	0	15,597,600	3,317,397	1,798,114	310,281	2,895,955
1989	7,847,029	6,233,325	5,956,130	0	13,645,200	4,082,012	1,961,757	347,515	3,243,470

Cumulative

Year	Sources				Applications			Working Capital
	Net Income	Depreciation	New Debt	New Equity	Capital Additions	Debt Payment	Dividends	
1979	$1,772,486	$1,682,585	$774,359	0	$2,986,800	$687,618	$443,122	$111,890
1980	3,525,345	3,408,055	774,359	0	5,012,400	1,576,815	881,336	237,208
1981	5,387,992	5,065,257	784,541	0	7,178,400	2,334,829	1,346,998	377,563
1982	7,869,707	6,836,681	3,310,768	0	12,421,200	3,093,768	1,967,427	534,761
1983	10,751,493	8,902,214	5,983,354	0	18,156,000	4,082,365	2,687,873	710,823
1984	14,161,286	11,282,298	9,300,273	0	24,981,600	5,313,924	3,540,322	908,012
1985	18,327,134	14,106,146	14,139,588	0	34,015,200	6,847,021	4,581,783	1,128,864
1986	23,623,482	17,789,881	21,881,180	0	47,192,400	8,820,056	5,905,871	1,376,218
1987	29,679,741	22,242,346	28,927,574	0	60,279,600	11,496,872	7,419,935	1,653,254
1988	36,872,197	27,662,524	37,338,332	0	75,877,200	14,814,269	9,218,049	1,963,535
1989	44,719,225	33,895,849	43,294,462	0	89,522,400	18,896,281	11,179,806	2,311,050

Minimum Working Capital in Base Year 1978 = 932,420

Increased at 12 percent per year

Dividends at 25 percent of net income

7 Changes in the U.S./ International Market, 1970-1980

Alan E. Pisarski

Introduction

The U.S./international air travel market changed significantly during the 1970s primarily because of a large shift in the composition of the market.[1] Over the past ten years, spurred by a falling dollar and other factors, foreign citizen travel increased much faster than U.S. citizen travel (see table 7-1). By 1980 the percentage of foreign citizens in the market was equal to the percentage of U.S. citizens in the market. This development is discussed in the first part of this chapter.

A second important change in the U.S./international market during the 1970s was an increase in the number of U.S. gateways, that is, U.S. cities from which a passenger could fly directly to foreign points. The number of gateways is ordinarily agreed on in bilateral negotiations between the United States and other countries. The number of gateways to be opened is thus a matter of the U.S. government's aviation policy. In the latter part of this chapter we examine changes in bilateral agreements during the 1970s and the economic effects of the new gateways that opened in the past decade. By looking carefully at the effects of these new gateways, one can see more clearly the economic ramifications of possible future U.S. aviation policies in bilateral negotiations.

Appendix 7A presents detailed data on individual U.S./international markets.

Changing Patterns of U.S. Citizen Participation in the International Air Market

In 1980, for the first time, the number of foreign visitors to the United States from overseas was equal to the number of U.S. citizens traveling abroad.[2] The decline in U.S. citizen participation relative to foreign citizen participation has important ramifications for foreign carriers, who stand to increase their markets, and for U.S. flag carriers, who stand to lose market shares.

147

Table 7-1
U.S.-Foreign Citizens Air Travel Trends, 1972-1979

Area	Percent Of Total Market 1979	Market Growth 1979/1972	U.S. Citizens as a Percent of Market			Foreign Citizens as a Percent of Market			U.S. Flag Share of U.S. Citizen Market			U.S. Flag Share of Foreign Citizen Market			Overall U.S. Flag Share		
			1972	1979	Change	1972	1979	Change	1972	1979	Change	1972	1979	Change	1972	1979	Change
Europe	38.4%	+ 41.1%	65.4%	53.1%	(12.2%)	34.6%	46.9%	12.2%	48.4%	46.7%	(1.7%)	29.7%	35.7%	6.0%	41.9%	41.5%	(0.4%)
South America	8.1	+127.4	41.0	29.4	(11.6)	59.0	70.6	11.6	41.9	51.7	9.8	37.6	40.8	3.2	41.8	44.0	2.2
Oceania	3.3	+ 86.5	47.7	39.2	(8.5)	52.3	60.8	8.5	65.7	57.7	(8.0)	48.9	46.4	(2.5)	57.0	50.6	(6.4)
Asia	14.5	+ 90.0	42.9	30.7	(12.2)	57.1	69.3	12.2	60.6	52.7	(7.9)	34.1	37.5	3.4	45.5	41.9	(3.6)
Central America & Caribbean	35.0	+ 55.5	67.8	61.4	(6.4)	32.2	38.6	6.4	70.5	64.7	(5.8)	58.2	53.4	(4.8)	66.6	60.4	(6.2)
Africa	0.1	+242.3	68.0	54.7	(13.3)	32.0	45.3	13.3	91.7	53.4	(38.3)	78.3	39.1	(39.2)	87.3	46.9	(40.4)
Total	38.4%	+ 59.0%	61.6%	50.4%	(11.2%)	38.4%	49.6%	11.2%	58.6%	55.5%	(3.1%)	40.6%	41.9%	1.3%	51.7%	48.7%	(3.0%)

Source: Immigration and Naturalization Service, *Reports of Passenger Travel Between the United States and Foreign Countries, 1970-1974;* and Department of Transportation, *U.S. International Air Travel Statistics, 1975-1979.*

U.S. Citizenship Trends

Figure 7-1 depicts the trends in the percentage of U.S. citizens in major world travel markets in the past decade.[3] Several points are evident from these data. First, the decline in the U.S. citizen share has occurred rather consistently throughout the decade. Second, the trend was worldwide in scope. All markets were affected, with only the Caribbean market not exhibiting a strong trend. Third, the original proportion of U.S. citizens in the market seems to have had little effect on the trend, in that the decline was as strong in markets in which the share was less than 50 percent at the beginning of the decade (South America, Oceania, and Asia) as in those where the U.S. citizen share was high (Africa, Europe, and the Caribbean).

Between 1972 and 1979, the U.S. citizen proportion of air travelers between the United States and foreign points fell from 61.6 percent to 50.4 percent, a decline of 11 percentage points. The U.S. citizen share in the Oceania and European markets declined about this same amount. Asian and African markets showed greater declines, about 20 percentage points in each case. South American and the Caribbean-Central American markets were most stable, declining approximately 5 percentage points each. Of course, the decline refers only to changes in market share. In absolute terms, U.S. citizen travel in 1979 in all world markets was greater than in 1972 despite a slight downturn in the mid-1970s. For the eight-year period, the annual growth rate was approximately 3.3 percent for U.S. citizens, although after 1975, the low point in the decade, the growth rate was approximately 7.3 percent.

Foreign citizen travel grew steadily and rapidly through the decade. Annual growth for the foreign citizen portion of the market averaged 9.4 percent between 1972 and 1975, and 12.1 percent between 1975 and 1979. Thus the declining U.S. citizen share of the market is attributable to the more rapid growth in foreign citizen travel in the decade.

These changes in citizenship composition have had two important effects. First, the changing mix of citizens in the market has led to necessary changes in how services are directed and marketing activities are focused. Figure 7-2 depicts the change in the mix of passengers on U.S. carriers as the share of U.S. citizens in the total market declined. The chart shows that 70 percent of the passengers on U.S. carriers were U.S. citizens in 1972. By 1979, U.S. citizens were only 57 percent of the passengers on U.S. carriers. This relationship, of course, varies considerably in individual markets. But in all markets the citizenship changes mandated placing much greater importance on successful marketing to foreign citizens.

A second effect of the changing citizen mix since 1972 has been a drop in the U.S. flag share of the market. Because foreign citizens fly more often with carriers from their own country than on U.S. flag carriers, the increase

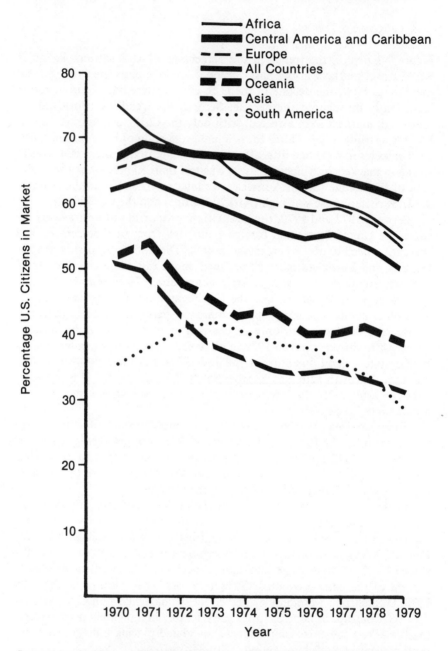

Sources: Immigration and Naturalization Service, *Reports of Passenger Travel Between the United States and Foreign Countries,* 1970-1974; and Department of Transportation, *U.S. International Air Travel Statistics,* 1975-1979.

Figure 7-1. U.S. Citizen Share of Major Markets, 1970-1979

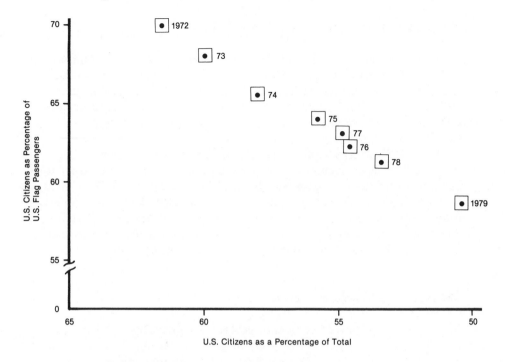

Source: DOT and INS data, 1972-1979.

Figure 7-2. Decreasing Percentage of U.S. Citizens on U.S. Flag Carriers as Percentage of U.S. Citizens in Market Decreases, 1972-1979

in the foreign citizen proportion of the market caused a decline in the U.S. carrier market share. A large part of the decline in the U.S. carrier market share since 1972 can be directly attributed to this effect of changing citizenship composition in the international travel market.

Surveys conducted abroad in the past have indicated that the United States is the number one destination in the preferences of foreign travelers of most countries when price is not a factor. As substantial as growth has been in some markets, considerable potential remains. The United States is the primary international destination of travelers from Canada, Mexico, and Japan, but ranks only seventh among destinations of travelers from the United Kingdom, and does not rank in the top ten destinations for France or West Germany, although it might rank higher than that when compared with other overseas destinations. The 1980s are thus likely to see a continuation of the traffic trend of the 1970s, with increasingly large numbers of foreign travelers in U.S./international markets, and with marketing to non-U.S. citizens essential to U.S. carrier profitability.

The Impact of New Direct Service to U.S. Points

In the second half of the past decade, there was an increase in the number of U.S. points served by foreign carriers. In 1974 there were twenty-two U.S. cities, exclusive of the territories, with foreign flag international service. By 1979 this number had increased to twenty-eight, exclusive of fourteen cities with international service to Mexico or Canada only. No more new cities were added in 1980.

Since 1977 liberal bilateral agreements and Civil Aeronautics Board (CAB) policy have given both foreign and domestic carriers authority to operate direct international service to the new inland points in the United States. Not all of this authority has been exercised, but several new points have been added. In the following sections we look at the effects of adding direct international service to inland U.S. points, and examine the ramifications of authorizing foreign flag carriers to offer this new direct service.

The Effects of New Direct Service

In the past several years a number of new gateways have opened with direct service to European points.[4] It is illuminating to examine in some detail what happened when three new gateways to London were opened: Atlanta, Dallas-Fort Worth, and Houston. These three markets were chosen as case studies for two reasons. First, the United States-United Kingdom market in recent years has been the largest U.S.-foreign nation market in passengers and passenger-miles.[5] Furthermore, these three gateways have been open long enough to get "before" and "after" statistics from standard federal sources.[6]

Instead of having U.S. and foreign carriers compete with one another head to head, the new U.S.-U.K. markets opened in 1977 were divided between the two countries, and exclusive nonstop rights were granted for three years. Thus Atlanta was reserved for a U.S. carrier, Dallas was reserved for a U.S. carrier, and Houston was reserved for a British carrier. In 1980 the nonstop exclusivity expired and nonstop service to all three points became competitive, but that was not the case in the period during which these data were developed.

Market Growth

The most dramatic effect of the new direct service was a tremendous growth in traffic between the new U.S. points and the U.K., as shown in figures 7-3, 7-4, and 7-5. In 1977, without nonstop service, scheduled passengers

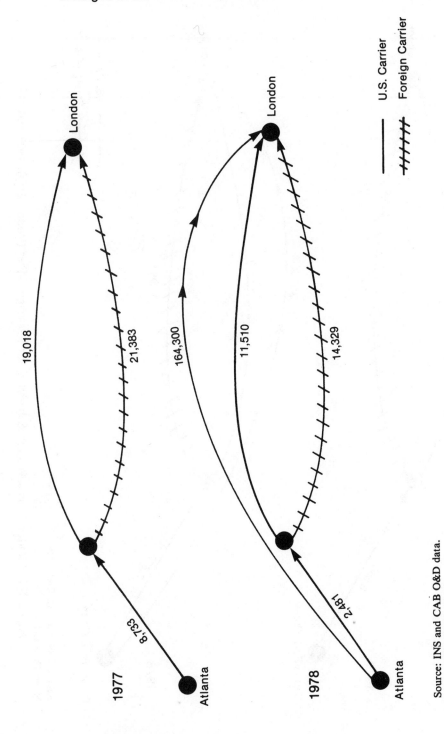

Figure 7-3. London-Atlanta Market, Scheduled Air Passenger-Miles (Round Trip), 1977 and 1978

Source: INS and CAB O&D data.
Note: Thousands of miles.

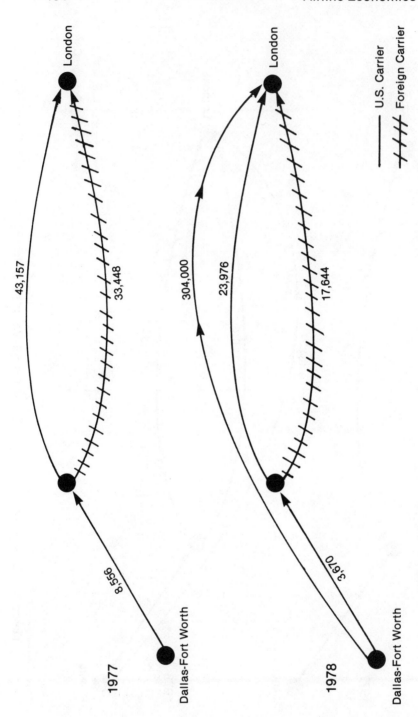

Figure 7-4. London-Dallas Market, Scheduled Air Passenger-Miles (Round Trip), 1977 and 1978

Source: INS and CAB O&D data.
Note: Thousands of miles.

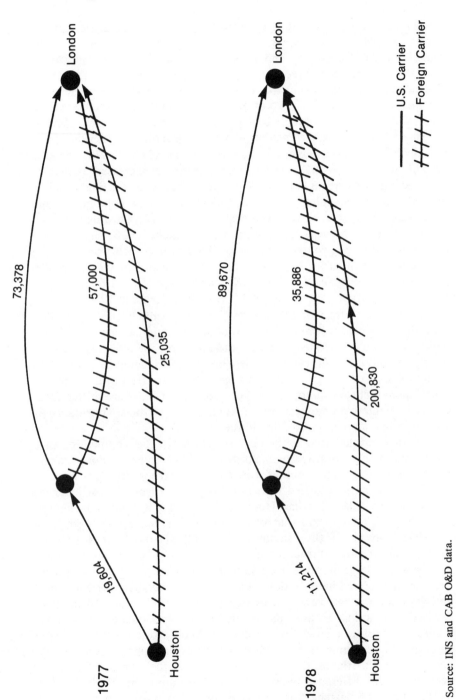

Source: INS and CAB O&D data.
Note: Thousands of miles.

Figure 7-5. London-Houston Market, Scheduled Air Passenger-Miles (Round Trip), 1977 and 1978

between the three points and the United Kingdom accounted for only 1.9 percent of all U.S.-U.K. passengers. After the gateways opened in 1978, this figure jumped to 5.4 percent, and in 1979 it reached 7.8 percent. The growth in traffic between the three U.S. points and the United Kingdom was phenomenal after the introduction of direct service. Scheduled traffic in the new markets increased 398 percent between 1977 and 1978, and 40 percent from 1978 to 1979, presumably because the new direct service was offered.

The U.S.-U.K. scheduled market grew faster than the total (scheduled and nonscheduled) market, increasing 42 percent from 1977 to 1978, and 12.2 percent from 1978 to 1979, while the overall market increased 24 percent and then only 4.4 percent in the same two years. Many factors might explain this growth in scheduled traffic, including growth in populations and economies, changes in service (especially a drop in nonscheduled traffic), and new fares. It appears that the opening of the new U.S. direct-service points was the largest contributing factor. Passenger growth from the three new points accounted for between 11 and 13.6 percent (155,000 to 197,000 passengers) of the increase in U.S.-U.K. scheduled traffic in 1977-1978, and approximately 20 percent of the total U.S.-U.K. increase in 1978-1979.

A significant effect of the new gateways is a shift in passenger-miles from the domestic account to the international account. When direct international service is provided to a U.S interior point, the previous domestic leg of international journeys from these points, which could be served only by domestic carriers, is lost to domestic carriage. One effect of this is purely statistical in that some amount of revenue passenger-miles are shifted from domestic to international accounts. This creates an artificial appearance of growth in one market and decline in the other.

Another serious effect is the opening to foreign flag competition of a market that was previously the sole province of U.S. carriers. For instance, regardless of flag shares out of J.F. Kennedy Airport in New York to London, U.S. carriers carried 100 percent of the first legs of those journeys starting in, say, Atlanta, Dallas, Houston, or any other inland points. Figures 7-3, 7-4, and 7-5 indicate that over 17 million revenue passenger-miles (RPMs) of travel in the three sample markets shifted from domestic to international carriage after direct service began. Table 7-2 summarizes the shifts.

Even these large numbers understate the full effect of the shift in traffic, because they represent only domestic traffic lost between the three new gateways and the gateways that existed previously. They do not measure domestic traffic lost because passengers from points outside of Atlanta, Dallas-Ft. Worth, or Houston flew through those cities instead of the old gateways. For example, if a passenger flew from Nashville to London connecting through Atlanta, these data do not record the domestic travel lost because of the difference between Nashville-Atlanta and Nashville-New York, where the passenger might have connected if Atlanta were not a gateway. Such linked traffic is considerable.

Table 7-2
U.S. Domestic Revenue Passenger-Miles, London Routes (Thousands)

	1977	1978	Decrease RPM	Decrease Percent
LON-ATL	8,733	2,481	6,252	72%
LON-DFW	8,556	3,670	4,886	57
LON-IAH	19,604	11,214	8,390	43

Source: CAB O&D data.

Table 7-3 gives an estimate of linked traffic using Immigration and Naturalization Service data as a measure of total direct traffic.

Notice that the linked traffic—that is, traffic arriving by air at these new gateways to connect to direct London service—was as large as or larger than the local service component. Since the CAB does not have Origin-Destination data for foreign carriers, it is impossible to make a hinterland or linked estimate for Houston, which was served nonstop only by a British carrier. To calculate the domestic RPM diversion from linked traffic, all of the differing distance of the old paths and new paths of the connecting traffic would have to be traced, using the CAB Origin-Destination tapes and computer network analysis. Even lacking that data, it is still clear that direct service sharply reduces domestic RPMs by diverting both local and connecting traffic from old gateways to new gateways.

Policy Options

The complicating factor in this diversion is the presence of foreign flag carriers. As pointed out previously, whatever the U.S. flag market share was out of the old gateways, the first leg of those journeys was the province of U.S. carriers alone.

Table 7-3
Direct-Service Passengers to London, 1978

	Total Customs Clearance as Measured by INS Data	Local Traffic Estimated From CAB O&D Data	Estimated Difference ("Hinterland," or Linked Traffic)
Atlanta	84,417	39,000	45,000
Dallas-Ft. Worth	131,649	64,000	67,000
Houston	76,007	N/A	N/A

Sources: INS and CAB O&D Data.
Note: N/A = Not available.

As domestic traffic is diverted, foreign flag carriers fly much of this previously domestic traffic. Moreover, because the domestic traffic has been diverted from the domestic to the international account, this new foreign flag traffic may not show up as an increased foreign flag market share.

This traffic diversion is seen by some as a sufficient reason for supporting a U.S. international aviation policy that does not permit foreign carriers to fly to interior U.S. points. However, the case against foreign service to interior points is not unambiguous. Whatever the effects of traffic diversion, both foreign and U.S. international carriers benefit from the tremendous traffic generated by the opening of service to interior points (points that could never enjoy direct service by U.S. carriers alone because of the need for bilateral agreement on direct service). And of course, in determining a national aviation policy, not only U.S. airlines but also U.S. consumers must be considered.

For consumers, the most obvious effect of new direct service is improved service. The average passenger flying between London and Atlanta, Houston or Dallas saved more than 15 percent of the total origin-destination trip time before direct service. Furthermore, many air travellers were spared the inconvenience of changing airlines or aircraft at some of the busier old gateways.

Another effect of direct service is the economy of nonstop service. The average air distance between the three new gateways and London decreased about 5 percent. Similarly, takeoffs and landings—the most expensive part of a flight—were halved. This reduction could translate into reduced operating costs and reduced fuel consumption per passenger. This reduction would be realized, however, only in those cases where both the new direct flights and the flights from old gateways have enough traffic to maintain load factors at their predirect service levels. If load factors on flights from the old gateways were to decrease because of reduced feed traffic, or load factors on the new direct flights were to decline, then average operating cost per passenger would not fall.

Notes

1. *International market* refers to the market composed of flights between the United States and foreign points. It does not include travel between two points, both of which are abroad. Basic data on the U.S./international market are presented in table 7-1.

2. The data in this section cover the period 1972-1979, the period for which detailed data were available at time of printing. The 1980 data are preliminary. Data for this chapter were developed by Gellman Research Associates.

3. Detailed market-by-market data on citizenship composition and market share are presented in appendix 7A.

4. Direct service means nonstop service hereafter.

5. Henceforth U.S.-U.K. market.

6. U.S. International Air Travel Statistics for calendar years 1976, 1977, and 1978, produced by the U.S. Department of Transportation, Transportation Systems Center, and based on Immigration and Naturalization Service statistics, from I-92 forms; and Origin-Destination Survey of Airline Passenger Traffic, International/Territorial, U.S. CAB calendar years 1976, 1977, 1978, based on 10 percent ticket sample.

Appendix 7A:
Data on Individual U.S./
International Markets

These figures and tables present additional data on U.S. citizen participation and U.S. market share trends both for the total international market and for the six individual markets that make up the total.

Figure 7A-1 represents the overall world market trend in U.S. flag shares of the two citizenship submarkets. The major market trends are visible—that is, a slight decline in U.S. flag share in the U.S. citizen market as the U.S. citizen market itself declines in market importance, while the smaller U.S. flag share of the foreign citizen market has improved slightly in that rapidly growing market.

Statistics for the total U.S.-international market and for individual markets are summarized in tables 7A-1 to 7A-7 (see also table 7-1 following the introduction).

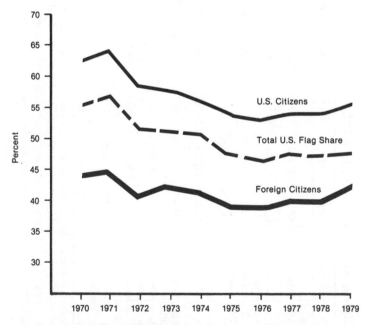

Sources: Immigration and Naturalization Service, *Reports of Passenger Travel Between the United States and Foreign Countries,* 1970-1974; and Department of Transportation, *U.S. International Air Travel Statistics,* 1975-1979.

Figure 7A-1. U.S. Flag Share of U.S. and Foreign Citizens in the World Market, and Total U.S. Flag Share

162   Airline Economics

Table 7A-1
U.S.-Foreign Citizens Air Travel Trends, 1970-1979—All Countries

Market Measures	1970[a]	1971[a]	1972	1973	1974	1975	1976	1977	1978	1979
Number of Passengers in Total Market (Thousands)	18,814	20,562	21,383	22,512	22,135	21,549	23,145	24,048	28,784	34,009
Number of U.S. Citizens in Total Market (Thousands)	11,722	13,101	13,169	13,503	12,828	12,042	12,605	13,201	15,406	17,130
Number of Foreign Citizens in Total Market (Thousands)	7,092	7,461	8,214	9,009	9,307	9,507	10,540	10,847	13,378	16,879
U.S. Citizens as a Percentage of Total Market	62.3%	63.7%	61.6%	60.0%	58.0%	55.9%	54.5%	54.9%	53.5%	50.4%
Number of Passengers on U.S. Flag (Thousands)	10,429	11,719	11,060	11,562	10,991	10,201	10,765	11,422	13,610	16,566
U.S. Flag Share as a Percentage of Total Market	55.4%	57.0%	51.7%	51.4%	49.7%	47.3%	46.5%	47.5%	47.3%	48.7%
Number of U.S. Citizens on U.S. Flag (Thousands)	7,324	8,405	7,722	7,755	7,176	6,519	6,699	7,123	8,318	9,490
Number of Foreign Citizens on U.S. Flag (Thousands)	3,105	3,314	3,338	3,807	3,815	3,682	4,066	4,299	5,292	7,076
Percentage U.S. Citizens Flying U.S. Flag	62.5%	64.2%	58.6%	57.4%	55.9%	54.1%	53.1%	54.0%	54.0%	55.5%
Percentage Foreign Citizens Flying U.S. Flag	43.8%	44.4%	40.6%	42.3%	41.0%	38.7%	38.6%	39.6%	39.6%	41.9%

Source: Immigration and Naturalization Service, *Reports of Passenger Travel between the United States and Foreign Countries,* 1970-1974; and Department of Transportation, *U.S. International Air Travel Statistics,* 1975-1979.

Exclusion: Statistics for travel to and from Canada have been excluded from figures.

[a]1970 and 1971 figures include charter services as well as scheduled.

Table 7A-2
U.S.-Foreign Citizens Air Travel Trends, 1970-1979—Europe

Market Measures	1970[a]	1971[a]	1972	1973	1974	1975	1976	1977	1978	1979
Number of Passengers in Total Market (Thousands)	8,515	9,456	9,244	9,355	8,310	7,826	8,490	8,850	11,135	13,043
Number of U.S. Citizens in Total Market (Thousands)	5,560	6,312	6,042	5,945	5,067	4,680	5,004	5,246	6,390	6,920
Number of Foreign Citizens in Total Market (Thousands)	2,955	3,144	3,202	3,410	3,243	3,146	3,486	3,604	4,745	6,123
U.S. Citizens as a Percentage of Total Market	65.3%	66.7%	65.4%	63.6%	61.0%	59.8%	58.9%	59.3%	57.4%	53.1%
Number of Passengers on U.S. Flag (Thousands)	4,084	4,538	3,874	3,912	3,311	2,931	3,270	3,559	4,470	5,416
U.S. Flag Share as a Percentage of Total Market	48.0%	48.0%	41.9%	41.8%	39.8%	37.4%	38.5%	40.2%	40.1%	41.5%
Number of U.S. Citizens on U.S. Flag (Thousands)	3,040	3,456	2,923	2,801	2,326	2,089	2,269	2,425	2,944	3,232
Number of Foreign Citizens on U.S. Flag (Thousands)	1,044	1,082	951	1,111	985	842	1,001	1,134	1,526	2,184
Percentage U.S. Citizens Flying U.S. Flag	54.7%	54.7%	48.4%	47.1%	45.9%	44.6%	45.3%	46.2%	46.1%	46.7%
Percentage Foreign Citizens Flying U.S. Flag	35.3%	34.4%	29.7%	32.5%	30.4%	26.8%	28.7%	31.5%	32.2%	35.7%

Source: Immigration and Naturalization Service, *Reports of Passenger Travel Between the United States and Foreign Countries*, 1970-1974; and Department of Transportation, *U.S. International Air Travel Statistics*, 1975-1979.

[a] 1970 and 1971 figures include charter services as well as scheduled.

Table 7A-3
U.S.-Foreign Citizens Air Travel Trends, 1970-1979—South America

Market Measures	1970[a]	1971[a]	1972	1973	1974	1975	1976	1977	1978	1979
Number of Passengers in Total Market (Thousands)	1,057	1,085	1,217	1,351	1,532	1,587	1,706	1,901	2,279	2,767
Number of U.S. Citizens in Total Market (Thousands)	374	411	499	566	621	613	649	693	762	814
Number of Foreign Citizens in Total Market (Thousands)	683	674	718	785	911	974	1,057	1,208	1,517	1,953
U.S. Citizens as a Percentage of Total Market	35.4%	37.9%	41.0%	41.9%	40.5%	38.6%	38.0%	36.5%	33.4%	29.4%
Number of Passengers on U.S. Flag (Thousands)	375	436	509	565	633	651	648	758	984	1,218
U.S. Flag Share as a Percentage of Total Market	35.5%	40.2%	41.8%	41.8%	41.3%	41.0%	38.0%	39.9%	43.2%	44.0%
Number of U.S. Citizens on U.S. Flag (Thousands)	168	200	239	271	295	286	286	329	388	421
Number of Foreign Citizens on U.S. Flag (Thousands)	207	236	270	294	338	365	362	429	596	797
Percentage U.S. Citizens Flying U.S. Flag	44.9%	48.7%	47.9%	47.9%	47.5%	46.7%	44.1%	47.5%	50.9%	51.7%
Percentage Foreign Citizens Flying U.S. Flag	30.3%	35.0%	37.6%	37.5%	37.1%	37.5%	34.3%	35.5%	39.3%	40.8%

Source: Immigration and Naturalization Service, *Reports of Passenger Travel Between the United States and Foreign Countries, 1970-1974*; and Department of Transportation, *U.S. International Air Travel Statistics, 1975-1979*.
[a]1970 and 1971 figures include charter services as well as scheduled.

Table 7A-4
U.S.-Foreign Citizens Air Travel Trends, 1970-1979—Oceania

Market Measures	1970[a]	1971[a]	1972	1973	1974	1975	1976	1977	1978	1979
Number of Passengers in Total Market (Thousands)	447	541	606	713	727	759	820	863	942	1,130
Number of U.S. Citizens in Total Market (Thousands)	232	289	289	324	309	327	325	341	388	443
Number of Foreign Citizens in Total Market (Thousands)	215	252	317	389	418	432	495	522	554	687
U.S. Citizens as a Percentage of Total Market	51.9%	53.5%	47.7%	45.4%	42.5%	43.1%	39.7%	39.5%	41.2%	39.2%
Number of Passengers on U.S. Flag (Thousands)	255	333	345	398	361	397	399	426	435	571
U.S. Flag Share as a Percentage of Total Market	57.0%	61.5%	57.0%	55.8%	49.6%	52.3%	48.7%	49.4%	46.2%	50.6%
Number of U.S. Citizens on U.S. Flag (Thousands)	160	205	190	209	180	207	180	186	212	255
Number of Foreign Citizens on U.S. Flag (Thousands)	95	128	155	189	181	190	219	240	223	316
Percentage U.S. Citizens Flying U.S. Flag	69.0%	70.8%	65.7%	64.6%	58.2%	63.3%	55.3%	54.5%	54.6%	57.7%
Percentage Foreign Citizens Flying U.S. Flag	44.2%	50.9%	48.9%	48.5%	43.3%	44.0%	44.3%	46.1%	40.3%	46.4%

Source: Immigration and Naturalization Service, *Reports of Passenger Travel Between the United States and Foreign Countries*, 1970-1974; and Department of Transportation, *U.S. International Air Travel Statistics*, 1975-1979.

[a]1970 and 1971 figures include charter services as well as scheduled.

Table 7A-5
U.S.-Foreign Citizens Air Travel Trends, 1970-1979—Asia

Market Measures	1970[a]	1971[a]	1972	1973	1974	1975	1976	1977	1978	1979
Number of Passengers in Total Market (Thousands)	1,937	2,209	2,589	2,743	2,826	2,895	3,320	3,559	4,060	4,919
Number of U.S. Citizens in Total Market (Thousands)	986	1,093	1,110	1,053	1,035	997	1,128	1,250	1,341	1,511
Number of Foreign Citizens in Total Market (Thousands)	951	1,116	1,479	1,690	1,791	1,898	2,192	2,309	2,719	3,408
U.S. Citizens as a Percentage of Total Market	50.9%	49.5%	42.9%	38.4%	36.6%	34.4%	34.0%	35.1%	33.0%	30.7%
Number of Passengers on U.S. Flag (Thousands)	1,071	1,235	1,178	1,037	1,312	1,174	1,343	1,455	1,567	2,060
U.S. Flag Share as a Percentage of Total Market	55.3%	55.9%	45.5%	47.6%	46.4%	40.6%	40.4%	40.9%	38.6%	41.9%
Number of U.S. Citizens on U.S. Flag (Thousands)	672	769	673	624	589	496	556	624	652	784
Number of Foreign Citizens on U.S. Flag (Thousands)	399	466	505	683	723	678	787	831	915	1,276
Percentage U.S. Citizens Flying U.S. Flag	68.2%	70.4%	60.6%	59.3%	56.9%	49.8%	49.3%	50.0%	48.6%	51.9%
Percentage Foreign Citizens Flying U.S. Flag	42.0%	41.8%	34.1%	40.4%	40.4%	35.7%	35.9%	36.0%	33.7%	37.5%

Source: Immigration and Naturalization Service, *Reports of Passenger Travel Between the United States and Foreign Countries*, 1970-1974; and Department of Transportation, *U.S. International Air Travel Statistics*, 1975-1979.

[a]1970 and 1971 figures include charter services as well as scheduled.

Table 7A-6
U.S.-Foreign Citizens Air Travel Trends, 1970-1979—Central America and the Caribbean

Market Measures	1970ᵃ	1971ᵃ	1972	1973	1974	1975	1976	1977	1978	1979
Number of Passengers in Total Market (Thousands)	6,793	7,216	7,655	8,277	8,649	8,368	8,688	8,706	10,168	11,907
Number of U.S. Citizens in Total Market (Thousands)	4,522	4,957	5,181	5,566	5,738	5,353	5,423	5,569	6,409	7,308
Number of Foreign Citizens in Total Market (Thousands)	2,271	2,259	2,474	2,711	2,911	3,015	3,265	3,137	3,759	4,599
U.S. Citizens as a Percentage of Total Market	66.5%	68.7%	67.8%	67.3%	66.3%	64.0%	62.4%	64.0%	63.0%	61.4%
Number of Passengers on U.S. Flag (Thousands)	4,583	5,128	5,092	5,320	5,306	4,978	5,037	5,122	6,044	7,187
U.S. Flag Share as a Percentage of Total Market	67.4%	71.1%	66.6%	64.3%	61.3%	59.5%	58.0%	58.8%	59.4%	60.4%
Number of U.S. Citizens on U.S. Flag (Thousands)	3,236	3,738	3,653	3,806	3,740	3,393	3,363	3,493	4,050	4,728
Number of Foreign Citizens on U.S. Flag (Thousands)	1,347	1,390	1,439	1,514	1,566	1,586	1,674	1,629	1,994	2,459
Percentage U.S. Citizens Flying U.S. Flag	71.6%	75.4%	70.5%	68.4%	65.2%	63.4%	62.0%	62.7%	63.2%	64.7%
Percentage Foreign Citizens Flying U.S. Flag	59.3%	61.5%	58.2%	55.9%	53.8%	52.6%	51.3%	51.9%	53.1%	53.4%

Source: Immigration and Naturalization Service, *Reports of Passenger Travel Between the United States and Foreign Countries*, 1970-1974; and Department of Transportation, *U.S. International Air Travel Statistics*, 1975-1979.
ᵃ1970 and 1971 figures include charter services as well as scheduled.

Table 7A-7
U.S.-Foreign Citizens Air Travel Trends, 1970-1979—Africa

Market Measures	1970[a]	1971[a]	1972	1973	1974	1975	1976	1977	1978	1979
Number of Passengers in Total Market (Thousands)	64	57	71	73	91	114	121	169	201	243
Number of U.S. Citizens in Total Market (Thousands)	48	40	48	49	58	73	74	101	117	133
Number of Foreign Citizens in Total Market (Thousands)	16	17	23	24	33	41	47	68	84	110
U.S. Citizens as a Percentage of Total Market	75.0%	70.2%	68.0%	67.1%	63.7%	64.0%	61.1%	60.0%	58.2%	54.7%
Number of Passengers on U.S. Flag (Thousands)	61	50	62	61	68	71	68	102	111	114
U.S. Flag Share as a Percentage of Total Market	95.3%	87.7%	87.3%	83.6%	74.7%	62.3%	56.2%	60.3%	55.2%	46.9%
Number of U.S. Citizens on U.S. Flag (Thousands)	47	30	44	43	46	49	45	67	72	71
Number of Foreign Citizens on U.S. Flag (Thousands)	14	14	18	18	22	22	23	35	39	43
Percentage U.S. Citizens Flying U.S. Flag	97.9%	90.0%	91.7%	87.8%	79.3%	67.1%	60.8%	66.3%	61.5%	53.4%
Percentage Foreign Citizens Flying U.S. Flag	87.5%	82.4%	78.3%	75.0%	66.7%	53.7%	48.9%	51.5%	46.4%	39.1%

Source: Immigration and Naturalization Service, *Reports of Passenger Travel Between the United States and Foreign Countries*, 1970-1974; and Department of Transportation, *U.S. International Air Travel Statistics*, 1975-1979.
[a]1970 and 1971 figures include charter services as well as scheduled.

8 The Airline Deregulation Act of 1978

James W. Callison

The Major Decreases in Regulation under the Airline Deregulation Act of 1978

To understand the deregulation law, it is necessary to compare the economic theory of the law prior to 1978, and the theory that Congress purported to adopt in the 1978 Act. This comparison reveals that Congress only partially embraced the new economic theories. A total commitment to deregulation would have compelled the abolition of the Civil Aeronautics Board (CAB) immediately, doing away with virtually all economic regulation of the transportation industry.

The Differing Theories of the Prior and Present Laws

The prior law was patterned on the theory of transportation economics and regulation that had existed in this country since before the twentieth century. The theory held that common carrier transportation was in many respects a public utility. As such, it was believed that fairly extensive economic regulation of routes, fares, rates, intercarrier agreements, interlocking relationships, mergers and acquisitions, with limited immunities from the antitrust laws, was necessary to ensure that all portions of the public, in both large markets and small markets, would be adequately served.

At the heart of this prior system was the franchise or the licensing program. In the airline industry, the CAB was mandated to encourage airline competition. The basic statute was procompetitive:

> It is significant that Congress, addressing itself to the air transport industry, deliberately fashioned this 1938 law (The Civil Aeronautics Act, later the Federal Aviation Act of 1958) so as to identify competition in express language as a key element of the public interest.[1]

This chapter is a revised and abridged version of my article, "Airline Deregulation—Only Partially a Hoax," which appeared in the *Journal of Air Law and Commerce* 45, no. 4 (Summer 1980), © by the School of Law, Southern Methodist University.

The competition envisioned by the prior law was not, however, to be unfettered competition:

(T)his was one of an emerging group of statutes that did not regulate the so-called "natural monopolies" that identified conventional public utility regulation, but instead called for "regulated competition," achieving the benefits of competition without the evils of unrestrained entry or undercost rate wars.[2]

Indeed, the CAB was also mandated by the prior law to foster sound economic conditions in the industry to assure continuation and stability of service.

In practice, while the CAB's policies were most often procompetitive, the Board limited the number of carriers in a given market to that level which it felt could operate economically. In this sense, the franchise system achieved the desired stability and continuity of service. This did, however, somewhat restrain competition, even though by the early 1970s, before the deregulation movement got underway, over 79 percent of the nation's scheduled air passenger traffic was already competitively served and, in most major markets, multiple carriers were certificated. Moreover, the prior law specifically prohibited the CAB from restricting the right of an air carrier, once certificated, to add to or change schedules, equipment, accommodations, and facilities for performing the authorized air transportation and service as the development of its business and the demands of the public required. Thus not only was competition fostered under the prior law, but once certificated the carriers were allowed to compete in whatever manner they desired, generally free of governmental dictation as to the quantity or quality of their service. The licensing system nevertheless imposed some restraint on new entrants and on entry by existing carriers into new markets.

In return for this competitively oriented yet somewhat restraining licensing system, the old law imposed firm public service responsibilities on air carriers. Such responsibilities included (1) obligations to serve both large and small communities and both large and small markets except where the CAB relieved a carrier of responsibility at a specific city;[3] (2) CAB control over airline rates and fares; (3) extensive control over airline accounts, with elaborate reporting requirements; (4) prohibitions against unfair practices and unfair competition; and (5) various other controls and monitoring of airline operations.[4]

It was a balanced system—mild restraints on entry and competition in return for firm public service obligations of the carriers.

The economic principles espoused by proponents of airline deregulation point 180 degrees in the opposite direction. These principles state that airlines are in no manner public utilities, but are just like any other business. The theories hold that these businesses are also of importance to the public, are not governmentally controlled, and yet their services and products are forthcoming at reasonable prices in an atmosphere where the absence of economic regulation and the interplay of free-market forces allows for maximum efficiencies and allocations of resources. Hence, the theory argues, air transportation will react similarly, and optimum air service will result if the government simply gets out of the way so that the marketplace determines the price, quality, variety, and quantity of services.

Senator Howard Cannon (D-Nev.), a principal architect of the Airline Deregulation Act, put it this way: the increased, if "imperfect," competition, which is supposed to result from extensive deregulation, should allocate resources better than the imperfect regulation that previously existed.[5] The imperfect regulation that existed under the prior law did produce the world's foremost air transportation system, with more service in more markets by more carriers with more competition with greater variety at lower rates and fares than existed anywhere else. Only time will tell whether the new law will improve on this system.

The Major Changes

In any event, Congress has adopted the new theory in major respects and, as Alfred Kahn predicted, the industry has been thoroughly "scrambled."[6] It is now too late to return to the prior system, whatever the results. There has, in fact, been deregulation in many areas, and as a practical matter many profound changes have resulted both in the governmental system and in the industry. The following are a few of the highlights.

Future Abolition of the Civil Aeronautics Board. The 1978 Act has scheduled two major diminutions in the CAB's power, leading toward its eventual abolition. As of January 1, 1982, the CAB will lose virtually all of its power to control entry into the air transportation business or entry by carriers into new markets. After that date, a regime of essentially free entry will exist within U.S. domestic air transportation.

One year later, on January 1, 1983, the CAB will effectively lose all of its power over airline passenger fares (it has already lost most of its power over air freight rates). At the same time the CAB's remaining authority over domestic airline mergers and interlocking relationships between domestic air carriers, and its remaining power to confer antitrust immunity with respect to agreements and arrangements between domestic air carriers, is scheduled to be transferred to the Department of Justice.

By not later than January 1, 1984, the CAB is required to report to Congress concerning the progress and effects of deregulation. Assuming that Congress does not change its mind because of these reports, or for some other reason, the agency is scheduled to go out of existence on January 1, 1985. At that time, the CAB's authority with respect to foreign air transportation will be transferred to the Department of Transportation, which will have to exercise this new authority in consultation with the Department of State. Simultaneously, the CAB's authority concerning mergers, intercarrier agreements, and antitrust immunities relating to foreign air transportation will be transferred to the Department of Justice, which will have earlier received similar authority concerning domestic air transportation; and the CAB's power to determine rates for the carriage of mail in interstate and overseas air transportation will be transferred to the Postal Service, which will be obligated to exercise such authority through "negotiations or competitive bidding." Jurisdiction over rates for foreign transportation of mail will be transferred to the Department of Transportation, which must exercise the authority in consultation with the Department of State.

Route Entry. In the short span of just over two years since the airline deregulation law was passed, the domestic air transport route system has been completely opened. In contrast to the entry restraints that existed under the prior law, air carriers can now fly virtually any place they choose. There are indications in the Conference Report[7] that Congress perhaps did not intend the transition to open route entry to proceed as rapidly as it has, but intended a gradual transition over the full period between 1978 and December 31, 1981.[8]

Under the revised law, a certificate is still technically required, but freely given in the case of a fit applicant despite the existence of statutory standards other than "fitness" that go virtually unnoticed. Utilizing the procedural reforms in the new statute, the current CAB employs expedited procedures with respect to most domestic route applications, and grants them in a matter of weeks after issuing the initial show cause order.[9] It soon became apparent that objections to show cause orders on grounds other than applicant's fitness (for example, that the proposed service "is not consistent with the public convenience and necessity") were futile. As a result, very few objections are filed today with respect to applications for expansion rights, and the "certification" process is especially swift.

In the months since the law was passed, thousands of city-pair authorizations have been granted to air carriers.[10] Multiple authorizations have been granted in numerous city pairs. While some of the former intrastate carriers and some of the former charter-only carriers have expanded into scheduled interstate markets, other new route awards have been made to commuter carriers and newly certificated carriers.[11]

Service Obligations. Interestingly enough, however, the bulk of the new certifications has not been utilized. By and large, air carriers are simply banking new authorities to have maximum flexibility until 1982, when the deregulation law strips the CAB of all authority over domestic airline route entry, except for determinations of fitness.

As this indicates, under the new law—much more than was so under the prior system—certificates carry no obligations either to begin or maintain services, except in the case of certain small communities:

> Under the new Act, mandatory authority, whether in domestic or foreign air transportation, no longer exists; airlines are not required to institute newly authorized service or obtain Board permission before terminating or suspending operations as long as they provide the statutory notice under section 401(j).[12]

Route Exit. The corollary to deregulation of route entry is freedom to exit markets. The basic economic theory that the government should step out of the way and that market forces should govern air services can be implemented only if air carriers have both exit and entry freedom. The marketplace cannot function unless carriers are given discretion not only to exit unprofitable markets, but also to shift resources from less profitable to more profitable markets.

The revised law does in fact afford air carriers increased flexibility to exit markets. In contrast to the prior law's requirement that an application for suspension or termination be filed, and that CAB approval first be granted after full administrative proceedings, including hearings, the new procedure allows an air carrier to terminate all services at a community simply by giving ninety days' advance notice.

While there are procedures that permit the registering of objections to proposed terminations and suspensions, in most cases the ninety-day notice is all that is required before a carrier can exit a community and its air transportation markets. This is true even though the CAB is authorized in certain cases to require continued service beyond the ninetieth day, where the exiting carrier is the last air carrier serving a particular community and a replacement is not readily forthcoming.

On the whole, and to the extent Congress permitted, the CAB has implemented a liberalized exit in accordance with the free-market economic theories. This has been beneficial to existing air carriers because, in many instances, new authorities obtained under deregulation have been exercised only as a result of a shifting of resources away from markets previously served. Indeed, in the first year after the new law was passed, notices affecting over 180 different points were filed by trunk and regional air carriers announcing that they were terminating all of their service at those cities.[13] In some instances, more than one carrier has terminated service at the same point, and at some of these communities service has dropped from two or three or more carriers to a single carrier. In some cases, replacements, mostly small commuter carriers, have stepped in to fill service gaps, though service is not necessarily to and from the same points previously served.

While exit rights have been significantly increased by the new law, the restrictions placed on exit exhibit serious misgivings by Congress about the free-market theories on which it professed to rely in passing the Airline Deregulation Act of 1978. These congressionally imposed restrictions have severely circumscribed exit rights at small communities.

During a ten-year transition period, the CAB (and after it goes out of existence in 1985, the Department of Transportation) has been given power to require the last air carrier serving any community to maintain what is called "essential air service" until a suitable replacement can be found and judged fit by the CAB.[14] This power exists even though the effects of free entry elsewhere on a carrier's system might dictate an earlier shifting of resources away from the community in question. Distrustful of the marketplace, Congress also gave the CAB new powers to define essential air service within parameters laid down by Congress itself, and authorized the agency to pay compensation to the incumbent for losses incurred during any period of required continuance of service beyond the carrier's planned termination date.

The first group of cities are those named in air carrier certificates, but which received service from one or no certificated carriers as of October 14, 1978, the date of the deregulation law's enactment. As of that date there were 555 such communities, including 228 points in Alaska. For these points, Congress guaranteed essential air service, including subsidized service where necessary. According to the statute, the CAB has the discretion to determine essential air service; but, for points other than Alaska points, the statute requires a minimum of at least two roundtrips five days per week, or the level of service in 1977 (whichever is less). The standard is lower for Alaskan points. Any carrier proposing to withdraw essential air service must provide notice of its intent (ninety days, if it is a certificated carrier; thirty days, if not), and the CAB may require it to continue serving the point until a willing replacement carrier can be found. Similarly, essential air service must be determined and guaranteed for any point whose service is reduced to one or no certificated carrier after October 24, 1978.

The second group of cities are those which the CAB designates as eligible points among communities that were deleted from carriers' certificates between July 1, 1968, and October 24, 1978. The agency has recently implemented procedures to determine eligible points under this phase of the Small Community Program. Like the other eligible communities, those made eligible under this program will have essential air service determined, with federal subsidy supporting the service where necessary, but in the normal situation the CAB cannot order a carrier to commence service at a point not being served by the carrier.

Still on the drawing board is a White House program to sponsor developmental air services for isolated or depressed areas of the country. Some discussions have taken place between administrative officials and other governmental (including CAB and congressional) officials concerning the prospects for development of federal/state or local cost-sharing arrangements to support such developmental services. No concrete legislative or other proposals have yet been advanced for such programs, however.

This Small Community Program was a major excuse for continuing the CAB in existence despite so-called deregulation, and the CAB is exercising considerable watchdog activities in this area. Indeed, as the number of service terminations has mounted, officials of small- and medium-size communities where the greatest loss of service has occurred, and their congressmen and senators have brought pressure to bear on the CAB to become more restrictive concerning exit. The CAB has endeavored to resist these pressures, but it nevertheless has gradually begun to impose stricter standards.

There are indications that efforts may be made to amend the existing statute to withdraw some of the new exit rights. Thus far the major congressional supporters of deregulation have resisted these efforts, but as air carriers exercise their exit rights added pressures to amend the statute could materialize.

Any such withdrawal of exit freedom would be damaging. It would be extremely difficult to operate successfully under a regime where entry was free but exit rights were severely curtailed. Senator Cannon has expressed the problem this way:

> An important understanding which I wish to emphasize . . . is that there is no half-regulation, half-deregulation solution which is feasible. We cannot, for example, go back and re-regulate exit, leaving entry and rates deregulated. Carriers cannot be told both that they must maintain services which result in losses, and that they are free to enter new markets at low fares to out-compete airlines which, in turn, cannot change their services in response to the new competition. Such an irrational economic basis would not be feasible.[15]

In theory a return to the prior system, where both entry and exit were regulated, would be preferable to a change that tightened up only the exit side of the equation. The nation's air transport system has been so transformed as a result of the deregulation, however, that there is no practical way to return to the past.

Rates and Fares. In domestic air transportation, air freight rates, airline all-cargo service, and in most respects cargo service provided on combination passenger/cargo aircraft, are now almost totally deregulated. Airlines have always acted individually in setting prices for domestic air freight and passenger service, rather than by conference as is done in some other transportation modes. Under the new law, however, airlines can set each individual air freight rate at any level any particular carrier desires, without significant governmental control or interference.[16]

Even the official air freight tariff system has been abolished, although airlines still maintain a private system of air freight tariffs. The private system, however, does not have the force of law that official CAB tariffs had, and the new tariff system is severely circumscribed by the antitrust laws.

Prior to the Act, new carrier tariffs were subject to immediate CAB suspension followed by an investigation that could declare the fares unlawful. Even if they were not suspended immediately, the CAB would still investigate them and find them unlawful on the grounds that they were predatory, discriminating, or prejudicial. With respect to passenger fares, the CAB's powers of suspension and investigation have been modified by providing for zones within which a carrier may raise or lower fares without CAB interference, subject to certain notice conditions and residual CAB jurisdiction over predation, unjust discrimination, and undue preference or prejudice. The law provides for an upward no-suspend zone in nonmonopoly markets of 5 percent above the Standard Industry Fare Level (SIFL), defined as the fares in effect on July 1, 1977, as adjusted for cost changes since that time. The law also permits carriers to reduce fares as much as 50 percent below the SIFL, unless the CAB finds that the reduced fares violate the federal antitrust laws.

Even before the new Act was passed, the CAB had revised its fare policies to permit increases in fares without CAB interference by as much as 10 percent above the then-prescribed ceiling fares in markets authorized to four or more carriers, by as much as 5 percent in markets authorized to two or three carriers, and up to 5 percent for fifty-eight days in one year in monopoly markets. Since passage of the Act, the CAB has expanded the zone of upward fare flexibility to 30 percent more than the SIFL plus $15 (with the $15 to be adjusted by the same amount as the SIFL) and has made the zone of downward fare flexibility unlimited. More recently, the CAB has also discussed another rule that would encourage peak and off-peak pricing by removing the ceiling altogether for 20 percent of the total seats in any given city pair. This would allow carriers to raise fares in a market on peak days such as a Friday to encourage travel on other days.

As indicated, the SIFL starts with the coach fares that were in effect July 1, 1977, adjusted on the basis of industry cost changes between that date and July 1, 1979, when these legislative provisions of the law took effect. From that date forward the CAB is obligated to raise or lower the SIFL semiannually for changes in reported airline costs, without any adjustment to those costs. The requirement that actual costs be considered without regulatory adjustment is essential to the establishment of airline managerial freedom and discretion over fares.

Under the prior law, even though the industry was characterized by low fares and extensive price competition, the CAB used many techniques to hold down the rate and fare level. The legal powers most often used were the powers to suspend proposed rates and fares, to investigate them, and to order changes in rates or fares believed by the agency after investigation to be unlawful under one or more of various statutory standards. These powers have been circumscribed by the "zone of reasonableness," within which the agency is powerless to suspend, investigate, or order changes. The practical device most often used under the prior law was to disallow airline costs that the agency concluded were improperly incurred. This device is no longer available to the agency with respect to the SIFL, which thus increases or decreases in accordance with general economic conditions and with the actual cost experience of the airlines.

Recently, because of the rapidly escalating cost of aviation fuel, the CAB has used its remaining powers over the passenger fare level to allow changes in the SIFL more frequently than semiannually. The SIFL is now adjusted semiannually to take account of all changes in airline costs, with interim modifications based solely on changes in airline fuel expenses. Although there are differences of opinion between the air carriers and the CAB as to whether the agency has actually permitted recovery of all increases in fuel expenses, or has acted speedily enough in view of the rapidity with which fuel costs have been escalating, these various adjustments in the SIFL are nevertheless the bases for the recent, necessarily repetitive increases in airline passenger fares.

This general condition of mildly increased freedom with respect to passenger fares will continue to exist until January 1, 1983, at which time the passenger tariff system will cease to exist and the CAB will lose virtually all control over airline fares.[17]

The foregoing related to the industry's basic fares—that is, day coach, night coach, and first class fares. In addition to the new and gradually increasing freedoms the industry has with respect to these fares, the new law increased the freedom that air carriers had under the prior law to engage in differential or discount pricing. Discounted fares are made available under limitations, rules, and regulations that distinguish the discounted fare traveler from the full-fare passenger (for example, by requiring advance purchase of tickets and restricting the times of permissible travel). The discount fares are designed to attract passengers who would not otherwise travel, to fill seats that would otherwise fly empty, to shift traffic from peak to off-peak travel, or to promote and develop a new market. The CAB's Bureau of Consumer Protection exhibits a growing tendency to engage in consumer protection regulation with respect to discount fares, but the freedom to engage in such differential pricing is essentially guaranteed and enhanced by the whole thrust of the new law.

Reduced Reporting Requirements and CAB Staffing. While the deregulation act itself did little to reduce the airline industry's burdensome reporting requirements, the CAB does appear to be moving in that direction on its own, through interpretation of the statute. Thus the CAB is conducting a comprehensive evaluation of its reporting requirements and financial and statistical information publications to restructure its regulatory information activities in light of the procompetitive directions of, and the hoped-for decrease in governmental involvement with, the industry. The CAB's efforts are designed to improve the quality of the information both received and disseminated by it, but it is too early to tell the results of those efforts. Indeed, the CAB has increased some reporting requirements while reducing others.

In spite of CAB chairman Cohen's announced objectives to dismantle the agency, the original CAB budget request for FY 1980 actually called for increased appropriations of $106.8 million (as opposed to $100.5 million actual budget for the prior year), and a reduction in permanent employee staffing of only 11 persons (830 persons in FY 1979 versus 819 requested positions in FY 1980). In May 1979 this request was amended to further reduce the staffing for FY 1980 to 743, a reduction of 87 from FY 1979. The budget proposal for FY 1981 shows a further reduction of 53 employees. Ironically, the CAB's projections in its original budget request for FY 1980 called for a staff of 500 persons even in 1985, the year the agency is scheduled to go out of existence.

Differing Carrier Reactions. Before turning to the subject of added regulation under the new law, and particularly the increased application of the antitrust laws to the air transport industry, it is both interesting and instructive to examine the varying reactions of air carriers to the new freedoms discussed here. The major reaction has been in the area of route entry. Because the CAB quickly gave the domestic air transport industry almost total freedom in this area, carriers have been able to move as rapidly or as slowly as they desired into new markets.

Some carriers have engaged in sharp modifications of their systems—expanding into new markets here, abandoning other markets there, and then abandoning some of the new markets. In some cases, the rationale for rapid system adjustments has been the belief that only large carriers will survive deregulation, as many opponents of deregulation predicted. This belief has led to some carriers making strong efforts to expand and change quickly to prepare for the onslaught of open competition and avoid merger or other extinction. Whatever the motivation, some of the carriers that have reacted to deregulation with erratic changes are suffering acute financial problems. Whether they will persist cannot yet be told.

The reaction of the local service carriers to deregulation can be viewed as a special case. Most of these carriers were opposed to extensive deregulation, believing that they could not survive in the absence of public-utility-type governmental protection and controls. Regardless of their survival chances in the long term, these carriers are generally growing faster thus far under deregulation than are the larger carriers, and generally are doing so with favorable financial results.[18] Deregulation has enabled these carriers to move rapidly into selected long-haul markets to balance their short-haul services, to enter vacation markets quickly, and to balance their business travel patronage with discretionary travel demand.

All of this is as it should be under the theory of airline deregulation. Each carrier should respond to market forces in its own way, and should enjoy or suffer the consequences of its decisions, as the case may be. Greatly liberated entry freedom (and relatively improved exit flexibility) are the principal regulatory changes that have made these varying carrier responses possible, and which do the most to validate the labeling of the new statute as "deregulation."

Federal Preemption

Until 1978, the federal statutes contained no specific provision preempting state economic regulation of air transportation. As a result, a few states exercised jurisdiction over intrastate air transportation, including operations within a state by an interstate carrier even when part of a continuous journey. This state authority was especially exercised in connection with rates and fares. For example, in California the state regulation sometimes required interstate carriers on flights between two points within the state to charge different fares for passengers whose flights were wholly within that state vis-à-vis passengers connecting to out of state flights. Nevada required carriers operating within the state to hold state certificates (or licenses), and regulated the carriers, including interstate carriers, in other ways as well.

The deregulation statute contains an express preemption provision. Section 105 provides that no state or political subdivision and no interstate agency shall enact or enforce any law or regulation concerning rates, routes, or services of any carrier having authority under Title IV of the Act to provide interstate air transportation. The statute further provides that, on receipt of authority from the CAB, an intrastate carrier is deemed to have obtained all of its authority from the CAB under Title IV.

The first judicial test of this preemption provision is pending in the Ninth Circuit Court of Appeals. After the deregulation act was passed, the California Public Utilities Commission (PUC) attempted to exercise rate jurisdiction (as it had in the past) by ordering Hughes Airwest (a federally certificated carrier) to maintain an existing level of fares in intra-California markets, despite CAB approval to increase such fares. Hughes Airwest, several other carriers, the CAB, and the Department of Justice filed suit against the PUC. In March 1979 a permanent injunction was granted, preventing the PUC from regulating the routes, rates, and service of the plaintiff carriers. The PUC has appealed the decision to the Ninth Circuit Court of Appeals.

International Air Transportation

In an effort to transpose some of the procompetitive principles and other provisions of the deregulation act to international air transportation, the Congress has recently enacted the International Air Transportation Act of 1979.

In addition to the strong enunciation of procompetitive policies and goals for international transportation like those now applicable to interstate and overseas transportation, the new law extends to international transportation fare flexibility and standard fare adjustment provisions similar to those adopted in the deregulation act. Thus the law creates a "standard foreign fare level" (SFFL) comparable to the standard industry fare level (SIFL) in domestic and overseas service. The SFFL is based on fares in effect on October 1, 1979, except that the CAB has discretion to establish a different SFFL for markets with as much as 25 percent of total traffic carried by U.S. carriers in foreign air transportation. Like the domestic SIFL, the SFFL must be adjusted periodically: in the case of fuel cost changes, every sixty days; and for other cost changes, at least semiannually. Within the zone of 5 percent above the SFFL and 50 percent below, carriers would be free to adjust fares with limited provision for suspension by the CAB.[19]

The new law makes it clear that international authority for U.S. carriers may not be altered, modified, suspended, or revoked through the simplified procedures now provided by Subsection (p) of Section 401 of the Act, if the certificate holder requests an oral evidentiary hearing or if the CAB determines that such a hearing is in the public interest. On the other hand, the law would give the CAB authority to revoke or suspend unexercised foreign rights, subject to certain notice requirements and an "opportunity" (without hearings) for the certificate holder to present its views.

The legislation also authorizes carriage of interstate and overseas traffic by foreign carriers, under certain highly circumscribed conditions. Thus foreign carriers may receive exemptions (not to exceed thirty days) to engage in overseas and interstate air transportation if the CAB finds, after consultation with the Department of Transportation, that an emergency exists "not arising in the normal course of business," and that all possible efforts have been made to have the traffic accommodated by U.S. carriers.

Other changes include a modification of modified standards used to determine the antitrust ramifications of intercarrier agreements—domestic and international—with some recognition of international comity and foreign policy considerations as public interest factors that may be sufficient to justify otherwise anticompetitive agreements. The revised law gives the Secretary of Transportation authority to permit foreign-registered aircraft to operate between U.S. points under a lease (without crew) to a U.S. carrier. The law also extends the prohibition against "part charters" (the comingling of charter passengers with scheduled passengers) until December 31, 1981.

Conclusion

The Deregulation Act of 1978 initiated the gradual deregulation of the U.S. commercial airline industry. As this chapter has shown, much deregulation has already occurred, and, as of now, there is a clear schedule for what remains.

The central question is whether the CAB actually will go out of existence. Congress has slated the abolition of the CAB for 1985, after two major reductions of its power—first, its loss of all route entry control after 1981; and, second, its loss of power over passenger fares after 1982.

Congress will, however, review the situation prior to 1985. There are substantial political constituencies that oppose deregulation and will fight the abolition of the CAB in 1985. On the other hand, there are other groups who are pressing for the abolition of the CAB even before 1985. Legislation proposing such an "early sunset" has been discussed in Congress, and the CAB itself advocates termination of its activities prior to the statutory deadline of 1985. The future of airline deregulation (or regulation) will depend on Congress in its review of the Airline Deregulation Act of 1978.

Notes

1. Continental Air Lines, Inc. v. CAB, 519 F.2nd 944, 953 (D.C. Cir. 1975).
2. Ibid.
3. Even then, this could be done only after due process, including hearings for all parties concerned, especially the communities involved.

4. For example, rules and regulations for the carriage of mail and the setting of the rate of compensation; CAB control over mergers, consolidations and acquisitions of control; prohibitions against interlocking relationships; CAB scrutiny of intercarrier agreements; and a number of broad investigatory and enforcement powers.

5. Speech by the senator before the National Association of State Aviation Officials, August 22, 1979, p. 1 of printed text.

6. Chairman, Civil Aeronautics Board, 1977 to 1978.

7. H. Rpt. 95-1179, 124 *Cong. Rec.* H 12636-64, part II (October 12, 1978); Senate Concurrence: 124 *Cong. Rec.* S 18796-801, part II (October 14, 1978); House Concurrence: 124 *Cong. Rec.* H 13444-50, part IV (October 14, 1978).

8. The statute does not call for totally open entry until January 1, 1982. Even after December 31, 1981, a certificate would still be required unless the law is amended to eliminate this technicality, but the only prerequisite will be that the applicant is "fit."

9. A show cause order is a CAB order that solicits any party to present to the CAB such reasons and considerations as one has to offer as to why a particular order of the CAB should *not* be put into effect.

10. The number of city pairs (markets) involved is smaller, although still substantial. The number in the text is the total number of new authorizations granted to all air carriers, many of which are duplicative as explained in the following text.

11. For example, Air Florida, whose operations were confined to the State of Florida prior to passage of the deregulation act; Air California and Pacific Southwest Airlines, which operated solely within California; and Southwest Airlines, which confined its operations to the State of Texas.

12. CAB Order 79-5-56, pp. 2-3.

13. About one-third of these were points at which the filing carrier's service was already suspended under the prior law. Also note that, while the procedures under the old law were much more involved and time consuming (because they afforded all interested parties, including the affected communities, an opportunity to be heard), there were nevertheless about 130 points that lost all certificated service in the ten-year period between 1968 and the time of passage of the revised law at the end of 1978. Normally this occurred because of the community's inability economically to support the service, a factor no longer considered in deciding under section 419(a) of the revised Act whether the CAB should compel continuation of service under the new Small Community Program discussed here (except in determining if subsidy is needed to support otherwise unprofitable service).

14. The Small Community Program of the Deregulation Act (49 U.S.C. 1398) guarantees essential air service to two groups of points that Congress

feared might lose vital air service if left to the mercy of market forces. See following text for details.

15. Hearing before the Subcommittee on Aviation, Committee on Commerce, Science and Transporation, U.S. Senate, 96th Congress, First Session, on Impact of Airline Deregulation on Service to Small- and Medium-Sized Communities.

16. The CAB retains jurisdiction over "unjust discrimination" and "undue preference or prejudice" (and now "predation") with respect to both rates and fares [49 U.S.C. § 1482(d)], but—in theory at least—this should not give it control over rate or fare levels per se.

17. As mentioned earlier, the law vests residual power in the CAB over predation, unjustly discriminatory, or unduly preferential fares, rates, and charges.

18. Thus during the twelve months ended 9/30/79, the regional carriers' total revenue ton-miles grew 21.9 percent, compared to only an 8.5 percent growth for so-called domestic trunk lines, and the smaller carriers' net income declined 14.1 percent compared to a 68.0 percent decline for the trunk lines (CAB Air Carrier Traffic Statistics and Quarterly Interim Financial Statements, September 1979). [This trend continued in 1980. Year over year, local service carrier RTMs were up 7.9 percent in 1980, while trunk RTMs fell 5.1 percent. Net income for the locals climbed 86 percent to $36 million, while net income for the trunks fell from $260 million in 1979 to a $45 million loss in 1980. Ed.]

19. Some suspension powers have been left with the CAB, including the right to suspend fares above the SFFL based upon findings of undue preference or prejudice, or unjust discrimination. Similarly, decreases below the SFFL can be suspended based upon predation or discrimination findings. In all cases, the CAB retains suspension power where it can find that the public interest demands suspension because of "unreasonable regulatory action of a foreign government."

9

The Coming Decade in Commercial Aviation

George W. James

1322
6150
US

Introduction

The end of the 1970s was tumultuous for the airline industry. Those years were highlighted by the Airline Deregulation Act of 1978, which began the process of passenger deregulation, to be completed with the scheduled phase-out of the Civil Aeronautics Board (CAB) in 1985.[1] By 1980 route deregulation was achieved (de facto if not de jure), and price deregulation had begun with the CAB allowing fares within a broad range. Deregulation of travel agent sales commissions was also in effect by 1980, and innovative commission plans were extensively offered in all quarters.

During the last half of the 1970s, the basic economics of the industry changed drastically. Fuel costs rose at an unprecedented rate, which raised variable costs in relation to fixed costs and forced airline managements to reconsider operating strategies based on the traditional high-fixed/low-variable costs of the industry. Four-engine aircraft, which consume jet fuel in great quantities, suddenly became uneconomical on many routes and had to be prematurely retired. Costs rose faster than yields or traffic, and the industry fell from a record profit year in 1978 to a record operating loss year in 1980, creating a capital shortage because obsolete planes needed to be replaced at a time when the industry was not earning sufficient profits to sustain large capital investment.

Early in the decade of the 1980s, change continues in the industry as the process of deregulation gains speed and costs continue to be volatile. This chapter is designed to put the events of the past few years in perspective and outline the challenges facing the industry in the 1980s.

Recent Developments in the Industry: A Perspective for the Future

For 1978, the airlines had an all-time high operating profit of $1.4 billion. Only two years later, the airlines sustained in 1980 an all-time record operating loss of $225 million (figure 9-1).

Both the profits of 1978 and the losses of 1980 demonstrate the enormous financial sensitivity of the airline industry to changes in certain key factors. The airline industry has long been noted as a highly cyclical industry.

185

There are four key elements of airline operations that, taken together, account for these rollercoaster-like changes in profitability. These four items, as analyzed in chapter 1 are:

1. Traffic—usually measured by revenue passenger-miles (RPMs).
2. Capacity—usually measured by available seat-miles (ASMs) or available ton-miles (ATMs).
3. Unit revenue—called yield and usually measured as cents per RPM.
4. Unit costs—normally measured as cents per ASM or ATM.

A significant change in either traffic, capacity, yields, or costs that is not offset by a change in one of the other three elements will cause a sharp swing in profits. To put it another way, uncompensated changes in either breakeven or actual load factor will sharply influence profitability. The events of the recent past can be used to illustrate this.

Source: CAB Form 41.

Figure 9-1. Operating Profit

The years 1975 through 1978 were characterized by steadily increasing costs. This inflation averaged about 7 percent per year and had to be offset by either increasing yield, increasing traffic, or decreasing capacity. In the years 1975 through 1977, yields increased at less than the pace of unit costs, but the slack was taken up by the fact that passenger traffic increased faster than capacity. In 1978 costs continued to increase (figure 9-2) and yields actually declined (figure 9-3). The combination of higher costs and lower yields raised the break-even load factor significantly, as shown in figure 9-4.

However, since traffic surged upward by 17 percent while capacity grew at a much slower rate (figure 9-5), actual load factors rose faster than break-even load factors. As figure 9-6 shows, average load factors increased about 5 percentage points while the break-even level grew only 3.6 percent. The result was record profits, indicating how sensitive the industry is to small changes in the spread between actual and break-even load factors.

The fare cuts of 1978 and the surge in traffic that occurred were seen by some to be the sure-fire key to airline profitability. But 1978 was an abnor-

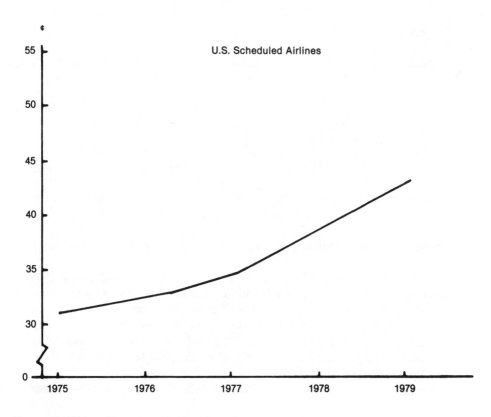

Source: CAB Form 41.

Figure 9-2. Operating Expense per ATM

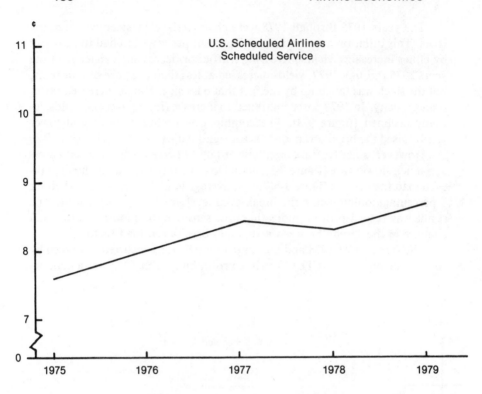

Source: CAB Form 41.

Figure 9-3. Yield per Passenger-Mile

mal and nonsustainable situation. The overall economy was very strong, and this plus the cut in fares produced a one-time surge in traffic and actual load factors. So long as load factors continued to increase at so rapid a rate, they could continue to override the pressures of inflation. But note that to keep that phase of the cycle going required continued extraordinary increases in average load factors, and those increases could not continue indefinitely.

In the first half of 1979, it looked as though the profitability of 1978 might continue. But fuel prices began to swing sharply upward, putting tremendous pressure on industry profits. For the year, unit costs increased by more than 14 percent (increases in the second half were over 25 percent). Load factors continued to climb, reaching 63.3 percent for 1979, but not all increases in costs could be recouped by the increasing load factors, and operating profits fell to $215 million.

Significantly, the financial decline of 1979 did not result from traffic

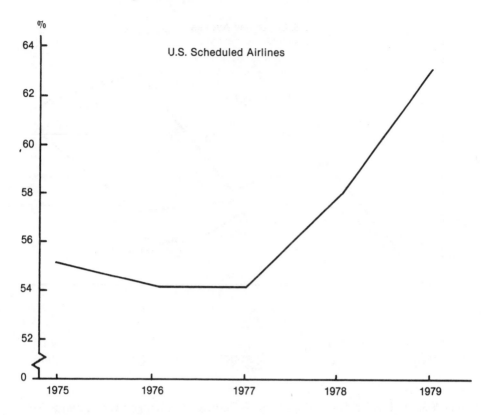

Source: CAB Form 41.

Figure 9-4. Break-Even Passenger Load Factor

softness, or an outright decrease in load factor. Passenger-miles in 1979 were still increasing at a double-digit rate, and load factors were rising, but the all important spread between actual and break-even load factors narrowed. Profits dropped sharply.

As part of this general picture also note that, even though 1978 profits were record breaking in absolute terms, they were not large in terms of the percentage margin they represented in relation to gross revenue (figure 9-7).

The operating profit margin in 1978 was only about 6 percent—much lower than the 13.5 percent margin that the industry had briefly enjoyed in the mid-1960s, and only slightly higher than the 4.7 percent margin experienced in the years 1972-1974 and in 1976-1977. For the rest of U.S. industry (900 companies) the operating margin averaged 13-14 percent each year during the decade of the 1970s.

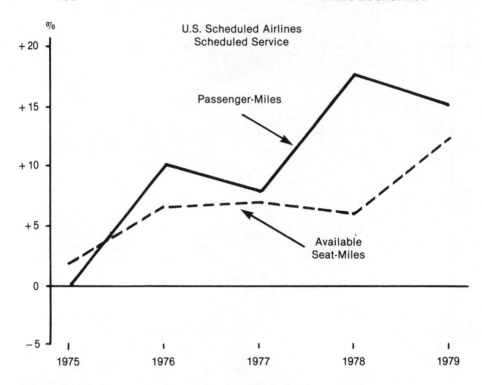

Source: CAB Form 41.
Figure 9-5. Airline Traffic and Capacity—Percentage Change over Previous Year

With the thin airline operating profit margin, it took only a moderate change in a few elements to plunge the industry into the sharp drop of earnings of 1979 and the record operating loss of 1980.

A further point to be noted in figure 9-7 is that the weakened results of 1979-1980 represent the first time in recent airline history in which the operating profit margin dropped to close to (or below) zero for two years in a row. This contrasts with other recent recessions in which the near-zero profit margin was a matter of only one-year duration (that is, 1961, 1970, 1975).

The cyclical experience of 1978-1980 provides important new insights into the economic dynamics that affect this industry. The results of 1978 were heralded by some as virtually the discovery of a self-perpetuating secret of airline success—that is, cut fares, increase the load factor, and improve profitability. Clearly this analysis was premature. The difficult job of managing costs, yields, traffic, and capacity remains. To see what is in store for the 1980s, we now have to look at the long-range outlook for those factors and the trends for the U.S. economy as a whole.

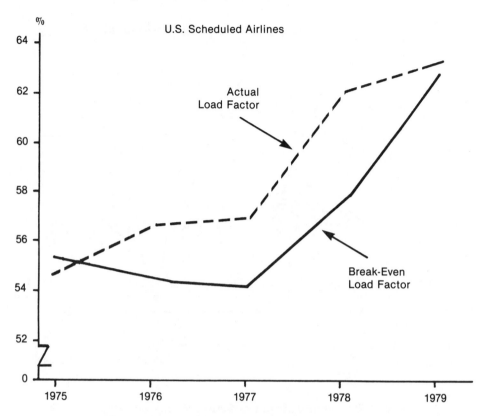

Source: CAB Form 41.

Figure 9-6. Actual versus Break-Even Load Factor

Future Factors Affecting Airline Development

The U.S. Economy during the Early 1980s

The losses of 1980 were attributable in part to a recession that had an adverse impact on airline traffic, particularly nonbusiness travel. Passenger traffic in 1980 showed the largest drop in aviation history, 3 percent. Traffic has declined from the previous year only twice before, in 1948 and 1975, and in each of those years the decline was less than 1 percent.

Over the next four to five years, the U.S. economy will be marked by continued inflation, concern over unemployment, difficulties in capital financing, and possible shortages in certain critical raw materials. Nevertheless, several long-range economic forecasts predict real GNP to rise at an average annual rate of 3-4 percent.

Airline Economics

Source: CAB Form 41.
Figure 9-7. Operating Profit as Percent of Revenues

   As the airline industry has matured, the industry has become more sensitive to national economic developments and the business cycle. Thus for
the airlines in 1981-1984 national economic environment will have important implications. The airlines will likely face slower market growth as a
result of slower national economic growth. Also, steps taken by the airlines
to cut costs and increase productivity in the 1970s will have to be pursued
with even greater intensity in the first half of the 1980s. The carriers will
have to be alert continually to possible shortages of critical resources, particularly fuel.

Outlook for Airline Costs and Fares

Few, if any, industries can match the airline record of past price improvement. When adjusted for inflation, airline average yields per passenger-mile
have trended consistently downward over the past three decades (see figure
9-8). The average yield (in constant dollars) was 11 percent less in 1960 than

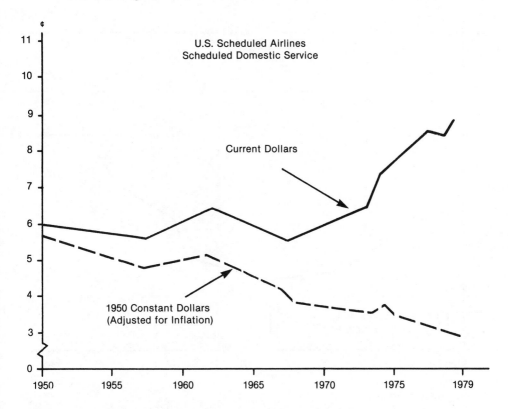

Source: CAB Form 41.

Figure 9-8. Yield per Passenger-Mile

in 1950—then dropped another 25 percent by 1970, and another 21 percent by 1979.

The ability to offer a steadily improving bargain in airline prices was a function of several factors. Most important was the increase in technological efficiency with the transition from piston to jets that started in 1960. This improvement produced a substantial decline in ATM costs—cutting such cost by about one-third during the 1960s (figure 9-9).

More recently, there were important productivity gains achieved by increases in seating density and in average load factors. Unfortunately, both of these were largely nonrecurring factors. At the same time, other pressures have developed to push airline costs upward.

The elements of the future cost outlook are discussed in the following sections.

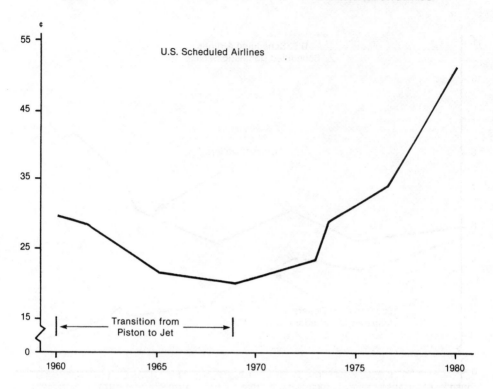

Source: CAB Form 41.

Figure 9-9. Operating Expense per ATM

Fuel Prices

Fuel has become more than 30 percent of total airline operating cost. Its price trend over the last few years is shown in table 9-1.

By the end of 1980, fuel prices had stabilized somewhat, but the long-term outlook has not significantly improved. In fact, sharp rises began again in early 1981 with President Reagan's decontrol of domestic oil prices, though they then leveled off again. Still, the underlying supply/demand forces that have enabled OPEC to boost prices so drastically have not been structurally changed.

Labor Costs

The bargaining power of organized labor is especially great in the airline industry. The inability to sell from inventory creates a problem for a struck airline that is considerably greater than that faced in most other industries.

Table 9-1
Trend of Jet Fuel Prices, 1967-1980—U.S. Scheduled Airlines

Year	Price per Gallon (Cents)
1967	10.4¢
1968	10.2
1969	11.2
1970	11.0
1971	11.5
1972	11.8
1973	12.8
1974	24.2
1975	29.1
1976	31.6
1977	36.3
1978	39.2
1979	57.8
1980	90.0

Source: CAB Form 41.

The Mutual Aid Agreement attempted to more nearly balance the bargaining power of labor and management in this industry.[2] With the termination of that agreement, the pressures grew for wage settlements (and other contractual provisions) that could push labor costs upward at a rate faster than general inflation.

In the twelve years between 1967 and 1979—while the Consumer Price Index was increasing at an average annual compound rate of 6.7 percent—the average compensation per airline employee was increasing almost half again as rapidly—that is, at an average annual rate of 9.9 percent (table 9-2).

Considering that this was the record while the Mutual Aid Agreement was in effect, it ought to be expected that the annual labor-cost increases would grow even more without the agreement. However, since deregulation, many new carriers have entered the industry and have provided a dampening effect because they typically have newer unions than the majors (or no unions at all) and less seniority on average than existing carriers. Also, if new entrants threaten the profitability (and hence total employment) of the large carriers, there will be pressure for established unions to accept less wage increases and more liberal work rules than in the past.

Airport Costs

At several major U.S. airports (Washington's National, Chicago's O'Hare, New York's La Guardia and JFK) the number of slots, or operations per

Table 9-2
**Trend in Average Compensation Per Airline Employee—Trunk and Local
Service Airlines**

Year	Dollars	Increase Over Previous Year
1967	$ 9,829	
1968	10,611	8.0%
1969	11,700	10.3
1970	13,235	13.1
1971	14,451	9.2
1972	16,085	11.3
1973	17,323	7.7
1974	18,710	8.0
1975	20,507	9.6
1976	22,682	10.6
1977	25,316	11.6
1978	27,891	10.2
1979	30,033	11.9
1980	33,580	10.1

Source: CAB Form 41.

hour, is limited. As traffic demand for slots has increased, these limitations
have become very important. The problem of slot allocation is compounded
by the number of new entrants, and the allocation of slots by agreement
among the airlines themselves (under CAB jurisdiction) is being altered.

If present proposals for "auctioning" slots at key airports were
adopted, the cost of airport access could escalate. A prime-hour slot at a
major hub can be one of the essential elements determining whether a $40
million plane and all associated support personnel and facilities are used to
optimum advantage.

Sales Costs

For many years commissions paid to travel agents were determined through
the Air Traffic Conference, an industrywide clearing house for travel agent
commissions that has CAB-conferred antitrust immunity for setting of
travel agent commissions, and all airlines paid the same commissions to all
agents. This period of stable commission rates has ended, and carriers are
now allowed to determine commission rates as they see fit. As travel agents
are large sellers of tickets, one can expect increases in travel agent commission rates as carriers try to "buy" agency patronage with liberal commissions.

There is also the possibility that, under more flexible rules, carriers will
eventually pay sales commissions to large buyers of tickets who are not

travel agents. Large corporations that do in-house ticketing are likely candidates for such commissions.

The amounts cannot be predicted in any meaningful way, but there is strong probability of higher costs in this general area.

Effect of Advanced Aircraft Technology

The acquisition of newer technology aircraft during the 1980s will partly offset the various upward pressures on airline costs. The 1980s will see the introduction of a number of new transport types, with advances in fuel and aerodynamic efficiency over the average of the current operating fleet. However, the degree of such improvement in the 1980s cannot be compared with that experienced in the 1960s with the initial change-over from piston to jets.

The most important source of improvement will, of course, be in jet fuel efficiency. As an example, one of the new technology jets to be introduced, the Boeing-757, will consume about 30 percent less fuel on a 1,000 mile trip than Boeing's comparable current-technology jet, the 727. On the other hand, these new planes may not bring comparable improvements in other components of operating cost, and depreciation and ownership cost will be much higher for the new aircraft. Moreover, the introduction of the newer planes will necessarily be on a gradual basis. It will be some time before the newer planes account for a high enough proportion of the total fleet to effect materially average costs. In short, benefits from aircraft technology will soften—but only marginally—the upward pressure of other cost factors. Modernization of fleets will be a vital need through the decade. Over the past decade the average age of the aircraft in U.S. carrier fleets has increased significantly, making the need to modernize an essential objective in the years ahead.

Effect of Load Factors, Seat Configuration, and Aircraft Utilization

Here again, the degree to which these elements will offset future inflation will be limited. The industry used up most of the potential productivity gains from these factors in the years between 1976 and 1979. There is a physical limit on how many seats can be crowded into the area of an aircraft cabin, and recent configuration changes have brought the industry very close to those limits.

As for load factor, there may be some slight further gain over the 1978/1979 level. As traffic continues to grow, the tightness of certain resources (planes, airport space, fuel) may force somewhat higher load factors. But two points should be kept in mind:

1. When systemwide industry load factors average in the 60s on a year-round basis, there have to be many individual schedules, on many routes, with load factors in the 80s and 90s—creating a problem of tight space and inconvenient service.[3]

2. Whatever degree of further load factor gain might prove to be feasible (that is, above the 63 percent average of 1979), it will still be a nonrecurring improvement. Possibly systemwide load factors later in this decade might get to some higher plateau, such as 65 percent or even higher. If so, the few percentage points of further gain above 1979 levels will provide a one-time further offset to inflation. But load factors cannot continue to increase indefinitely; so this cannot be counted on to mitigate substantially the continuing inflation of airline cost elements.

A similar comment applies to aircraft utilization. An increase in utilization (hours flown per plane per day) was part of the productivity gain achieved by the airlines in the past few years. While some further increases may be achieved in the future, the gains already realized in 1978/1979 make it unlikely that further increases would be substantial. At the same time, the sharp rise in the cost of fuel has changed the fixed cost/variable cost ratio in the industry. With fuel and other variable costs now very high, it is no longer safe for the airlines to assume that *any* aircraft utilization improvement is to their advantage. Unless demand is high enough to cover the now-higher variable costs, increases in utilization are not economical. Given these pressures, further increases in aircraft utilization are not likely to be large.

Airline Yields

Combining the preceding considerations, it is clear that the industry is entering a new phase in the relationship of its fares to the overall purchasing value of the consumer's dollar. For decades, the marketing of air transportation was aided by the fact that air fares represented a steadily improving bargain in comparison with almost all other goods and services.

That past trend was made possible by (1) developments that have already been largely exploited (for example, increased seat density and load factor), or (2) factors that are not likely to be as potent in the future as they were in the past (for example, the degree of technological cost improvement for new aircraft).

During this coming decade, the industry faces substantial inflationary pressure, employee compensation, and other costs—without as much ability as in the past to offset these upward pressures through productivity increases alone.

Outlook for Airline Traffic Growth

The long term trend of air traffic growth is indicated in table 9-3 and figure 9-10. During the decade of the 1960s (with the first impact of the jet transition), the average annual compounded growth rate was 12.7 percent. During the 1970s, the average annual rate was 6.5 percent.

There has been a general consensus that the long-term growth rate during the present decade would average about 5-7 percent per year.

The recession of 1980 resulted, of course, in a deviation from the basic trend. For 1980 as a whole, a traffic decline of 3 percent occurred, and 1981 is likely to be soft as well. However, by 1982 an upward trend should reassert itself.

Some recent forecasts have projected more conservative growth rates than the 5-7 percent level. For example, a recent projection by McDonnell-Douglas placed the average annual growth rate in the 1980s at 5 percent. Also, the latest FAA forecast shows an average annual growth rate of 5 percent. By 1990 the number of airline passengers is expected to be about 500 million, compared to 317 million in 1979.

In air freight, of course, the untapped market is greater than in the passenger business. Many commodities (for example, fashion items, flowers, and so on) are perishable or of such high value that air transportation is the preferred mode even at much higher rates than surface. Still, today there exists a large volume of these air-eligible commodities that are not moving by air.

Since the deregulation of air cargo in 1977, many new entrants have been permitted to operate provided they were "fit, willing, and able." There has been an increase in direct transportation of cargo by air freight forwarders. The all-cargo carriers have expanded domestic routes and thus intensified competition with combination carriers and freight forwarders. Over the decade of the 1980s air cargo, based on current FAA and other forecasts, is expected to grow at a rate a little higher than that for passenger traffic.

In the 1980s, freight will be transported to air hubs by truck from over a broader area. There may be more cases of companies owning both airline

Table 9-3
Airline Traffic Growth Rate—U.S. Scheduled Airlines

Period	Annual Growth Rate
1960s	12.7%
1970s	6.5%
1980s—Forecast	5-7%

Source: CAB Historical Data; ATA Forecast.

and trucking operations. The continuing problem of fuel supply and price will remain challenges for those seeking to expand the air freight market. Long-haul international air freight markets are likely to present the most promising growth opportunities throughout the 1980s.

Fleet Modernization and Expansion

The year 1979 marked the twentieth anniversary of the start of commercial jet operations. During the decade of the 1980s, a high proportion of the aircraft now in service will have to be retired because of federal noise restrictions, poor fuel economy, or old age.

Specifically, it has been estimated that by the end of the 1980s roughly half of the current industry capacity will have been retired.

In the meantime, total available capacity will need to be substantially increased over current levels because of expected traffic growth. By 1989, traffic growth could create the need for about twice as much seat-mile capacity as was operated in 1979.

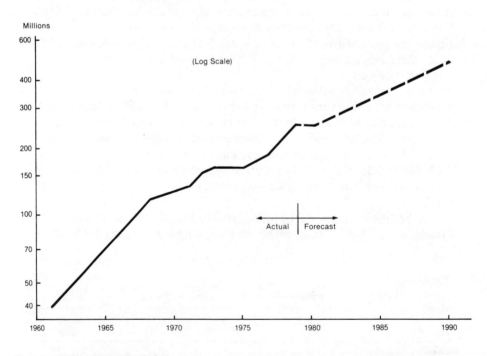

Source: Air Transport Association.

Figure 9-10. Past and Projected Trends of Revenue Passenger-Miles

The combination of expanded total requirement and substantial retirement of current planes produces an enormous need for new aircraft acquisition. The effect of these two factors is shown graphically in figure 9-11. The amount of lift that must be newly acquired during these ten years is substantially greater than the total capacity operated in 1979. However, the total number of aircraft in the scheduled airline fleet is not expected to change sharply over the next ten years because the new aircraft being delivered will, on average, be larger than those being replaced.

The Air Transport Association's (ATA) latest projection of equipment requirements through the 1980s was prepared in mid-1979.[4] Its basic dimensions are summarized in table 9-4. It projects a requirement near $90 billion (current dollars) in aircraft investment in this period. To place that requirement in perspective, figure 9-12 compares it with the aircraft capital expenditures in the preceding two decades. As indicated in this figure, the amount required in the 1980s will exceed by nearly nine times the amount spent in the 1960s, and will exceed by more than five times the amount spent in the 1970s.

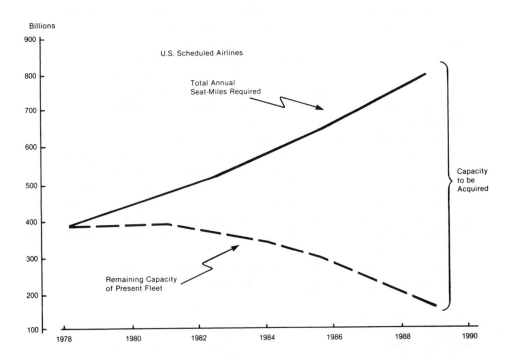

Source: Air Transport Association.

Figure 9-11. Seat-Mile Capacity Needed by 1990—Passenger Aircraft

Table 9-4
Airline Capital Requirement for Aircraft Acquisition, 1980-1989—U.S.
Scheduled Airlines
(Millions of Dollars)

Year	Passenger Aircraft	Freighters	Total	Cumulative Total
1980	$ 1,830	$ 196	$ 2,026	$ 2,026
1981	1,785	381	2,166	4,192
1982	4,494	749	5,243	9,435
1983	5,236	499	5,735	15,170
1984	6,239	587	6,826	21,996
1985	8,311	722	9,033	31,029
1986	12,319	857	13,176	44,205
1987	12,355	732	13,087	57,292
1988	14,655	943	15,598	72,890
1989	12,174	1,471	13,645	86,535

Source: Air Transport Association.
Note: Current dollars assumes 7 percent annual inflation rate.

Even with optimistic assumptions of retained earnings, airlines will need a substantial amount of external financing to handle this large capital outlay.

The ability to finance this program of capital expansion depends upon a return on investment (ROI) substantially above anything the industry has achieved on an ongoing basis in the past—an ROI in the neighborhood of 13-15 percent. Figure 9-13 shows how this required ROI compares with the actual ROI experience of the industry to date.

These projected equipment requirements were based on an average annual passenger traffic growth forecast of 7 percent. As indicated in the preceding section, the possibility of somewhat lower growth rate must be considered. This would lower the capital equipment needs, of course. On the other hand, an inflation rate above 7 percent and aircraft service lives below eighteen years would raise the capital requirements. The net result of these possibilities is a capital requirement in the range of $80-100 billion for the decade of the 1980s.

In short, the capital requirements faced by the airlines for aircraft acquisition in the 1980s present a challenge of substantial magnitude.

Principal Challenges for Airline Planners and Policymakers

Effective Management of Capacity

The most critical leverage in the airline financial equation is that exerted by load factor. The sensitivity of this element is indicated by the fact that the

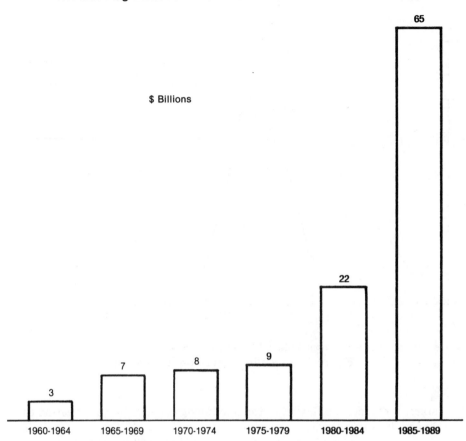

$ Billions

	65
1960-1964	3
1965-1969	7
1970-1974	8
1975-1979	9
1980-1984	22
1985-1989	65

Source: Air Transport Association.

Figure 9-12. Airline Capital Investment

record profits of 1978 were generated by a load factor margin of only 4.3 percentage points above break-even. If load factors had been just 2 percentage points lower, that would have cut the industry's profit approximately in half.

The fine tuning of capacity, so as to get those last few points of load factor, has always been difficult because airline capacity comes in such large, indivisible units. The new environment of deregulation will in some ways render this challenge more difficult, and in a few ways will make it easier. Management of capacity will be more difficult because of the increase in number of carriers on many routes, and the fact that, as a market gets subdivided among many carriers, the flexibility of each carrier to add or cancel on a fine tuned basis is reduced.

Another factor making capacity management more difficult will be the increase in aircraft size. As each unit of capacity addition or deletion gets

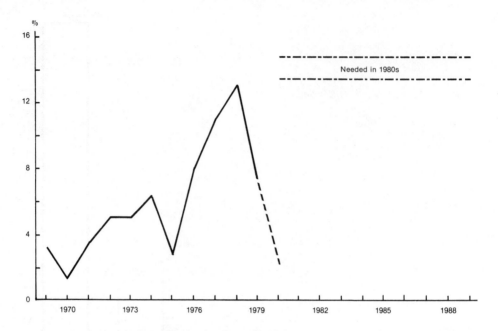

Source: Air Transport Association; Historical Data CAB Form 41.

Figure 9-13. Airline Return on Investment

larger, it reduces the flexibility for fine tuning capacity in close relation to changes in traffic levels.

On the other hand, one aspect of deregulation will ease somewhat the challenge of capacity management, namely, that carriers will not be as locked into routes as in the past. With free entry and exit, there may now be somewhat greater willingness for a carrier to simply drop out of a market in a situation of overcapacity, because there will remain the opportunity to get back in should future conditions change.

In any event, the effective management of capacity, so as to achieve and maintain an adequate load factor spread above break-even, clearly will be one of the major challenges facing the industry in the 1980s.

Challenge of Seat Inventory Management

One of the important remaining areas for increased productivity is in connection with more effective management of seat inventory. In addition to the possibilities for improved seat utilization through sound promotional pricing, there is the opportunity to reduce the "spoilage" of seat inventory created by no-shows.

For most carriers, the ratio of no-shows has recently been about 20 percent as an average, with the ratio getting much higher than that on some particular routes and in some seasons.

The waste that is represented by no-shows has been rendered even more significant in recent years by the fact that load factors have moved to higher levels. The higher the load factor, the greater the chances that the no-show has displaced a potential revenue passenger who had called for a seat and had been rejected because the flight was ostensibly booked.

Challenge of New Sales Distribution Flexibility

As part of deregulation, the matter of travel agency sales commissions has already been removed from the process of industry agreement. This has led to various carrier initiatives, which have raised the level of such commissions.

But beyond this, the industry now faces the possibility of totally new sales distribution relationships. For example, with large corporate accounts the possibility of commissions (or discounts) for in-house travel departments will surely loom large. Indeed, in the new deregulated environment, there appears to be no barrier against volume discounts whether in-house traffic-department activities are involved or not.

The recently established General Services Administration arrangement for discounts on government travel is another indication of what can happen in the future.

Airlines are especially reactive to the bargaining power of volume purchasers of transportation—whether in the personal travel market (that is, tour operators) or in the business travel market (that is, government agencies or large corporations). This vulnerability stems from the uniquely low marginal cost of selling a seat that would otherwise be empty. The almost zero marginal cost of the otherwise empty seat places carriers in a position where they can seek the larger purchasers of transportation to the point where full-cost economics are ignored.

Indeed, there would seem to be no barrier to companies forming air-purchasing cooperatives to increase their bargaining power. Also, companies supplying goods and services to the airlines may now be paid, in part or whole, through free or reduced air transportation.

It will be an enormous challenge for the industry to find the delicate balance at which it is able to benefit from the new flexibilities in sales distribution options—while refraining from selling below costs.

The Challenge of Airport Access

The issue of access to airport slots has become the subject of reexamination by both the CAB and the FAA. In the past, "slots," or the right to take off or land, have been allocated at busy airports by the airlines themselves under the jurisdiction of the CAB. There are only a few airports where the number of slots available is less than the number desired, but the airports involved are important ones. With new carriers starting operations and requesting slots at those airports, it has become more difficult for the carriers to agree on slot allocations.

Various proposals have been advanced for new methods of allocating such slots to replace the airline scheduling committees. Such new methods involve some form of auction.

The free-entry aspect of deregulation makes it important to seek solutions to airport access. In particular, it will be important to improve traffic control technology to increase acceptance rates at key airports.

Conclusion

All businesses, of course, face challenges as they prepare for the decade ahead. The challenge of balancing costs and revenues exists uniformly. However, for the airlines certain unique challenges are evident, including the continued adjustment to the deregulated environment and the unusually large impact of jet fuel prices on the basic economics of the industry. These two factors alone initiate or accentuate other challenges of new technology, airport access, capacity and yield management, and redistribution of sales outlets.

Maintaining its historical record for unusual achievements, the U.S. scheduled airline industry can be expected to meet the new and exciting challenges of the 1980s and continue to provide outstanding service in the future.

Notes

1. Air freight deregulation occurred in 1977.
2. The Mutual Aid Agreement, which existed for many years before the Deregulation Act effectively ended its utility, provided for a return to a struck carrier of those revenues earned by other (nonstruck) carriers principally because of the strike. That is, those revenues earned by transporting passengers who otherwise would have flown with the struck carrier were returned to the struck carrier on the premise that this would tend to bring

greater balance between labor and management powers—a union's power to threaten or implement a strike contrasted with a carrier's inability to "take a strike" in the absence of any revenue whatsoever. The intent of the Mutual Aid Agreement was to allow a carrier to assume the strike risk instead of granting what it considered unwarranted increases in compensation, thus strengthening the industry's bargaining position with labor and forcing some restraint in union wage demands.

3. For more on this point, see chapter 3.

4. See chapter 6.

Part III
Airline Planning:
The Air Transport
Association/Stanford
University Symposium

10 Strategic Cargo Planning

6150
US

William M. Caldwell IV

The air freight industry differs in important respects from the air passenger industry. The differences make the job of the air freight company planner quite different from that of his air passenger counterpart.

General Characteristics of Air Freight

Table 10-1 contrasts air freight and air passenger companies. While the air passenger company concentrates its marketing effort on the private consumer, the air freight company focuses on the industrial customer. Although both passenger and shipper value the speed and safety of air transportation very highly, passengers give less weight to the cost of air transportation than do shippers (or receivers) of freight. Accordingly, air is the dominant mode of intercity passenger travel, while air is merely a relatively small complement to surface movement of freight.

To accommodate its customers, the air passenger company provides a fairly homogeneous service. Passengers typically buy round-trip tickets, prefer to fly nonstop during the day, and move themselves to and from the airplane. Shippers (or receivers), on the other hand, require a variety of services. Their shipments typically go one-way, may fly on multistop flights at night, and require handling both to and from the airplane.

Air passenger transactions are generally single-party transactions with simple documentation. The rate structure is complex. Air freight transactions are generally multiparty transactions with complex documentation. The freight rate structure is even more complex than the passenger rate structure.

Freighter aircraft have special characteristics that differ from those of passenger aircraft. Freighters require large doors and large cargo areas to handle efficiently shipments of varying size and density. Because freight is their principal source of revenue, freighter aircraft are equipped with very efficient types of containers. They are also equipped to provide safe handling of hazardous materials. In operation, aircraft must be scheduled to meet demand; for freighters this means predominantly night schedules to provide late-day shipment and early morning delivery. The system provides for later cut-off and faster recovery. As was said earlier, freight shippers are very price sensitive and hence ship relatively few goods by air. However, for those

211

Table 10-1
Air Freight versus Air Passenger

	Passenger	Freight
Market	Consumer	Industrial
Relative value	Highest	Highest
Relative price	Lowest	Highest
Market share	Dominant mode	Complementary mode
Services required	Homogeneous	Varied
	Round trip	One way
	Nonstop	Variable
	Daylight	Night
	Self-handling	Passive
Transactions		
Number parties	Single party	Multiparty
Documentation	Simple	Complex
Rate structure	Complex	More complex

products that are shipped by air the speed of air freight is usually considered a necessity, so air freight users tend to be even more sensitive to service than to price. Products that move by air often have a high value per pound and are sold in markets that tolerate high markups. They may be highly perishable (for example, flowers); the market may be fleeting (for example, Christmas gifts); they may be needed because of short deadlines or factory breakdowns; they may need special security to prevent theft, damage, or other loss; or they may be candidates for market expansion in distant lands.

As mentioned earlier, air freight is a complementary mode of transportation, employed when surface transportation is unpredictable or when peak loads require rapid supplements to regular surface shipments. Most price-sensitive products move by surface. In fact, air freight carries only about 0.2 percent of the tonnage shipped domestically, but 16 percent of the dollar value.

Table 10-2 shows the principal commodities shipped by air within the United States and across the Pacific. With the exception of the westbound transpacific shipment of printed matter, all of the leading commodities have a high ratio of value to weight.

Evolution of a Strategic Plan

It is a truism that strategies must adapt to changes in the environment. And one of the biggest changes in the air freight environment was the Air Cargo Deregulation Act in 1977—a change that opened new domestic route oppor-

Table 10-2
Air Freight Commodity Mix
(Revenue)

Domestic

1. Auto parts
2. Electronic/electric equipment
3. Machinery and parts
4. Wearing apparel
5. Printed matter

Transpacific

Eastbound

1. Wearing apparel
2. Electrical
3. Optical
4. Machinery
5. Auto parts

Transpacific

Westbound

1. Machinery
2. Electrical
3. Aircraft/auto parts
4. Chemical/drugs
5. Printed matter

---

tunities and new pricing freedom. Flying Tigers adapted to the new environment by developing new strategic plans.

Our first step was to reexamine and set forth strategic objectives for growth, market control, and competitive posture. As table 10-3 outlines, we set our sights on profitable growth, achieved by increasing both our yield and our market share. We decided to seek better market control by providing door-to-door service for our retail customers and by attracting a larger number of customers. Our competitive posture was designed to achieve superiority by offering differentiated services, by expanding our domestic system geographically, and by improving our operational efficiency.

In recent years (with the exception of the recession years of 1974 and 1975) our operating revenues have exceeded our operating costs, but by a margin too small to provide an adequate return for financing continued profitable growth. Figure 10-1 depicts operating revenue and costs for the years 1970-1976, inclusive. One reason for the low profit margin in those years was the concentration of our business with a relatively small number

Table 10-3
Strategic Objectives

Profitable growth

  Increased yields
  Increased market share

Market control

  Door-to-door retail customer interface
  Expanded customer base

Competitive superiority

  Differentiated product
  Geographical expansion
  Operational efficiency

of customers. As table 10-4 shows, 65 percent of our scheduled freight revenue was derived from forty-one customers: United Parcel Service, twenty freight forwarders, and twenty commercial accounts.

Flying Tigers was in the position of a regulated carrier in a market that was rapidly becoming deregulated. U.S. international airlines were being awarded domestic fill-up rights. Supplemental carriers were receiving dual certification; that is, they were being certificated to fly scheduled service as well as the charter service for which they had been originally certificated. Freight forwarders were being authorized to charter freighter aircraft. Air taxi and commuter carriers, such as Federal Express, were being allowed to use larger aircraft than those to which they had previously been restricted. CAB control of cargo rates prevented selective price increases to counterbalance the effects of the added competition that was driving prices down in selected markets. Simultaneously, new bilaterals were opening major U.S. interior cities to foreign carriers, thus reducing the potential for domestic connecting traffic. Despite the new competition, regulation was still in place, making expansion of a domestic route system a slow and uncertain process that required at least three years of procedural delay.

Before deregulation, direct air carriers such as Flying Tigers were limited to specific airport cities plus a twenty-five-mile pickup and delivery zone. Substitute truck service was permitted only to those cities that the carriers were certificated to serve. Regulation effectively eliminated cargo service in short-haul and small-volume markets by keeping prices too low in those markets to permit carriers an adequate profit. Indirect carriers, on the other hand, were permitted unlimited geographic coverage and pricing freedom.[1] In that environment, Flying Tigers served ten domestic cities with direct air service and five with over-the-road trucks. In all, 210 city pairs were served.

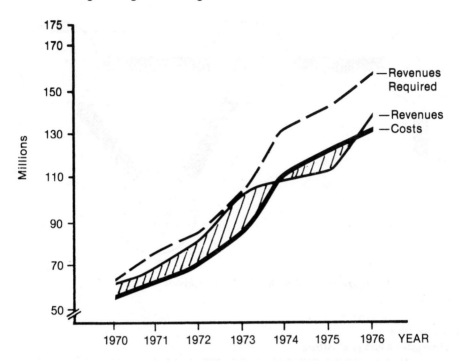

Figure 10-1. Current Market Position, Domestic Operating Profits

As we faced the new deregulated domestic environment, we identified two alternative strategies for the future:

1. Conservative: limit the domestic system to feed international routes.
2. Aggressive: pursue domestic opportunities produced by deregulation.

To help us select the best path for Flying Tigers, we undertook market research that would tell us which factors are most important to customers in their selection of carriers.

Figure 10-2 is a framework for evaluating our findings. It portrays the air freight decision process as a multilevel decision tree. First comes the mode decision: to use air or surface. Next the customer who elects the air mode must decide whether to use a direct air carrier like Flying Tiger or a freight forwarder. If the former, then he must decide which airline to use. If the latter, the customer first decides on a specific freight forwarder who then selects the airline to be utilized.

Our query about reasons for using air freight produced the following responses:

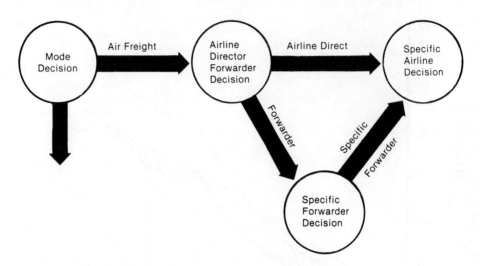

Figure 10-2. The Air Freight Decision Process

Table 10-4
Domestic Market Position

Concentrated customer base
  Freight forwarders
    35% of scheduled freight revenue
    29% from top 20 freight forwarders
    Average yield = $27.35 cwt

  United Parcel Service
    20% of scheduled freight revenue
    Average yield = $30.31 cwt

  Commercial accounts
    34% of scheduled freight revenue
    16% from top twenty accounts
    Average yield = $25.21 cwt

Urgency or emergency (various definitions)   34.5%
    Deadlines
    Breakdowns
    Back orders
    Low inventories

Service   27.0%
    Security from theft, loss, damage

Control, tracing
High dollar value

Cost/Revenue Consideration	16.0%
Marginal revenue	
Air freight comparable or less	
Cash flow, total cost	
Expanded Market Philosophy	13.0%
Product life-cycle	
Perishable	
Other	9.5%

The decision between use of a freight forwarder or a direct carrier was strongly influenced by whether the shipment was domestic or international. As figure 10-3 shows, 79 percent of shippers selecting West-bound

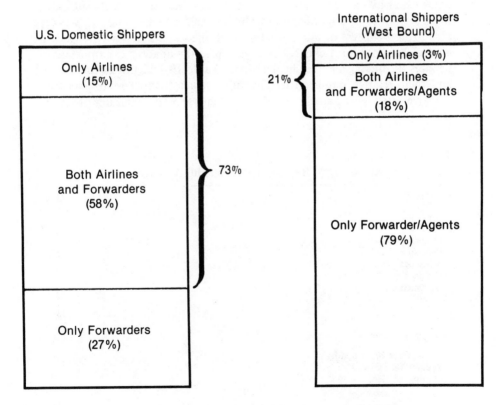

Figure 10-3. Use of Forwarders versus Airlines

transpacific air used only forwarders or other agents, whereas only 27 percent selecting domestic air used only forwarders or other agents.

Our survey of carrier "brand" loyalty revealed the following behavior patterns among shippers:

32% did not switch carriers

42% switched carriers only when a serious problem arose with their customary carrier

17% switched frequently

9% switched on periodic review

Table 10-5 displays the reasons shippers gave for switching carriers. 71 percent switched for service reasons, 13 percent for cost reasons, 13 percent for psychological reasons, and 3 percent for other reasons.

Respondents to our survey cited thirty-five service reasons for selecting a particular air carrier. Table 10-6 enumerates these reasons. By subjecting these responses to a mathematic technique called factor analysis, we were able to find clusters of attributes by which the shipper defines the value of air freight. Four such clusters emerged from the analysis as important attributes in making air freight decisions. Table 10-7 identifies the clusters and their relative importance. The first cluster (factor) represents time-sensitive attributes: namely, handling of emergencies, handling of late-in-

Table 10-5
Shipper Brand Loyalty—Reasons for Switching Carriers

Service	71%
Tracing	
Reliability	
Damage and loss	
Pick-up and delivery	
Schedules, locations served	
Claims	
Documentation	
Cost	13%
Psychologial Benefits	13%
Personal service, empathy	
Reputation, carrier size	
Multiple carriers	
Other	3%

Table 10-6

Service Reasons for Carrier Choice—Domestic Air Freight

1. Reliablity	19. Truck driver's attitude
2. On-time performance	20. Salesman's knowledge
3. Most professional	21. Container programs
4. Carrier's customer service	22. Good delivery service
5. Computer tracing system	23. Handling of late in the day shipments
6. How often salesman calls	24. Handling of emergencies
7. Total cost considerations	25. Assistance on special problems
8. Daylight rates	26. Most cities served
9. Prime night-time departures	27. Frequency of service
10. Door-to-door time	28. Ability to trace
11. Advertising	29. Accurate documentation service
12. Carrier's knowledge of your problems	30. Freedom from worry
13. Accurate billing	31. Keeping the shipper informed
14. Insurance and claim service	32. Honest and straightforward
15. Time between call and pickup	33. Best informed on new prices and schedules
16. Security	34. Good pick-up service
17. Best price	35. Size of carrier
18. Size of shipment	

the-day shipments, good delivery service, door-to-door time, prime night-time departures, and assistance in handling special problems. The second cluster represents price-sensitive attributes: namely, price, total cost considerations, availability of information or prices and schedules, and daylight rates. The third cluster represents information-sensitive attributes: namely, keeping the shipper informed, honesty and directness, freedom from worry, availability of information on prices and schedules, ability to trace, accuracy of documentation, assistance in handling special problems, and salesmen's knowledge. The fourth cluster represents pick-up-sensitive attributes: namely, good pick-up service, time between call and pick-up, and truck drivers' attitudes.

Translating the results of our survey and factor analysis into desirable attributes for air freight carriers, we identified four variables that would form important inputs to our strategic plan: geographic coverage, door-to-door responsibility and control, delivery time, and shipment size capability.

Figure 10-4 depicts our measure of the importance of various levels of geographic coverage. If serving the top fifty cities in the country is assigned a preference index of 100, then our analysis shows that serving only the top twenty cities reduces the preference index in the eyes of the customer to a value of 48. Serving only the top ten cities reduces the preference index to 24.

Figure 10-5 is a measure of the importance of various levels of door-to-door responsibility and control. If full responsibility (operating our own trucks and aircraft) is assigned a preference index of 100, then operating our own trucks and assuming responsibility reduces the preference index to 84,

Table 10-7
Domestic Factor Analysis of Benefits

Factor I "Time Sensitive"   (6.22)

    (.68) Handling of emergencies
    (.62) Handling of late in the day shipments
    (.47) Good delivery service
    (.47) Door-to-door time
    (.42) Prime night-time departures
    (.41) Assistance on special problems

Factor II "Price Sensitive"   (2.04)

    (.81) Best price
    (.77) Total cost considerations
    (.40) Best informed on new prices and schedules
    (.33) Daylight rates

Factor III "Information Sensitive"   (1.67)

    (.70) Keeping the shipper informed
    (.66) Honest and straightforward
    (.57) Freedom from worry
    (.53) Best informed on new prices and schedules
    (.49) Ability to trace
    (.45) Accurate documentation service
    (.34) Assistance on special problems
    (.33) Salesman's knowledge

Factor IV "Pick-up Sensitive"   (1.63)

    (.81) Good pick-up service
    (.75) Time between call and pickup
    (.55) Truck driver's attitude

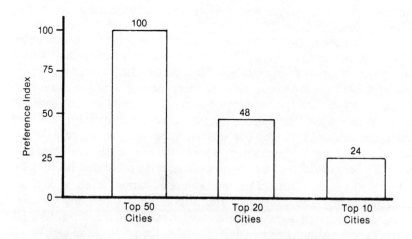

Figure 10-4. Service Attribute Values, Geographic Coverage

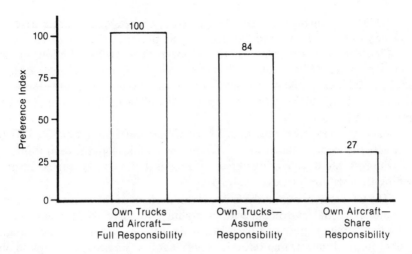

Figure 10-5. Service Attribute Values, Door-to-Door Responsibility and Control

while operating only our own aircraft and sharing responsibility with truckers reduces the preference index to 27.

Figure 10-6 depicts the importance of various delivery times. If delivery before 9 a.m. is assigned a preference index of 100, then offering delivery only before noon reduces the preference index to 62. Offering delivery only

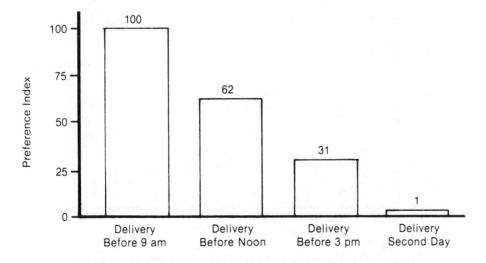

Figure 10-6. Service Attribute Values, Delivery Time

before 3 p.m. further reduces the preference index to 31, while offering delivery only on the second day reduces the preference index to 1.

Figure 10-7 is a measure of the importance of various limitations on shipment size. If the carrier has no limitations on shipment size, a preference index of 100 is assigned. Imposition of size limitation reduces the preference index to 33, while imposition of weight limitations reduces the preference index to 23.

Each of these four measures of service-attribute values enabled us to estimate the value of better service so that we could weigh the desirability of providing some degree of better service against the costs incurred in providing that service improvement.

The next step in our analysis was a comparison of the needs of our present and potential customers with our ability to serve those needs. Table 10-8 lists some of those comparisons. If we were to elect to become a major factor in the domestic market, it became clear that we needed to expand our route system to conform to the market and to take advantage of the pricing and service options that deregulation would now permit. It was also clear that our performance met customer needs within the limits of our existing system.

In the deregulated environment, direct air freight carriers may serve any city by air or by substitute truck service. Direct air freight carriers may also price their services at levels that support cost of any service, regardless of distance or volume. As a result of our decision to proceed aggressively into the domestic market, Flying Tigers now serves twenty-two domestic cities

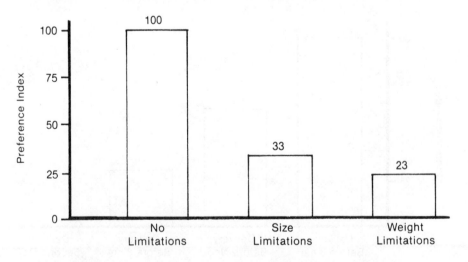

Figure 10-7. Service Attribute Values, Shipment Size Capability

Table 10-8
Flying Tigers and Deregulation

FTL's Abilities Versus Customer Needs

Customers	FTL
Fastest growth in sunbelt	Northern tier
Geographic coverage	Fourteen markets
Single-party responsibility	Geographically limited
Pick-up and delivery times	Good where limited volumes justified
Shipment size capability	Good
Reliability	Good
Variety of service-price options, flexibility	Rigid, limited utility concepts of CAB
Demand growing	Industry freighter service declining

with direct air service, compared with ten before deregulation. We also serve seventy-four domestic cities with over-the-road truck, compared with five before deregulation. At the same time, our competition has expanded to a present total of eighty-two Part 418 carriers, including such operators of large air-craft as Emery and Evergreen International.[2]

The goal is to exploit our advantage as the lowest cost, most efficient air freight operator by providing single carrier service in all major domestic markets. The decisions on which markets to enter by direct air service and on the order of entry are affected by:

Efficiency of available aircraft.

Available traffic in each market; including traffic generated from truck feeder service in adjacent markets.

Operating costs of new service.

Competitive considerations.

Fuel availability.

Capital availability.

Human resources.

Two alternative methods of setting up a route system also needed to be considered in setting priorities for route expansion. One of these is a linear system that connects city pairs directly with each other. The other is a hub and spoke system that feeds traffic from many cities into a central hub to connect with flights to final destinations. Figure 10-8 illustrates the two systems. The hub and spoke system has the dual advantage of minimizing aircraft investment and operating costs while maximizing operating flexibility and reliability. Figure 10-9 further illustrates the huge potential for

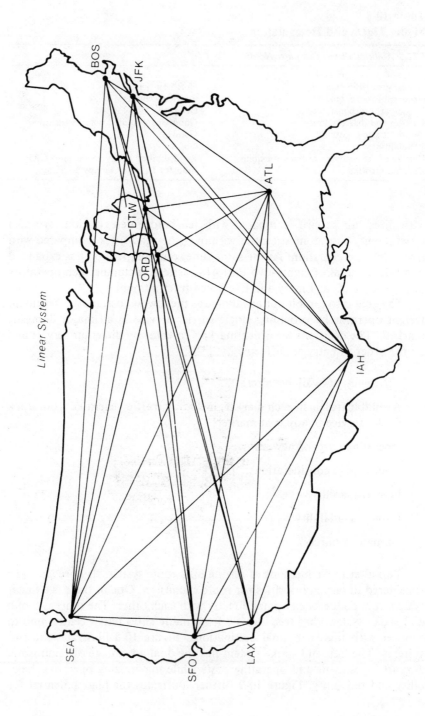

Linear System

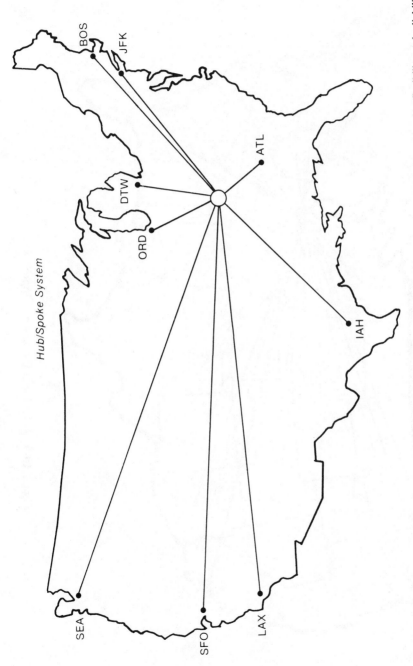

Note: The hub/spoke system minimizes aircraft investment and operating costs. The hub/spoke system maximizes operating flexibility and reliability.

Figure 10-8. Linear versus Hub/Spoke System

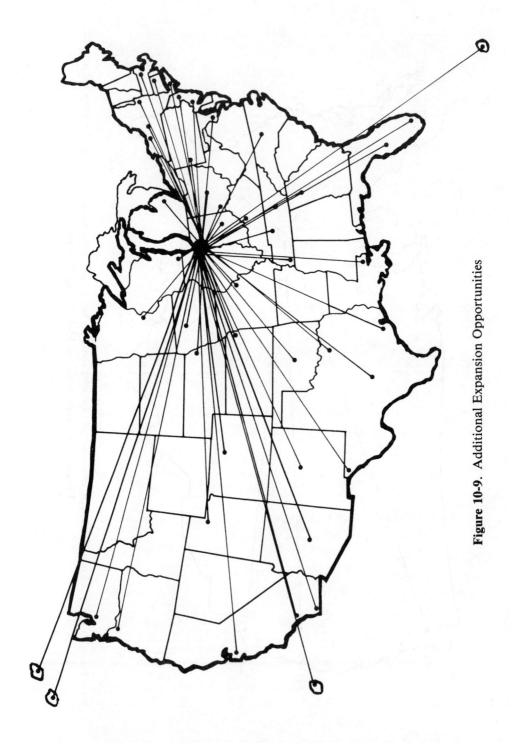

Figure 10-9. Additional Expansion Opportunities

connecting many markets through a central hub with far fewer flights than would be required to connect each pair of cities in an extensive system.

From this analysis emerged our grass roots (or channel improvement) strategy: to improve the Flying Tiger channel structure by establishing new customer service centers and by expanding sales coverage to smaller cities surrounding a hub. In this way, we achieve additional penetration in existing wholesale and commercial segments and expedite new product expansion. The rationale for this strategy is as follows:

1. Migration of industry is toward smaller cities.
2. Therefore, air freight must shift from concentration in twenty-five major markets to smaller cities.
3. This is accomplished by strengthening our channel structure; that is, channeling traffic into hubs by truck or by DC-8 aircraft.
4. Finally, we improve the Flying Tiger product line through expanded trucks, air feeders, and pick up and delivery to sixty-seven additional cities by 1980.

Our plan for putting the strategy into operation has three phases. In Phase I we plan to initiate service to and from the top Standard Metropolitan Statistical Areas (SMSAs). These are grouped into terminal areas, based on size and ability to achieve 10 a.m. to 2 p.m. delivery. SMSAs are then ranked by expected traffic volume and composition. In carrying out Phase I, we seek broad geographic coverage with emphasis on fast delivery, retaining door-to-door responsibility in as many markets as possible.

In Phase II, by 1983, we expand coverage in each of the terminal areas set up in Phase I by including more cities. As we proceed, we seek to determine when markets become large enough to warrant direct air service—replacing truck or even bypassing hubs. This part of the plan also identifies further service and sales potential needs and new vehicle needs.

In Phase III we implement the service standards model that guides phase-in of other market areas and the build up of service and sales capability.

A final commentary on the benefits of deregulation for Flying Tigers relates to the international portion of our system, where regulation by many governments still constrains our operation. In international operations, shippers consider second-day delivery possible and practical. However, regulation makes this level of service impossible in many places. Bureaucratic obstacles in Taipai, for example, result in average delays of nine days. JFK airport in New York is little better. The most prevalent regulatory constraints are:

1. Custom clearance procedures.
2. Documentation required.

3. Antiquated requirements.
4. Antiquated data processing.

In addition, U.S. flag carriers when operating abroad are usually handled by a monopoly handling group of the host country's flag carrier, thus giving nonhost country carriers low handling priority. Furthermore, cargo often must be offered to the host country's flag carrier and refused before an American carrier can transport it. American carriers often have to operate in very restricted space and with limited access to the market. On top of all of these regulatory constraints, a host of government restrictions exist in many countries. Table 10-9 identifies a number of these. This pattern of restricted freedom served as an additional reason for concentrating on the opportunities afforded by deregulation of U.S. domestic air freight.

In summary, we concluded that Flying Tiger should continue a balanced, controlled expansion of its domestic service. Details of the systemwide implication of this conclusion are displayed in table 10-10.

Table 10-9
Government Restrictions

	Hong Kong	Japan	Korea	Singapore	Taiwan	USA
Restrictive bilateral	X	X			X	
Government/carrier ownership of ground handling agent	X	X	X	X	X	
Monopolized warehousing	X	X		X	X	
Limited fifth freedom rights	X					
Regulatory restraints		X	X		X	X
Export/import license constraints		X	X		X	X
Slot, curfew, or aircraft type restrictions		X				
Facilitation obstructions			X	X	X	
Lengthy customs procedures			X		X	
Large number of clearance documents required			X		X	
Prohibitive airport fees		X	X			
Warehouse fees unrelated to costs	X	X	X	X		
Extra charges—security, airline documents, parts, maintenance, etc.	X	X				
Currency remittance constraints			X		X	
Government interest/ownership in the national carrier		X		X		
Totals	6	9	10	4	10	2

X = Yes; substantial.

Table 10-10
Summary and Recommendations

			FTL Should Continue a Balanced, Controlled Expansion of Its Domestic Service			
Market	*Geographic Expansion*	*Service/Price Options*	*Reliability*	*Pricing*	*Sales*	*Promotion*
Backdoor/Industrial • Direct Retail • Wholesale	• FTL A/C (markets) • Feeders (truck, air, taxi)	• PU&D • Small Package • Priority • Reserved	Improved - • HUB • Schedule Reliability • Customer service Standards	• Keep All Options • Price Selectivity	• Expand Sales Force • Reorganize: - Wholesale/ Retail - Zip Code Territories	• Personal • Direct Mail • Promotional Events • HDQ or terminal Executive Contacts
Front Door/ Consumer	• Key off Expansion of Backdoor Service/Production Capability	Door-Door	Must Be Excellent Initially	• Competitive but Profitable	• Few High-Level • Emphasis on Drivers • Separate from Industrial Sales Force. Different Compensation and Measurement	• Mass Media • PR

The two markets can be pursued compatibly, but one should not be permitted to interfere with the other.

The Critical Initial steps are:

1. Get the feeder services implemented.
2. Get the PU&D Service expansion implemented.
3. Get up Service Assurance/Administrative System.

Notes

1. Indirect air carriers are the same as freight forwarders.
2. Part 418 carriers are all-cargo carriers. Such carriers are certificated according to criteria detailed in Part 418 of the Federal Aviation Act.

11 Marketing Planning

Robert L. Crandall

At American Airlines, the market planning process and the overall planning process are inseparable. They encompass the following major activities:

1. Defining corporate objectives.
2. Establishing broad strategies to satisfy those objectives.
3. Formulating specific plans to implement strategies and integrating plans through all departments.
4. Executing plans and modifying them as experience dictates.
5. Appraising results.

The planning process involves a continuous interplay between the short, intermediate, and long term. The short-term plan, with a three- to five-month horizon, must be responsive to current economic, traffic, and competitive intelligence. The intermediate-term plan looks ahead twelve to eighteen months and includes an annual operating plan (budget). Finally, American develops a five- to ten-year long-range plan for the purpose of testing alternative fleet, route, and competitive plans. Aircraft fleet, facility requirements, and traffic volumes in the long-range plan are predicated on forecasts of the economy, industry traffic, and American's market share.

The planning process requires coordination of activities among many departments. Table 11-1 is an outline of some of the principal planning functions in the marketing, operations, and finance departments and lists other American Airline activities that interact in the planning process.

Planning Overview

Many factors must be considered in the planning process. Some of these factors are subject to control by American Airlines: routes, fleets, facilities, schedules, and administrative and cost considerations. Other factors are external and outside the airline's direct control: government policy, the competitive situation, the economy, and technological advances. A few words about each of these areas will help place the planning process in perspective.

Routes

In determining the routes that American will fly in the planning period, we consider a number of factors. These include stage lengths, a critical cost

231

Table 11-1
American Airlines—The Planning Process
(A Continuous Interplay—of Many Departments)

Marketing	Operations	Finance	Others
Product definition	Flight resources	Budgeting	Properties and facilities
Product pricing	Maintenance and engineering support	Financial analysis	Purchasing
Sales and advertising		Profitability analysis	Data processing
Monitor and refine		Revenue accounting	Sky chefs
			Public relations

issue. We examine recent trends in boarding volumes in each of the cities the airline serves. Interdependence of routes is a very important factor, since our strategy is focused on developing patterns that help us strengthen our exchange complexes. And demographic trends (for example, changing age distribution of the public, and changes in regional population and economic activity) also provide important inputs to the route planning process. The route structure is considered semifixed in the short-term plan, but for intermediate and long-range planning we assume that American's route structure can be expanded or contracted to meet our profit objectives.

Fleets

American's fleet of aircraft varies in size from Boeing 727-100s to 747s, and in range from less than transcontinental to international. With new aircraft on order and older aircraft being retired from the fleet, the available mix of aircraft varies from year to year. Because plane-mile and seat-mile costs vary from plane to plane and with distance flown, careful matching of aircraft characteristics to market demand pays off. In recent years, fuel efficiency has been important in aircraft fleet decisions as jet fuel prices have skyrocketed since the 1973 oil embargo. Older planes, in addition to being less fuel efficient than the newer planes, are too noisy to meet the environmental constraints adopted by the Federal Aviation Administration (FAA).

This mix of factors—size, cost, fuel economy, and the environment—plays a key role both in aircraft assignment and in procurement of new aircraft. Future aircraft types must be useful and economic on present and expected future routes, economical (and fuel efficient) to operate, available from the manufacturers at dates the airline requires the new capacity, acceptable (even preferred, if possible) by passengers, and reliable.

Facilities

To move its aircraft efficiently through its route structure, the airline needs access to gate facilities at each airport served. Behind these facilities at the airport are crew locker and briefing rooms, office space, maintenance facilities ranging from modest to major, ticket counters, and a vast array of powered vehicles for towing, fueling, provisioning, lifting, and so on. And backing the whole system are ticket offices in major cities, a reservation system that can keep track of many flights on many airlines, many hotel rooms, and a myriad of other details. A vast communications network ties the system together. For every dollar invested in flight equipment, nearly twenty cents is invested in ground property and equipment in the scheduled airline industry. In the rapidly changing environment in which we now operate, providing adequate facilities at times and places needed is a major planning challenge.

Schedules

Flight scheduling sets the short-term pattern of operations. For each segment to be flown, the scheduler must consider how large a market is expected and how it will fluctuate by day of week and hour of day. At some airports, he must adapt to a shortage of slots for landings and departures. At others, curfews may shorten the flying day. The scheduler considers onboard loads by looking at local traffic, through traffic, and traffic that connects at some intermediate point with another flight, and must pay particular attention to building efficient complexes with multiple cross-feed. Aircraft must be scheduled to end their day's flying at the point of origin of the next day's flight pattern, and that pattern must bring the aircraft into maintenance shops on a predetermined schedule. To further complicate the task, schedulers try to maximize stage lengths, since short-hauls are more expensive per mile and require a proportionately larger share of the aircraft's day on the ground.

Traffic

In analyzing traffic, the planner looks at the total market and the route-by-route breakdown. He further breaks down traffic estimates by presumed purpose of trip and by probable fare base. Fares, tour packages, and promotional campaigns are aimed at attracting particular categories of travelers. Traffic on some routes is seasonal, and plans for airline operation must take advantage of that variation in demand for travel. Finally, the economic environment affects the demand for travel, whether for business, for visiting friends and relatives, or for other purposes.

Administrative and Cost Constraints

At least for short-term planning, much of the airline's infrastructure is fixed, thus putting constraints on planning. Some examples: a crew schedule that leaves flight or cabin crews overnight away from home base involves expenses (meals and hotels) plus hours of pay ("pay and credit") even though the crews are not flying. Some airports are not equipped to handle widebody aircraft because of lack of proper jetways or inadequate runways and taxiways. Each aircraft must be at a maintenance station every few days, and each maintenance station must have a specific number of aircraft available each night.

Government Policy

Among the factors over which the airline has virtually no control, government policy ranks high. Regulatory policy has been in a state of flux since passage of the Airline Deregulation Act of 1978. The Civil Aeronautics Board (CAB) is scheduled to be abolished by 1985, although many of its functions will probably be shifted to the Transportation, State, and Justice departments.

Environmental concerns have fostered federal regulations that forbid use of aircraft not meeting specified noise and emission standards. As a result, some aircraft are being retrofitted to meet the regulations, and others are being prematurely retired. This problem has been exacerbated by some local governments, which have responded to aircraft noise by instituting curfews forbidding late night and early morning departures. Some local governments have even tried to outlaw particular aircraft types in the name of noise and safety. Others have established quotas or limited slots to reduce airport traffic.

In response to consumerism the government has also elected to intrude in selected areas rather than let the market provide the regulatory mechanism. Mandatory smoking/no smoking sections in aircraft are an example of government response to strong consumer pressures. The price and availability of jet fuel is also influenced by government policy in addition to other factors.

Competitive Situation

The planner must also assess his competitors. Different carriers offer different quality of service. Some offer special inducements to business travelers; some, to bargain hunters. Some airlines seek to attract business by lower fares, some by frequent schedules, some by attractive accoutrements. Different competitive philosophies are reflected in different market responses.

Airline cost structures also differ, depending in part on aircraft type and configuration, in part on organization and route structure. Therefore, the planning process must take into consideration the cost structure of competitors.

New carriers entering the airline field pose special competitive problems. Although these neophytes lack the image of the established carriers, they start with low costs because of below-market labor cost caused by the absence of unions and the low seniority of crews and other personnel. Because the new carriers often serve only a limited market area, and because they do not participate in the interline system, they have simpler (hence less-expensive) overhead structures. Because of their low-cost operation and concentration in limited high-density markets, they may cut deeply into historically profitable markets that established carriers depend on to support operations in lower density, less-profitable markets.

Technological Advances

A final area of consideration for the planner is new technology. As airframe and engine manufacturers bring out new and improved models, airlines must consider which to buy for growth and for replacement of less-efficient, older aircraft. The fuel efficiencies of the newer aircraft result in substantial operating cost advantages at today's cost of jet fuel, while the high capital cost of the new equipment imposes significant financing costs.

Technological advances in competitive modes must also be watched. In some short-haul markets, high-speed rail service competes with air for passengers. The Northeast Corridor rail improvements, for example, are expected to make further inroads on air travel in that market. Overall, however, these inroads are not significant.

Telecommunications, especially closed circuit television for business conferences and videophone service, may also replace some business travel. Many companies are now experimenting with these newly developed communication systems with the objective of reducing travel for their executives. Airline planners will continue to monitor these developments.

Data Sources

Because of regulatory reporting requirements, there is probably more information on the airline industry than on any other. For planning, airlines make extensive use of CAB industry filings, consumer research programs, and competitive data gleaned from the market place.

CAB Industry Filings

Table 11-2 outlines the principal sources of data available as a result of regulatory agency reporting requirements. The Origin and Destination Survey provides detailed data on a 10 percent sample of travelers, showing itineraries and carriers used, not merely origins and destinations. The service segment data enable the planner to determine how traffic on each segment is distributed among all certificated route carriers. Used in conjunction with the Official Airline Guide (OAG), these data enable a planner to determine how traffic on a busy segment was distributed by time of day. Finally, the Form 41 data provide some quarterly cost information on each carrier, monthly traffic and capacity data, plus a plethora of other information.

Recent data for all of these CAB sources are readily accessible through any of several time-sharing services. Older data are available in report form. Note, however, that once the CAB ceases to exist some of these data sources may disappear.

Internal Corporate Sources

Each airline has detailed information on its own operations. American, for example, has load messages that provide traffic and capacity data by flight leg, summarized to various levels of aggregation. The reservations system, in addition to performing the function of maintaining booking information

Table 11-2
Data Sources—CAB Industry Filings

O&D (Origin & Destination) Survey	— Quantifies market size, long-term (thirty-five years) history of all city-pairs
ER586 Service segment	— Monthly flight by flight traffic and capacity
Form 41	— Aggregate traffic and capacity results, plus costs and revenues

Note: The continuation of some of these data sources is questionable once the CAB ceases to exist.

on future flights, enables planners to ascertain patterns and levels of bookings for future flight planning.

One of the most detailed sources of internal information is the marketing information reporting system, elements of which are shown in table 11-3. Passenger flight coupons, collected by the airline as each passenger boards, are the basic source documents. Each flight coupon provides information on revenue, type of fare used, point of ticket sale, and which flight was taken on which day and hour. The millions of flight coupons collected each year provide a rich source of information about the airline's system. Many routine reports are prepared regularly, special reports can be generated as needed, and real-time access via computer terminal makes it possible to examine details at will.

Consumer Research Programs

American's marketing approach requires substantial communication with our customers. Our research is designed to tell us what our customers want and to guide us in developing the product that they will buy. We have over 200,000 annual respondents to our customer surveys, giving us direct access to passenger opinion—a major input for market planning, pricing, services, schedules, and sales and promotion. Table 11-4 outlines the types of consumer research programs used at American: quarterly in-flight surveys, competitive airline surveys, attitude and awareness interviews, panel discussions with frequent travelers, and special surveys. These programs provide an invaluable input to the planning process.

Development of the Plans

As table 11-5 illustrates, American Airlines develops many different plans—some long term and some short term. The content and development of each are discussed in the following sections.

Table 11-3
Data Sources—Internal Corporate Sources

Marketing information reporting system	
— Source:	Passenger flight coupons—Revenue accounting system
— Contents:	Traffic, revenue, and yields by flight and class, detail by fare basis, identifies point of sale and specific account
— Time:	Date, day of week, weekly, month, or annual
— Availability:	Routine reports on paper or microfiche exception reports as generated real-time CRT access

Table 11-4
Data Sources—Consumer Research Programs

Quarterly in-flight survey	— Service ratings, purpose of trip, elasticity, demographics, special analyses—150,000 respondents annually
Competitive airline survey	— Competitive service ratings, blind mail-back questionnaires, twice annually
Attitude and awareness	— Evaluates public perception of American and competitors, advertising effectiveness, three times per year via telephone interviews
Frequent travelers	— Panel discussions concerning American's services
Special surveys	— Custom-designed surveys to determine passenger's perception of a particular feature or service, approximately twenty five—thirty per year

Route Plan

American's route plan is based on the airline's existing route structure, expanding on known strengths and compensating for identified weaknesses. In developing the route plan, we consider such questions as:

What traffic flows can we expect on a candidate route?

How would it mesh with the existing and contemplated system of hubs?

How would it benefit the quality of American's service?

Is the route seasonal; if so, does it aggravate or alleviate other system seasonalities?

The plan is first developed without reference to the present fleet or to anticipated changes in the fleet, to reflect what we would like to do. Subsequently, the plan is adjusted to reflect a realistic matching of desires and resources.

Table 11-7
Fleet Plan—Increased Aircraft Seat Densities

Long-Term Plans	Operational Plans	Derivative
Route plan	Traffic	Manpower (budgets)
Fleet plan	Schedules	Service
Facility plan	Pricing	Sales and advertising
Balance sheet		
Operating margin		

The route plan identifies the most likely competitive situation; that is, the expected number of competitors and their relative strengths and weaknesses. The plan also reflects the planner's judgments on such general route characteristics as:

Market size—local and total.

Market growth—historical and potential.

Accessibility and support via other routes.

Stage length.

Seasonality.

Since passage of the Deregulation Act of 1978, American has taken advantage of the greater ease in adding or subtracting routes from its system. As table 11-6 shows, we have suspended almost as many routes as we have added since deregulation, thus altering the basic route structure signficantly. We have added fourteen new cities while terminating service at four. As can be seen in the table, route additions were oriented toward destinations in the sunbelt, the Caribbean, and Mexico.

Fleet Plan

American's fleet plan begins with mission requirements, which are derived from the route plan. The fleet plan identifies candidate aircraft for each mission by examining existing and new aircraft types, their mission capabilities, and their cost characteristics. The final step of the fleet plan is optimization of fleet mix, subject to corporate financial constraints. In selecting the most profitable aircraft mix for the fleet, many issues are considered:

Table 11-6
The Route Plan since Deregulation

Non-Stop Routes		*Cities*	
Suspended	42	Terminated	4
Added	44	Added	14
Sunbelt	19	Sunbelt	5
Caribbean	8	Caribbean	3
Mexico	2	Mexico	2
Other	15	Other	4

Wide body versus narrow body.

Range and mission capability.

Plane-mile and seat-mile costs versus revenue potential.

Fleet retirement plans.

Minimization of number of different aircraft types.

In recent years, American and other airlines have increased fleet capacity by increasing seating density—a less-expensive way to increase capacity than buying new aircraft. Table 11-7 displays the added capacity American has achieved by this method.

One aspect of fleet planning is the necessity to comply with Federal Aviation Regulation Part 36 (FAR 36), which specifies maximum fleet noise levels. Noncomplying aircraft must be either retrofitted to meet FAR 36 requirements or disposed of by specified dates. Table 11-8 shows American's compliance plan, indicating the phasing out of B-707s, retrofitting or replacing B-727-100s, and retrofitting noncomplying B-747s and B-727-200s. The DC-10s were in compliance when manufactured.

Facility Plan

American's facility plan identifies the facilities required to accommodate the planned level of operation presumed by the fleet plan. The facility plan quantifies requirements such as the number of gates and the square feet of terminal facility needed at each airport. Facility planning involves close coordination with such outside groups as airport authorities, city governments, other carriers (especially commuters) with whom interline connections are contemplated, and the Air Transport Association (ATA).

Table 11-7
Fleet Plan—American Airlines Fleet Compliance Plan for FAR Part 36

	1976	*1980/1981*	*Difference*
747	338 Seats	396 Seats	+ 58 Seats
DC-10	240	269	+ 29
707-323	144	retire	
707-123	133	retire	
727-223	125	144	+ 19
727-100	91	115	+ 24

Table 11-8
Fleet Plan—   American Airlines Fleet Compliance Plan for FAR Part 36

Passenger and Freighter Aircraft

January 1977

Aircraft Type	Baseline Fleet	Non-FAR 36 Aircraft	Non-FAR 36 Aircraft at			Compliance Program
			1/1/81	*1/1/83*	*1/1/85*	
B747-123	10	10				Retrofitted in 1979
DC-10-10	25					
B-707	89	89	45	9		Replace with B727-223 and B767
B-727-223	58	42	22			Retrofit
B-727-023	57	57	37	—	—	Retrofit/Replace
Total	239	198	104	9		

The facility plan must also provide for facilities at locations other than airport terminals. These include facilities for administration, training, reservations, maintenance, crew bases, and ticket offices.

Traffic Plans

A key input to the overall planning process is the traffic plan. American's traffic plan begins with a forecast of the overall economy. Then separate forecasts are made for industry passenger, freight, and mail traffic. These plans take account of such factors as:

Expected state of the economy.

Historic growth rate of airline traffic.

Known factors causing change (for example, route expansion).

Elasticity of demand (demand levels vis-à-vis expected changes in price and income levels).

Forecast industry capacity.

American's traffic is then projected as a share of aggregate industry traffic, considering historical share levels, the identity and number of competitors, anticipated share of industry capacity, planned levels of service, and new routes. A macroforecast is then developed by geographic entity. To accomplish this step, passenger traffic is estimated by fare basis, by type (business, pleasure), and by length of haul. This traffic is then priced to develop revenue estimates. As a check on this process, we construct a micro-forecast, built up from origin and destination markets. The macro- and microforecasts are reconciled to ensure reasonableness.

Traffic forecasts are the foundation for all long-term planning and for the annual operating plan. The level of detail, of course, varies with the requirements of the plan. Forecasts may be either demand limited or capacity limited; that is, there may be too few passengers or there may be too little capacity for the number of passengers seeking transportation. As external conditions change, forecasts are updated.

American utilizes a single, unified traffic and revenue forecast for all purposes. That is, a single forecast is used for schedule planning, station manning, sales quotas, and for financial, operations, and maintenance planning.

Schedule Plans

American's schedule department integrates the ideas, proposals, and levels developed in the route, fleet, and traffic plans into an airline schedule.

An intermediate schedule plan is developed to generate operating statistics necessary to the work of other departments who plan for:

Needed levels of crew manning.

Hours, routings, and overnights for maintenance work load accomplishment.

Budget development.

Probable new schedules requiring special sales and advertising support.

Short-range schedule planning develops the actual schedule by fine tuning the intermediate schedule plan for gate availability and by adjusting times to facilitate passenger connections. The short-range schedule can also react to market conditions. Figure 11-1 illustrates, for example, how 1980 schedules were curtailed from original plans as market conditions deteriorated in 1980. Finally, the planner must ensure that schedules are published on time and that planned capacity is available for sale as early as possible.

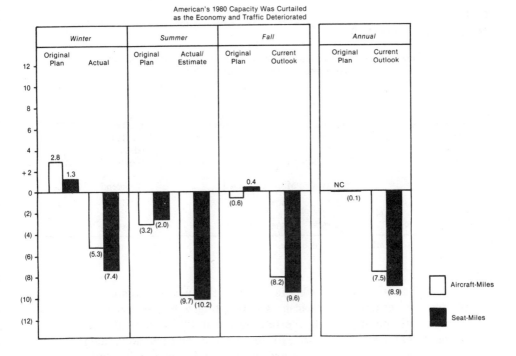

Figure 11-1. American Airlines Schedule Plan, August 1980

Pricing Plans

In considering a new pricing plan incorporating a discount, whether system-wide or in an individual market, the planner must assess the impact of the discount on *traffic generation*—the number of new passengers who will be induced to travel by the availability of the proposed fare; and on *dilution*—the amount of money a carrier will lose by allowing passengers who would have traveled anyway, at a higher fare, to make use of a discount fare.

American's pricing plans include both American initiatives (super saver, night fares, market-specific fares, and special premium flight fares) and defensive action (unrestricted "peanut" fares, $99-129 transcontinental fares, and introductory fares). During the summer of 1980, super saver fares became so liberalized that dilution outweighed generation, leading to a tightening of conditions by autumn and even tighter conditions promised for December. Table 11-9 charts some of the recently changing terms of super saver fares.

Table 11-9
Pricing Plans, August 1980

*Current Super Saver Conditions Have Become So Liberalized that They
No Longer Prevent Excessive Dilution*

		Summer 1978		Summer 1980	Fall 1980	
Advance purchase		30 Days		7 Days	14 Days	
Minimum stay		7 Days		1st Saturday	1st Saturday	
Maximum stay		45 Days		60 Days	60 Days	
Capacity limits		35% of aircraft		Carrier discretion	Carrier discretion	
		Weekend	Midweek	Daily	Weekend	Midweek
Discount	Day	30%	40%	35%[a]	35%	45%
from						
Coach fares	Night	40%	50%	45%[a]	45%	55%

[a]Discounts in selected markets vary by distance.

American is planning further innovations that will lead to more rational pricing. For example, American is conducting a limited experiment in flight-specific pricing during the fall season of 1980. This will allow the airline to charge a different price (or set of prices) on each individual flight, meaning that fares will differ on a given segment by time of day and day of week *for the same class of service.*

The plan calls for premium charges for flights with peak demand, in the hope that peaks and valleys in demand may be somewhat leveled and that, in any event, the high-demand flights will help to repay losses on low-demand flights. To accomplish flight-specific pricing on all flights, we must have new and better automation capabilities. The new proposal would greatly expand the number of fares from a current 8,000 to a proposed 280,000 (table 11-10). Moreover, the interline reservation system must be reprogrammed, since current computer communications between airlines transmit only minimal flight-specific pricing information. The industry's dependence on interline bookings requires that all carriers have comparable reservations capabilities.

Manpower Plans

Manpower plans are developed to service traffic and operating plans at established levels of quality. Statistics from the fleet and operating plans are provided to appropriate departments to be used in their manpower plans. The flight department then hires and trains pilots. The maintenance department establishes plans for line and base workloads. Staffing levels for flight

Table 11-10
Pricing Plan—Flight-Specific Pricing Issues

New proposal will contain a premium or discount by specific flight

Current Situation	Proposed Situation
O&D Market	O&D Market
Routing	Routing
Midweek/weekend	Day of week
Season	Time of day (specific flight)

New proposal would greatly expand the number of fares

Current Situation		Proposed Situation	
O&D Markets	800	O&D Markets	800
Routings	1	Routings	1
Fares/market	10	Fares/market	10
Total fares	8,000		8,000
		Daily flights/market	×5
		Days per week	×7
		Total fares	280,000

attendants, for airport and reservation agents, and for fleet service employees are set in accordance with expected traffic, planned flight frequency, and desired quality of service levels.

Service Plans

American's service planning is based on the assumption that we should provide a perceptibly better passenger service, and resources are provided to accomplish that goal. Consumer research and correspondence from our customers provide ideas for new service features. Service planning covers all areas of passenger contact—reservations, airport ticket counter, boarding point, and in-flight. In the past two years, American has introduced several new passenger service features:

Positive name check in.

Round-trip check in.

Connection check in.

Advance check in.

Service planning is a part of the new aircraft selection process as well. For example, service planners are now designing new in-flight service for the

B-767 aircraft on order, evaluating ticket vending machines, and planning service patterns for new airports.

Service planning also coordinates our involvement with the many industry agreements that ensure minimal customer inconvenience, such as interline baggage handling and ticketing agreements. American's service commitment is evidenced by its on-time performance over the years; we were third among trunks on on-time performance in 1975, we were second in 1976 and 1977, and we led all other trunks during 1978 and 1979.

Sales and Advertising Plans

American's sales and advertising planning is intended to assure that the public understands the intended results of all our other plans. We seek to convince all travelers that American is the best airline, and to build an image as the standard of excellence in domestic commercial aviation. American's advertising is directed to motivate customers to call us first, communicating the message that our prices are competitive and our service superior.

The advertising planning process determines appropriate spending levels based on analysis of historical and competitive ratios of advertising to sales and on expenditures per available seat-mile and per revenue passenger-mile. The plan also allocates funds between strategic and tactical expenditures. In 1980, for example, several special tactical programs included reintroduction of the family plan fare, an on-board lottery game, and various fare wars. Finally, the plan considers the most effective means of reaching potential customers through demographic segmentation of the message and the medium, adjusting for seasonal changes in travel interests.

Sales planning ensures that corporate and field sales efforts are integrated and are consistent with the various operational plans and with the advertising effort. Sales plans focus on major customers and their special needs:

Travel agencies.

Corporate travel departments.

Military and other government.

Other travel entities, such as car rental companies and tour wholesalers.

Credit card marketing.

American's sales plan recognizes the advantages of having these major customers tied into American's reservation system. The growth in subscribers to American's automated system (SABRE) is shown in table 11-11

Table 11-11
Sales Plans

Sales Planning Recognizes Subscriber Automation as an Effective Merchandising Vehicle	
	Subscriber Automation Installations Cumulative Locations
1976	130
1977	405
1978	840
1979	1706
1980 (June 30)	2457
1980 (December projected)	3200

to have reached 3,200 locations by the end of 1980, from an early start in 1976 of only 130 locations.

The sales promotion plan supports and augments the sale and advertising plan. It includes planning such things as displays, direct mailings, tour brochures, and customer impact items.

The planning process described so far in this chapter can be visualized in various ways, one of which is shown on figure 11-2. Of the several steps shown there, we have yet to discuss postappraisal.

Postappraisal

Postappraisal is an objective evaluation of the results of an action taken. Postappraisals compare actual with anticipated results. Some examples of activities that are subjected to postappraisal are:

Revenue and traffic on a new flight.

Telephone answering time.

Consumer research results.

Traffic generation of a new fare.

American has learned from its postappraisals and applied its findings to refine the planning process and its implementation. American's continued expansion of sunbelt routes, our recent decision to purchase fifteen B-727-200 aircraft from Braniff (to replace less-efficient B-727-100 and B-707 aircraft), our reductions of 1980 capacity from original plan, our efforts to restructure super saver fares to reduce dilution, and our continuing

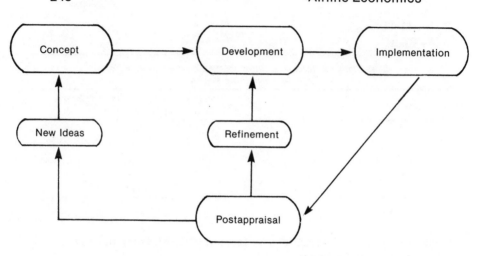

Figure 11-2. The Planning Equation

effort to sell travel agency automation systems are all the results of the post-appraisal built into the planning process.

Market Planning in Action—American's Hawaiian Route

Having described the planning process at American, I now turn to an example of this process: our analysis of whether we should reenter the U.S. mainland-Hawaii market. When the analysis led to a positive decision, plans for implementation began to be formulated.

American originally gained access to the Hawaiian market during the trans-Pacific case, decided in 1969. American's authority, won in the case, included restrictions that prevented profitable operation. For example, we were permitted no West Coast gateways, and our Hawaii frequencies were limited by the requirement that flights serve points beyond Hawaii (that is, Australia, New Zealand, Fiji, and American Samoa). Inadequate bilateral route authority seriously limited the number of flights we could offer. In addition, airport curfews on the long-haul flights forced American to serve Hawaii at unpopular hours. Accordingly, American reluctantly abandoned that route, trading it to Pan American Airways for several Caribbean route authorities.

In considering reentry, American's planners studied, among other things, the impact of Hawaiian traffic on United Airline's mainland routes. As table 11-12 illustrates, we felt that approximately 5 percent of United's mainland traffic was Hawaii related. Exclusion of that traffic from

Table 11-12
Hawaiian Route Planning Perspective

Traffic analysis routinely demonstrated the benefits of Hawaiian traffic flow on United's mainland routes. We estimated the following situation:

Traffic on all mainland routes	100%
Less Hawaiian thru passengers	1%
Less Hawaiian intraline connections	4%
True mainland traffic	95%

This flow had a very positive impact on United's forty-eight-state load factor and share of market. For example, in 1976:

	Actual	Excluding Thru	Excluding Thru and Connections
Load factor	57.6%	57.0%	54.7%
Share of market	21.1%	20.9%	20.0%

United's mainland routes would have reduced United's forty-eight-state load factor in 1976 from 57.6 percent to 54.7 percent—a huge revenue loss —and would have reduced United's forty-eight-state market share by over 1 percent (as shown in table 11-12).

In other words, United's domestic system received substantial support from operations beyond the forty-eight states. Similarly, other U.S. carriers receive support from operations beyond the contiguous states, whether from Hawaii, South America, or European operations. American was the only major East-West carrier without beyond-forty-eight-state support, and we felt that the Hawaiian operation was a perfect support for American's system, allowing us to fill empty domestic seats with flow traffic bound from or to the Hawaii-Los Angeles segment.

The CAB's interpretation of the Deregulation Act of 1978 made reentry possible without the restrictions of the earlier route authority. Preliminary route planning, accomplished in the summer of 1979, established the feasibility of reentering the market, but raised questions about profitability. Reevaluation in spring and summer of 1980 convinced us that reentering the Hawaiian market would increase system profitability.

Detailed planning for December implementation followed. Local Hawaiian activities were planned and coordinated, including:

Airport facilities.

Fuel.

Catering.

Local sales.

Crew accommodations.

Reservations.

Traffic flows and schedules were coordinated, based on an evaluation of competitive traffic results, analysis of Hawaii Visitors Bureau statistics, information from the field sales organization, and aircraft availability. Schedules were set to provide maximum flow and connections. We concluded that about 27 percent of the revenue passenger-miles (RPMs) associated with the Hawaiian routes would be flown on the mainland, and that about 60 percent of the overwater RPMs would flow from interior points.

Flight crews had to be trained and the route incorporated into the crew bidding process. In-flight services with a special Hawaiian motif had to be readied. Flight attendants had to be trained. Sales and advertising programs were developed to introduce the new service. Sales promotions were designed to reach travel agents, wholesalers, and interliners. Advertising was designed for a broad reach within the pertinent geographical areas, and with demographic characteristics of Hawaiian visitors in mind. Meanwhile, the pricing department reviewed existing tariffs and evaluated various introductory fares.

Schedules were finalized and put into the SABRE system and the OAG for sale. The sales force went to work.

Freight planning followed a similar pattern. The wide-body aircraft to be used on the route provided significant belly capacity for freight. It was necessary to ensure that necessary airport facilities would be available. Potential shippers were identified and contacted. Appropriate sales and advertising programs were developed.

The Hawaiian plan shows the integration of many departments under marketing's leadership: maintenance and flight plans by the operations department, fuel plans by the purchasing department, facilities plans by the property and facilities department, planning evaluations and cost assumptions by the finance department, and communications network planning by the data processing department. The Hawaiian operation will become part of the base of all future route, fleet, and facility plans. Careful follow-up of all aspects of Hawaiian start-up service is planned. Traffic will be tracked from its origin, with sales managers held accountable. Competitive action will be monitored. If necessary, the service will be fine tuned.

Planning in a Deregulated Environment

As the CAB's influence decreases over the next few years, the airlines will be operating in an environment that is only now beginning to emerge. A number of questions face planners in this new era. For example, with the sunset of the CAB in 1985 (or possibly earlier), will airline reporting requirements be discontinued or modified? Which data will be provided, and to whom will it be reported? Will there be new sources of data for planning purposes?

Another crucial issue will be assessing potential competitors in the coming years. How many airlines will remain by 1990? Will we see horizontal transportation conglomerates that cover all modes—air, rail, and truck?

Other questions abound. With long-term facilities and equipment no longer supported by route franchises, how will long-term planning for airport expansion be accomplished, and how will long-term financial agreements be arranged? What will the sales distribution network look like ten years from now? Will net fare plans emerge? What will be the impact of open commissions? Will travel agents retain the exclusive right to distribute the airline's product? How important will new carriers be—and how will the trunks and other established carriers compete?

This chapter has reviewed the planning process at American Airlines. We have seen that for American the marketing plan and the overall plan are identical: all other planning is derivative and in support of the marketing plan. For in the end, all planning is profit planning and profits flow only when we sell what we produce.

12

Financial Planning for Fleet Acquisition

Charles L. Glass

6150
5210
US

This chapter discusses planning for acquisition of Eastern Air Lines' new aircraft and financing of Eastern's capital acquisitions. Like most trunk airlines, Eastern serves a variety of markets, some of which have high enough traffic density to require large aircraft; some can economically support only small aircraft; other markets lie between these extremes. Figure 12-1 shows Eastern's fleet of 137-seat B-727-200s, 240-seat A300-B4s, and 293-seat L-1011s. Eastern also flies DC-9s and B-727-100s, though they are not shown on this chart. For markets too large for the B-727-200 but too small for the A300-B4, Eastern's choice today is to underutilize the larger aircraft or to overschedule with the smaller one. The B-757 fills that capacity gap and was, therefore, a candidate for consideration in our fleet planning.

Planning for New Capital Acquisition

Eastern's fleet of smaller aircraft is approaching old age. The B-727-100s, purchased between 1964 and 1968, will have their twentieth birthdays beginning in just a few years, as shown on figure 12-2. The DC-9 fleet is only slightly younger and, by the end of the decade, the B-727-200s begin to celebrate twenty years with Eastern. The importance of age is that aircraft maintenance and the related unproductive downtime increase significantly.

Even though fully depreciated, the aging B-727-100 aircraft have higher direct operating costs per seat-mile than do the new A-300s, as depicted in figure 12-3. This cost differential is due to a number of factors:

Larger aircraft are more economical (per seat-mile) than smaller aircraft, given identical technology and age.

The A-300s have only two engines, the B-727s have three.

A-300 engine technology, especially the high bypass ratios, provides substantial fuel economy.

Maintenance costs increase with age for any type of equipment, including aircraft and engines.

Figure 12-3 also illustrates that the cost differential will increase over the decade.

253

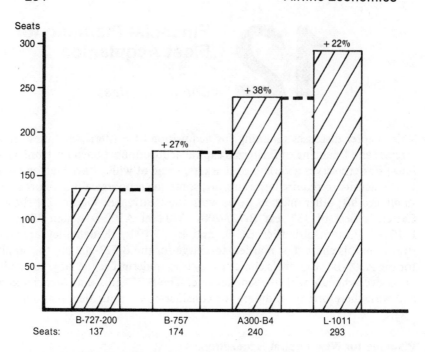

Figure 12-1. The Capacity Gap Filled by B-757

At this point one might conclude that cost per seat-mile is the only criteria.. That conclusion would lead an airline to buy wide-body aircraft only. That conclusion also ignores a reality of airline economics—the marketplace must be able to accommodate the very large number of seats generally offered by low seat-mile cost aircraft. Many markets cannot, so aircraft-mile costs *coupled with* seat-mile costs are important. Figure 12-4 illustrates these relationships. Cost per seat-mile is plotted on the vertical axis along with cost per aircraft-mile on the horizontal axis (seats are shown in parentheses). The key is to find the right mix of low seat-mile and low aircraft-mile costs for the total markets to be served. For example, note the B-727-100 versus the A-300-B2. If a market has a demand for only 100 seats, the low seat-mile cost A-300, with 280 seats, is much less desirable because its aircraft-mile cost is approximately $14.00, whereas the 107-seat B-727-100 aircraft-mile cost is only $8.00. Yet both aircraft can fulfill the market demands. In actual aircraft procurement, the ultimate goal is to have the right mix of small and large aircraft in total for the markets to be served, with each of the several size groupings consisting of the lowest seat-mile and aircraft-mile cost aircraft in the size group.

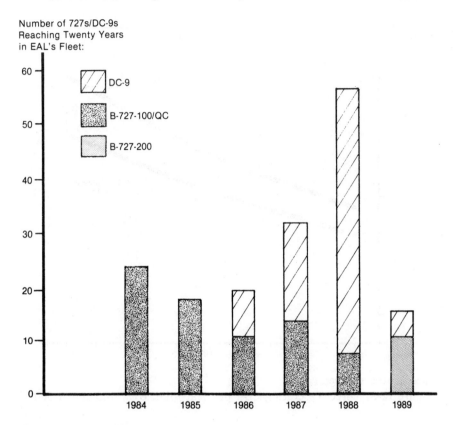

Source: Eastern Air Lines.

Figure 12-2. Chronology of B-727s and DC-9s Attaining Twenty Years in Eastern's Fleet

In light of these cost differentials and the need to retire or retrofit those older aircraft that do not meet federal noise regulations, Eastern undertook a study of routes to determine how a combination of B-757s and additional A-300s might fit into the fleet. Figure 12-5 illustrates some of the results of the detailed fleet planning study. It shows that the added A-300s would be used in three ways—to expand service on existing and newly acquired routes, to replace L-1011s on some routes for which the slightly smaller A-300 would be of suitable size, and to replace B-727-200s (as traffic grows sufficiently on routes served by those aircraft to make substitutions of a larger aircraft economical).

Some B-757s would also be used to replace B-727-200s that had become too small in a growing market. These displaced B-727-200s would then per-

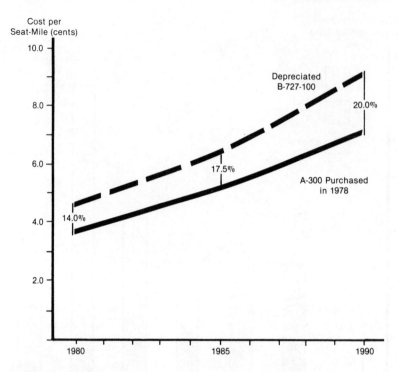

Source: Eastern Air Lines.
Figure 12-3. Direct Operating Cost per Seat-Mile, B727-100 and A-300

form the same replacement function for the smaller B-727-100s. The latter, in turn, would be retired or put on to new low-density routes.

Financing Eastern's Capital Acquisition

Rather than attempting to forecast for you how Eastern will finance its next aircraft and other equipment, I will relate our history in financing some 251 aircraft and associated ground equipment over the course of the past thirteen years. A total of $3.2 billion went into those purchases from 1967 through 1979. Funds to pay for this equipment came partially from internal sources—profits, depreciation, and aircraft sales—and partially from sources outside the company—equity, subordinated debt, leasing, manufacturers' financing (for the A-300s, supported by foreign governments), and senior debt.

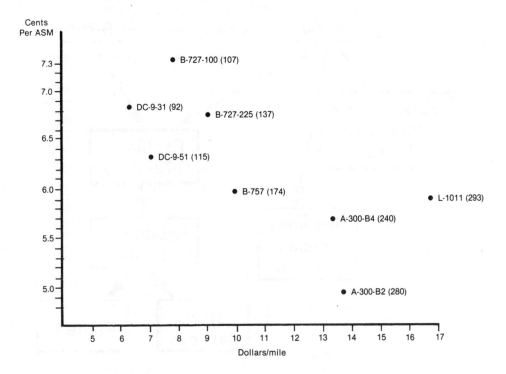

Note: Fuel at $1.25/Gallon.
Figure 12-4. Aircraft Cost Comparison, 500-Mile Stage Length

Table 12-1 displays details of the internally generated funds. It shows, among other things, that the first ten years of the thirteen-year period generated about $130 million a year, while the last three years generated over $240 million a year.

The accelerating pace of investment requirements posed serious—but soluble—problems for Eastern. In the thirteen-year period, profits were far too low to support the growth requirements of the company. In fact, of the $2 billion of internally generated funds, profits accounted for little more than 3 percent. Equipment sales provided about 18 percent and the remaining nearly 80 percent came from depreciation charges. Even if aircraft are not fully depreciated, it is impossible to buy aircraft at 1980s price levels with depreciation charges on aircraft that were purchased at 1960s or 1970s price levels.

In table 12-2, we see the details of the aircraft acquisition program. Total capital addition for the thirteen-year period, as previously noted,

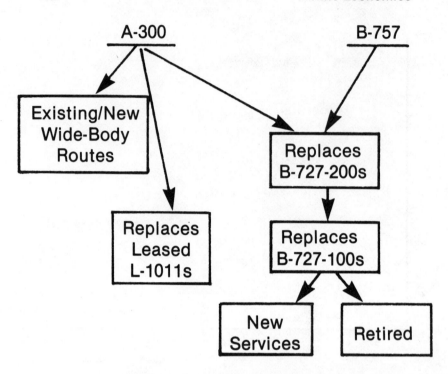

Figure 12-5. A-300 and B-757 Missions

amounted to about $3.2 billion. About $2 billion of that amount was financed by internally generated funds, as noted in table 12-1. However, debt retirement required nearly $2 billion in funds over that thirteen-year period, leaving Eastern with a need for outside financing of over $3.1 billion, *approximately the entire sum of the planned capital addition.*

Sources for the outside financing are itemized on table 12-3, amounting to about $220 million a year between 1967 and 1976 and about $320 million a year between 1977 and 1979. About one-third of the funding was accomplished by leasing aircraft instead of purchasing them. Another one-third (or slightly less) came from increases in senior debt. Eighteen percent came from aerospace companies and, in the case of the A-300s, export financing arranged through their government. About 10 percent came from selling additional shares of Eastern stock, while another 10 percent came from a net addition to subordinated convertible debentures.

To sum up our financing arrangements for the thirteen-year period, internal sources were just about enough to meet debt retirement needs, leav-

Table 12-1
Internally Generated Funds
(Millions of Dollars)

	1967-1976	*1977-1979*	*Total*
Profits	$ (90)	$155	$ 65
Add noncash charges (depreciation)	1,095	505	1,600
Equipment sale and other	290	65	355
Total	$1,295	$725	$2,020

ing Eastern in the position of going to outside financing for approximately the entire cost of fleet acquisition of more than $3 billion.

The obvious conclusion to be drawn from this chapter is that a capital-intensive industry or company cannot continuously replace its assets without meaningful profits. This is particularly true in an inflationary economy where replacement assets cost far more than the depreciation allowances based on historical acquisition cost. While it can be done for a while, the outside financial markets will not permit it indefinitely.

Table 12-2
EAL's Fleet Acquisitions and Other Expenditures, 1967-1979
(Millions of Dollars)

		1967-1976	*1977-1979*	*Total*
Acquisitions				
Aircraft acquired	Number			
DC-9	91			
DC-8	23	$ 1,905	$ 855	$ 2,760
B-727	88			
A-300	12			
L-1011	37			
	251			
Ground equipment		265	160	425
Total capital additions		2,170	1,015	3,185
Debt retirement and other		1,300	670	1,970
Financed by internally generated funds		(1,295)	(725)	(2,020)
Remaining—use outside financing		$ 2,175	$ 960	$ 3,135

Table 12-3
Outside Financing
(Millions of Dollars)

	1967-1976	*1977-1979*	*Total*
Amount needed	$2,175	$960	$3,135
Sources:			
Leasing	655	385	1,040
Manufacturer/export financing	260	275	535
Senior debt	940	50	990
Subordinated convertible debentures			
Original issue	205	200	405
Converted	(90)	(50)	(140)
Equity	205	100	305
Total	$2,175	$960	$3,135

Further compounding the problem is technological obsolescence and related cost obsolescence. A capital-intensive company cannot expect to generate adequate profits if its competitors are operating more-efficient aircraft because ultimately fare levels are based on cost plus a return element.

Thus consistent profitability is still the key to the ability to remain a viable competitor.

13 Government Affairs Planning

Harvey J. Wexler

All too often the language of Washington reduces itself very quickly to the bureaucrats versus the lobbyists. The former are perceived as not fully understanding and, as a result, thwarting the efforts of private economic initiative. The latter are perceived as urging a well-meaning cause, and are sometimes called "self-serving." This is a gross oversimplification of the real world. It obscures the true relationship between the public and private sectors. Political democracy and private economic enterprise cannot inherently be natural adversaries. In fact, they must be complementary forces if the system as a whole is to work.

It must be conceded that the ultimate and ideal objective of a private corporation and a national government cannot, and indeed should not, be identical. The word *ideal* is used in the sense of a vacuum in which there are no countervailing factors. A corporation is concerned with its own bottom line—indeed, it would be irresponsible if it were not (bottom line is hard to define with precision—it can mean this year, or five or ten years hence). The government, on the other hand, is concerned with the immediate bottom lines of all those industries (agriculture not excluded) that make up our total national productive effort and the general welfare of the nation at any point in time.

It is all too easy for the vested interests of any particular group or industry to become the basis for day-to-day activity and advocacy. To draw an analogy in the political area—and only as an observation, not as a personal statement one way or the other—it is easy to see the increased complexity and futility brought about by what is today commonly called "single-issue politics."

Such a perspective will get us nowhere. What is needed—the crucial ingredient—are ideas, a plurality of ideas from all vantage points. Ideas are generated by listening and by espousing on all sides. Each of us must search for the "art of the possible" in the context of the capabilities, ambitions, and limitations of others. Each must develop ideas and approaches that can blend with the objectives of both—or at least do violence to neither. For example, at any point in time, our industry interest in aviation negotiations with another country may have to take a secondary role in the broader national interest.

This is where the government affairs planner comes in. He must discern trends in public policy and, most important, the reasons behind them. He

261

must always keep in mind his company's objectives and articulate them persuasively. He must listen and learn—synthesize and interpret—advise his company of government policies that may impinge upon the freedom of executive decisions. The interests of a private corporation, or even those of an entire industry, may not (or even perhaps should not) coincide with those of the public sector. A former chairman of the Civil Aeronautics Board (CAB) said it very simply and well when he stated that the airlines have their responsibilities and the CAB has its responsibility. He noted that, if the Civil Aeronautics Board agreed with the airlines all the time, there would really be no reason for the existence of the Civil Aeronautics Board at all.

Admittedly, that was said before the era of deregulation. But it highlights the essential job of planning—to mesh private corporate objectives with broad public objectives. The essential function of the government affairs planner is as an advisor—a consultant—a person detached from the day-to-day (albeit vitally critical) operating, marketing, and financing aspects of corporate existence. In a word, he should be the government's de facto internal corporate voice. But equally, he must be his corporation's day-to-day Washington spokesman.

Concerning airline deregulation, it is also intriguing to note that deregulation has, in effect, broadened the constituent base of airlines. No longer can an airline rely primarily for its destiny on an image, sometimes very artfully designed, as perceived by a panel of five people. Its product is more directly on the line. Its destiny rests essentially with its customers, its management, and employees—the public at large.

One of the basic challenges (of dealing with the government) arises from the inherently conflicting objectives of the respective government departments and agencies. A tremendous competitive element exists within the government. It is a highly limited-entry market since it takes legislation to create a new entrant. Each agency has its own goals—both by statute and by human ambition. There is no reason to believe that human beings employed by the federal government are any less ego-affected than those in the private sector.

The creation of the Department of Transportation resulted from a very logical notion that all things relating to transportation might be most effectively dealt with under the same roof. As a result, that department since its inception has felt that it should play a more dominant role in international air transport negotiations. Repeatedly, the analogy is made that foreign transport ministries conduct such negotiations—not ministries of foreign affairs. Recently the Department of Transportation hired a private consultant to advise it on how to obtain this enhanced role in shaping the U.S. international air transport system. The selection of a consultant was impeccable—a man who had for a number of years chaired the U.S. delegation in international air transport bilateral negotiations as a member of the Department of State. It is not suggested that personal ambition should not go public—that would be ridiculous, but only that the government affairs planner must keep his ear to the ground for this, among many other factors, which can and does affect public policy.

Similar conflicts can exist within an individual agency. There is no doubt that the CAB is dedicated to the deregulation of air transportation. Underlying this objective there must certainly be the sincere and genuine belief that open, free, and unimpeded forces of competition will do two things: provide the most rational allocation of limited economic resources, and at the same time provide the consumer with the best possible product or service at the lowest possible price.

The underlying theory dictates that competition (actual and/or potential) protects the consumer, and does so in the objective marketplace. The economic concept on which deregulation is founded in no way contemplates or justifies subjective consumer protection in the form of government edicts. It is not accidental that nowhere in the index of Alfred Marshall's classic text, *The Principles of Economics,* is there a reference to "consumer."

The existence of the CAB's Bureau of Consumer Protection must be prima facie evidence that someone in authority lacks anything like full confidence in the effective role, function, and purpose of open competition— at least in the air transport industry. The very existence of a Bureau of Consumer Protection under deregulation is totally inconsistent with the economic rationale for deregulation. By way of illusration, there is no such tax-payer-funded bureau overseeing the hotel industry—and understandably so.

The government's policies change, as indeed do those of individual airlines and just plain individual people. For the government affairs planner perceiving timing is extremely important. Sometime it can be as important as the substance itself.

For example, the transition to deregulation was more rapid than initially expected. Just imagine the rupturing effect on airline operations caused by having to move from a highly regulated and structured environment to a deregulated situation in roughly a thousand days. To many deregulation seemed a sudden occurrence. But deregulation of some form was clearly in the clouds of Washington well before enactment of the deregulation bill. At the first deregulation hearing, Senators Kennedy and Thurmond were in total agreement (albeit for totally different reasons) and the idea—for good or evil—had arrived.

This is mentioned only to suggest the rather unique sensitivity and perception a government affairs planner should have. Without a sort of instinctive (and sometimes seemingly esoteric) function, it would be doubly difficult for those on-the-line operators of a company to plan their respective programs and contribute to that corporate enterprise that ends up as the total company.

The tenor of this analysis is very much "all the problems we have with the government." The airline industry does have problems with the government—but it must be conceded that the government has a few with the industry. Often the government affairs planner is in an uncomfortable position because of the dichotomy of a corporate desire for government protection or assistance and laissez-faire freedom.

Certainly many government officials have been bewildered when receiving two entirely different positions on a given matter from the same company; and surely are similarly bewildered when a company has one position on Monday and a different position on Tuesday.

The government affairs planner must constantly ask himself or herself the question of how to best represent the company and how best to personify its image. He or she must never forget that his or her personal reputation—particularly as regards integrity and honesty—becomes the company's reputation.

It is necessary to be exposed to Washington to understand just how it works. Just one example: nothing is worse than being confronted with a question and having to say, "I'll have to check with my company." That response conveys the message that the Washington representative is not in the scheme of corporate life. He or she doesn't even know what the corporation thinks, so why should official Washington listen. That person is not only useless to the government; worse, he or she is useless to the corporation.

Airlines will be increasingly turning to long-range strategic planning as a result of deregulation. It is a natural consequence of freedom of entry, exit, pricing, unrestricted competition, and so on. How well that long-range planning is performed will determine in no small way the bottom line five or ten years hence. The quality of overall corporate planning is, in turn, highly dependent upon the inputs of the government affairs planner. As stated earlier, government is always going to be an influence in our lives—in our corporate lives, in our private lives. It is incredible that this is not altogether accepted, no less understood.

14 Airline Fleet and Schedule Planning

Russell Thayer

The analysis that leads to schedule plans and to fleet plans begins with examination of an airline's route system. This chapter, therefore, first deals with Braniff's route restructuring following passage of the Airline Deregulation Act of 1978. Next it treats some aspects of schedule planning and then proceeds to a discussion of factors to consider in fleet planning.

The Route System

Braniff, like most airlines, has a mix of route segments of varying profitability. Table 14-1 illustrates the characteristics of a good route—long haul, low break-even load factor, and good profit potential. But Braniff's prederegulation route system left much to be desired. Figure 14-1 shows a route map of those U.S. city pairs over which more than 400,000 true origin-destination passengers traveled in 1974. Figure 14-2 shows Braniff's domestic route system at the moment of passage of the Deregulation Act. Comparison of these two maps makes it clear that Braniff had little access to the high-density markets in the country.

Another way to illustrate that isolation from high density markets is to look at Braniff's top ten city pairs, measured in number of origin and destination (O&D) passengers. Table 14-2 shows how each of these ten city pairs ranks among total U.S. domestic city pairs. Dallas-New York, Braniff's fifth-best city pair, is thirty-fifth in rank for the whole country. Others of the Braniff top ten are even lower density markets.

To strengthen its route system, Braniff took advantage of the dormant route authority provisions of the Deregulation Act to add many new routes to its domestic system. Figure 14-3 shows Braniff's domestic route structure after this took place.

At the same time, the international route system was subject to re-examination as bilateral air agreements were renegotiated. Prior to June 1979, Braniff's transatlantic service consisted only of a Dallas/Fort Worth-London route. But, because Dallas and London are major connecting hubs, that limited segment offered Southwest U.S. travelers on the route access to 156 cities in twenty-four countries, while offering European travelers to the United States access to 180 cities in twenty-four states. Addition of a Boston gateway in the United States and Amsterdam, Brussels, Frankfurt, and

265

Table 14-1
Braniff Airways B-747 Hawaiian Operations Scheduled Service, 1975

Aircraft-miles (thousands)	2,498
Revenue passenger-miles (thousands)	462,314
Available seat-miles (thousands)	864,933
Passenger load factor	53.5%
Break-even load factor before income taxes	44.5%
Profit spread	9.0% Points
Unit costs—total operating expenses	
Per available seat-mile	2.14¢
Per revenue passenger-mile	4.00¢
Yield per revenue passenger-mile	4.07¢
Average flight segment length (miles)	3,764
Aircraft utilization—block hours per day	14:01

Paris gateways in Europe opened many new travel opportunities in both directions.

On routes with relatively low traffic densities, such as the new Braniff transatlantic routes, there is a considerable advantage in having two or more origins and two or more destinations, so that different combinations

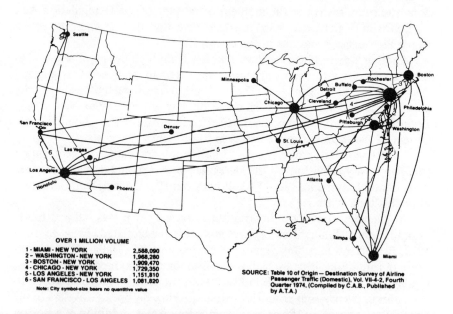

OVER 1 MILLION VOLUME

1 - MIAMI - NEW YORK   2,588,090
2 — WASHINGTON - NEW YORK   1,968,280
3 - BOSTON - NEW YORK   1,909,470
4 - CHICAGO - NEW YORK   1,729,350
5 - LOS ANGELES - NEW YORK   1,151,810
6 - SAN FRANCISCO - LOS ANGELES 1,081,820

Note: City symbol-size bears no quantitive value

SOURCE: Table 10 of Origin — Destination Survey of Airline Passenger Traffic (Domestic), Vol. VII-4-2, Fourth Quarter 1974, (Compiled by C.A.B., Published by A.T.A.)

Over 400,000 True Origin-Destination Passengers
Figure 14-1. Leading U.S. Domestic City Pairs, 1974

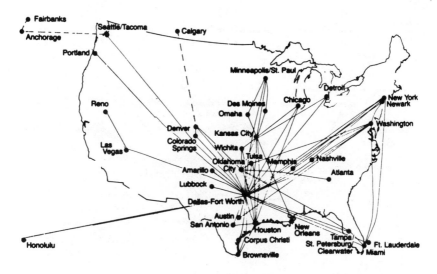

Figure 14-2. Braniff's Domestic System, 29 October 1978

of origins and destinations can be served on different days. On a route with low traffic density, such as Dallas-Frankfurt, there may not be enough demand to justify many nonstops each week, but by adding other U.S. or European points to the route more frequent one-stop flights can be provided through one-stop service, because demand for service between the intermediate points (Dallas-Brussels; Boston-Frankfurt) helps support the thin demand between Dallas and Frankfurt. In later discussions of flight scheduling, this technique is referred to again and its value to the airlines is illustrated quantitatively.

Table 14-2
Market Density—Braniff Top-Ten City Pairs

Pairs of Cities	Braniff Ranking	Industry Ranking
Dallas-Houston	1	51
Dallas-San Antonio	2	203
Dallas-Denver	3	111
Austin-Dallas	4	149
Dallas-New York	5	35
Chicago-Dallas	6	60
Chicago-Kansas City	7	47
Dallas-Kansas City	8	193
Chicago-Houston	9	77
Dallas-Oklahoma City	10	213

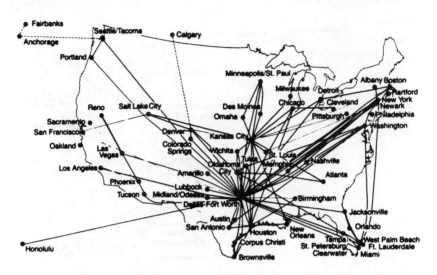

Figure 14-3. Braniff's Domestic System, 27 April 1980

The new international opportunities also made it possible for Braniff to expand its Pacific operations beyond Honolulu, adding Guam, Hong Kong, Singapore, and Seoul. This new route authority made it possible for travelers from the Far East to make connections not only in the United States, but also to Braniff's Latin American destinations, while Americans could now have new ways to reach Far Eastern destinations. The new trans-pacific and transatlantic routes stretched the Braniff system from Singapore across the United States and into continental Europe.

To conclude this discussion of the expansion of Braniff's route system, it is pertinent to take note of the network from the United States into South America, a long-time Braniff stronghold. Figure 14-4 sketches the entire international route system that Braniff had developed by April 1980.

Schedule Planning

The task of the schedule planner is to serve the cities on the route system in a way that meets the demands of travelers and that return a fair profit to the airline. To accomplish that task it is necessary to balance capacity against the demand at the price at which the capacity is offered. Selection of the proper aircraft type for each part of the route system in the fulcrum of this scheduling concept. This balance is achieved by operating at a low cost per seat-mile, accomplished in part by high utilization of equipment and high

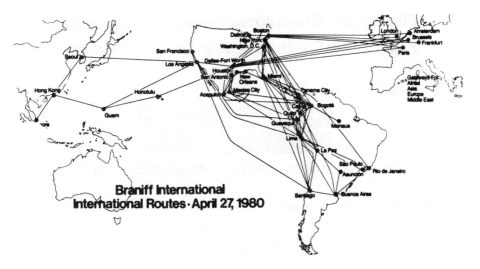

Figure 14-4. Braniff's International Routes, 27 April 1980

productivity of both equipment and manpower, by frequent service, and by flow-through traffic.

Operating a nonstop flight between cities A and B serves only one market. If, however, the flight goes on beyond B to C, that one-stop flight from A to B to C serves three markets: A-B, A-C, and B-C. If, in addition, the flight proceeds on to D, that two-stop flight serves six markets: A-B, A-C, A-D, B-C, B-D, and C-D. Figure 14-5 is a hypothetical example to illustrate how we make through traffic work. If traffic between A and B is insufficient for profitable operation, and if traffic between B and C is also insufficient, putting the two flights together and attracting additional passengers between A and C can make both segments profitable.

To illustrate more specifically, let's consider Braniff's Flight 21 from Newark to Houston in December 1975. Only nineteen passengers a day flew on BN 21 that month between Newark and Houston. But, because of the intermediate stop at Dallas/Fort Worth, many more passengers were served by BN 21—fifty-five per day between Newark and Dallas and sixty-four per day between Dallas and Houston. Instead of a nonstop Newark-Houston flight with nineteen passengers a day, we had a one-stop flight with seventy-four passengers on the first segment and eighty-three on the second. The intermediate stop makes the flight economically feasible.

As another example, table 14-3 shows how a very light-traffic flight between Albany and New York's LaGuardia Airport is profitably added to a flight that would otherwise have served New York-Dallas-San Antonio.

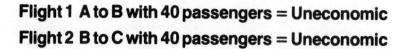

Flight 1 A to B with 40 passengers = Uneconomic

Flight 2 B to C with 40 passengers = Uneconomic

Flight 3   A   to   B   to   C

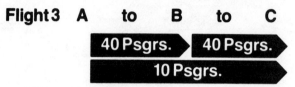

50 passengers over both segments = Profit

Figure 14-5. Braniff Airways: How We Make Through Traffic Flow Work

The seventeen Albany passengers who proceed to Texas on the flight bring in an equivalent of 190 Albany-New York passengers as measured in revenue passenger-miles (RPMs).

As an airline acquires authority to serve new city pairs, the schedule planner finds opportunities to put together new aircraft routings that will take advantage of through traffic. For example, Braniff acquired authority to serve Houston, Memphis, New Orleans, and New York City from Birmingham as a result of the dormant route provision of the Deregulation Act. This provided four new city-pair markets. But, because it now became possible to tie these four markets into the existing route network, twelve additional city-pair markets were added through use of one-stop routings over Birmingham, as shown in figure 14-6. In figure 14-7 the market progression is carried even further by adding a Birmingham-Dallas segment, thus adding another sixteen cities that could be served (with two stops enroute) from Birmingham.

Table 14-3
Value of Through Traffic

Flight	Average Passengers per Flight	Revenue Passenger- Miles (RPM)	ALB-LGA RPM Equivalents
ALB-LGA	31	105,400	31
ALB-DFW	15	568,452 ⎫	190
ALB-SAT	2	76,110 ⎭	
Totals	48		221

Note: The seventeen passengers traveling beyond New York are equivalent to 190 Albany-LaGuardia passengers.

Acquired Under Dormant Route Authority

Four Markets

Figure 14-6. Market Progression Opportunities

Addition of new cities can provide the schedule planner with the means to strengthen the airline's prime markets. For example, addition of Boston, Hartford, and Albany to Braniff's route system provided an opportunity to carry passengers and cargo from those cities through New York to Dallas. The traffic over New York from these gates allowed us to add new flights from New York to Dallas, thereby strengthening that market.

Schedule planners have many other variables to consider in producing an airline schedule. Each aircraft must eventually return to its starting point. Aircraft must be scheduled through maintenance bases at predeter-

Added One Stop Possibilities

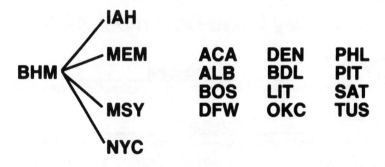

Increases Markets by 12
A Total of 16 City Pairs

Figure 14-7. Market Progression Opportunities

mined times. Crews must be available at the right places and, to the extent possible, returned to home base at night. And aircraft sizes must be matched as closely as possible to market sizes. This is difficult to accomplish because a typical domestic aircraft routing will serve markets both large and small in the course of a single day. An example of a day in the life of a Braniff airplane is shown in figure 14-8. Four separate flights encompassing nine segments take that particular aircraft from Corpus Christi in the morning to Amarillo in the evening. The following day, that same aircraft would follow a different routing, starting at Amarillo in the morning.

Fleet Planning

The mix of aircraft best suited to an airline's requirements is determined by a complex process of analysis. Basic to the analysis is the distribution of aircraft sizes and range capabilities required to serve the airline's route system now and into the future. Figure 14-9 shows the distribution in 1972 of our aircraft seats, varying from 31 percent in small, short-range aircraft, to 14 percent in large, intercontinental-range aircraft. By 1985, we expect that this distribution will have changed dramatically, as illustrated in figure 14-10. A fleet purchased to meet the 1972 distribution would be ill-suited for the 1985 distribution—it would have too many small, short-haul aircraft, medium-range aircraft that are too small, and it would have no large aircraft with just transcontinental range. Those differences in requirements led the aerospace companies to size their new aircraft offerings to fill the

One–Day Cycle·December 1975

Flight 12
Long-haul
Corpus Christi—Dallas-Fort Worth—Washington, D.C.—New York

Flight 15
Long-haul
New York—Washington, D.C.—Dallas-Fort Worth—San Antonio

Flight 194
San Antonio—Dallas-Fort Worth

Flight 198
Dallas-Fort Worth—Lubbock—Amarillo

Figure 14-8. Braniff Airways Aircraft Routing No. 16

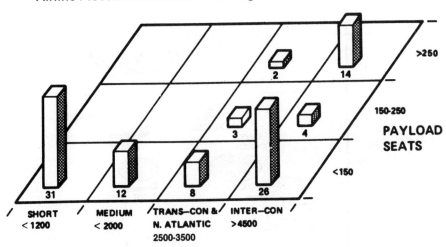

Figure 14-9. Percentage Distribution of Seats Based on Lift Requirements—1972

gaps that exist today. Braniff decided to examine in detail, from among these offerings, an advanced B-727, the B-757, and the B-767. These aircraft fit into the oval spaces shown in figure 14-11 as the gaps in today's distribution of aircraft sizes and range.

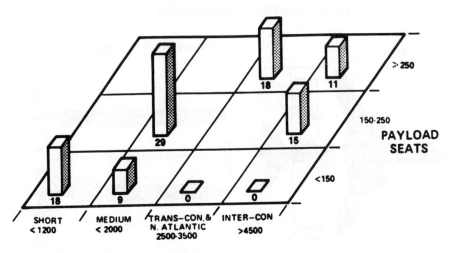

Figure 14-10. Percentage Distribution of Seats Based on Lift Requirements—1985

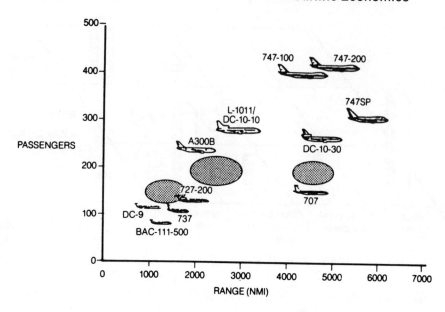

Figure 14-11. Size and Range Caps in Current Fleets

Since its introduction nearly twenty years ago, the B-727 has grown in size and range. A contender to replace the 727, the B-757, is shown in figure 14-12 to have a shorter wing span with length nearly identical to the 727-200, yet it carries more passengers.

One way of analyzing alternative aircraft types is to compare performance on a variety of routes that span the relevant types of segments to be

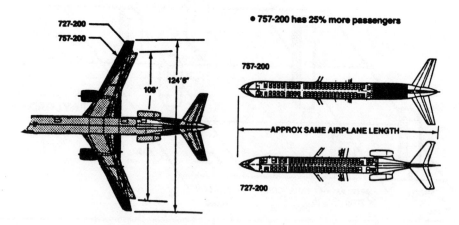

Figure 14-12. Size Comparison, B-757-200 and B-727-200

flown. A combination of "design routes" for domestic service would include segments with high-altitude, hot weather take-off conditions, long-haul segments, and over-water trips. The maps in figures 14-13 to 14-16, inclusive, show range capabilities of the advanced 727-200, the 757-200, and the 767-200 when taking off on a hot day from LaGuardia, from Denver, from Mexico City, and from Bogota. A comparison of figures 14-13 and 14-14 illustrates how the range of the 727-200 and 757-200 is reduced by the high altitude at Denver, while the range of the 767-200 is less out of New York than out of Denver because of the short runway at LaGuardia.

Fuel consumption is another important consideration in aircraft selection. An important issue to consider is the effect of increasing fuselage cross section (and hence aerodynamic drag) on fuel consumption for a particular flight pattern. Technological improvement in fuselage design coupled with changes in wing and engine design have resulted in reduced fuel consumption with succeeding generations of aircraft. These improvements are continuing, but at a diminishing rate, as shown in figure 14-17. In general, fuel consumption increases with aircraft size. A quantitative measure of that difference, as shown in figure 14-18, makes the 727-200 look good as a fuel conserver on routes for which it is large enough.

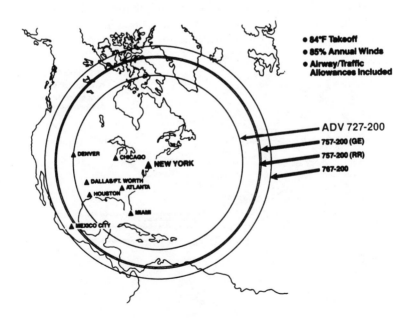

Figure 14-13. Range Capability from New York (LGA)

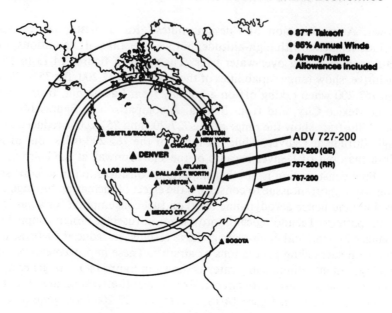

Figure 14-14. Range Capability from Denver

Fuel is a large element in total operating costs—about thirty percent of total cash operating expenses and over half of the direct operating costs. Nevertheless, cost comparisons must be made in terms of all direct operating costs and, when affected by the decision, *all* operating

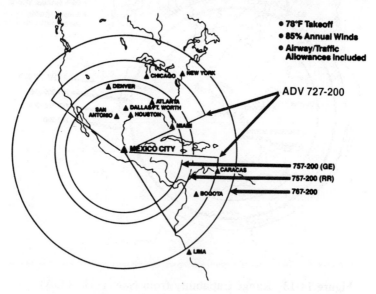

Figure 14-15. Range Capability from Mexico City

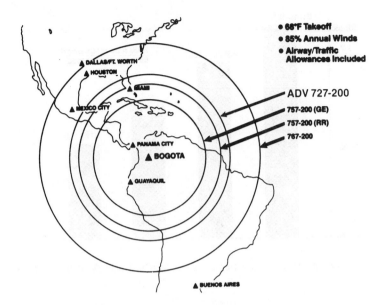

Figure 14-16. Range Capability from Bogota

costs—both direct and indirect. Figures 14-19 and 14-20 show comparative direct operating costs per seat-mile and per aircraft-mile for the L-1011-1, A-300B4-220, A-310-220, and B-727-200 aircraft. On a seat-mile basis the 727 is slightly more expensive than the other three. But in markets not

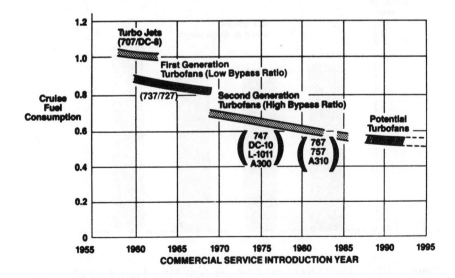

Figure 14-17. Fuel Consumption Improvements, 1958-1995

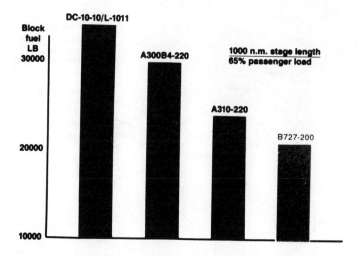

Figure 14-18. Block Fuel per Stage Length, Four Aircraft Types

requiring the greater seating capacity of the other three, the 727 is more economical, because its aircraft plane-mile costs are much lower than the others.

Another aspect to consider in selecting new aircraft types is commonality, which affects maintenance costs, spare parts, inventory levels,

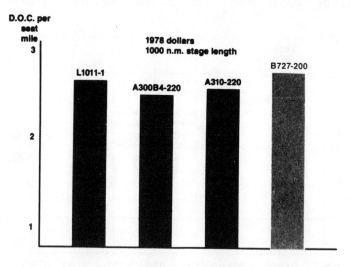

Figure 14-19. Direct Operating Cost per Seat-Mile, Four Aircraft Types

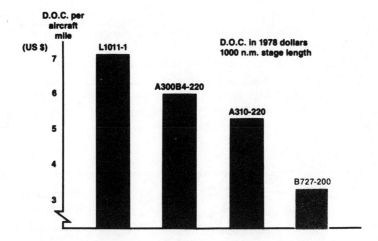

Figure 14-20. Direct Operating Cost per Aircraft-Mile, Four Aircraft Types

and training costs. Figure 14-21 illustrates the commonality principle in a family of Boeing aircraft.

In sum, for Braniff's domestic route system and for some of our Latin American routes, the advanced 727-200 fills the needs well. This aircraft meets the requirements of markets with low density and heavy business

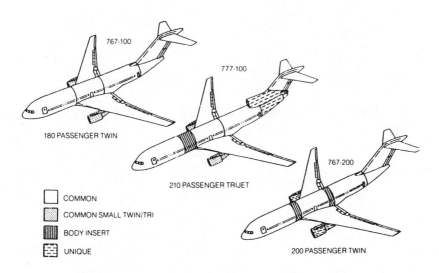

Figure 14-21. Twin-Twin-Tri Family Commonality

travel; it meets schedule requirements of multiple frequencies and limited capacity per trip; and it meets equipment requirements of low operating cost and appropriate capacity.

Looking at longer range aircraft to serve Braniff's long-range international routes brings back a familiar map as a way to compare range capabilities of long-range aircraft. Figure 14-22 shows the superior range capabilities of the B-747SP aircraft Braniff has recently purchased for these routes.

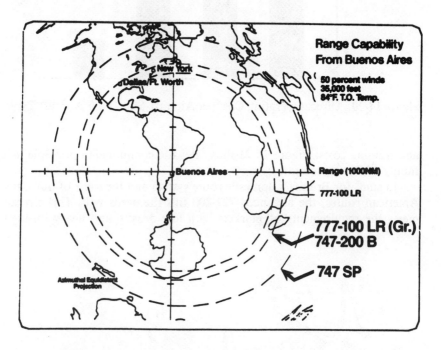

Figure 14-22. Range Capability from Buenos Aires

15 International Planning

William H. Waltrip

It is clear that, because of a confluence of causes, our industry is in a major upheaval. Under these circumstances, long-range planning is not so much a set of fixed goals as an effort to transform the decision-making process to cope with the daily changes. As somebody put it, "maintaining a rigid state of flexibility."

This does not mean that you don't have to know where you are going and where you want to be in three to five years. The challenge is to integrate short-term, tactical decision making with this vision of the future.

Let me try to sketch the environment we operate in. Although I will look at it from the viewpoint of an international carrier, the starting point has to be domestic deregulation, not only because it foreshadows developments in the international arena, but also because the new Pan Am is now a major domestic carrier.

Contrary to some myths, this has never been a placid industry. In our history, spanning half a century, we have never gone a decade without a major improvement in our basic equipment, the airplane. It is these innovations that have made air travel ever safer, faster, more comfortable, and cheaper. The technological breakthroughs have gone hand in hand with innovations in marketing, selling, advertising, pricing, and distribution. Product improvement has been constant and continuous both on the ground and in the air.

Yet what we are witnessing today is something entirely new. It is new partly because of the kinds of changes we are witnessing: where they used to be marginal and gradual, today they are fundamental and radical. What is also new is the frequency and rate of change. For instance, significant schedule and fare changes used to occur every two to three years. These days they seem more like every two to three months.

We may get an idea of how far and fast we have come by looking back just three or four years. The conventional wisdom, taken for granted and virtually unchallenged, and, in the minds of most people, elevated to the status of natural laws—valid forever—included the following:

1. A basic tenet held that airline pricing is different from the pricing of any other product and service; for instance, you couldn't experiment with new concepts in a limited test market.

2. Similarly, it was assumed that introductory offers of the kind used by manufacturers of new products are not applicable in our business. Yet

the last two years have seen a rash of such introductory offers. Today, for an airline inaugurating new service, it is more the rule than the exception.

3. More than two classes of service on the same airplane were held to be unworkable, both operationally and from the standpoint of marketing and public acceptance. Now the experiences of some carriers have borne out that judgment, but those of Pan Am and some other carriers have proved that three classes of service can be offered efficiently and to the satisfaction of all passengers.

4. It was an article of faith that competing carriers on a given route must offer the same fare types. Indeed, during the International Air Transport Association's (IATA) reign, it couldn't be otherwise. Yet carriers lately have selectively withdrawn or failed to match certain fares, and the world hasn't come to an end.

5. It was entirely unthinkable that competing airlines offering the same fare classes on the same routes would price them at different levels. It has happened now on more than one route, and the carriers with the higher fares seem to be surviving.

6. Another standard and unquestioned rule was that a round-trip promotional fare must not be less than the one-way normal economy fare. In other words, the largest discount may not be more than 50 percent of the normal economy fare. Thanks to new fare concepts and new classes of service, this law has become obsolete, too. Fares with 60 or even 70 percent off the normal fare abound.

7. Fares had to be identical on a given route in both directions. You couldn't charge $1,000 from Australia to the U.S. and $800 from the U.S. to Australia. Now you can and do.

8. Fare structures in markets that are closely related geographically had to be the same, or else massive traffic shifts would occur, it was said. Now we have structural differences between France and Belgium, and between Italy and Austria, and the dire predictions haven't materialized.

9. It was an iron law that fare levels in adjacent markets had to be related. A certain fare to a more distant point could not be lower than the same fare to an intermediate point. Yet some fares from the United States to Italy, for example, have been lower than those to Switzerland, but the disparities do not cause any particular problem.

10. It was taken for granted that all carriers had to be price competitive in all markets, even if they didn't serve that market on line. For instance, a passenger going from New York to Amsterdam by taking TWA from New York to London and British Airways from London to Amsterdam, paid the same fare as a passenger who took KLM's nonstop New York-Amsterdam flight. The price parity kept TWA in this market despite its disadvantage in service. However, since it had to share the fare with KLM, it netted less from this passenger than from a regular New York-London passenger. Now

there are quite a few promotional fares that do not permit interlining, and thus carriers in off-line markets are uncompetitive for sizeable segments of those markets. Yet, overall, perhaps we're all better off for it, as we all cater to the traffic we can most efficiently carry.

11. In the charter market, do you remember the time when you had to belong to a club or association to be eligible for one? These days, getting on a charter is as easy as visiting your nearest travel agent. Yet the widely predicted disintegration of scheduled service has not materialized.

12. Then we have our budget fare, where the passenger selects the week of travel but the airline tells the passenger which day and flight the traveler will have to take. For years, we were alone in believing that there was a market to be served profitably with this fare. Three years, half a million passengers, and $150 million later, we can safely say the others were wrong.

These examples make my point that in pricing, as well as in every other facet of our operation, what conventional wisdom held unthinkable yesterday is happening today. Nor are these minor changes. They alter the way we do business.

The other hallmark of the new era is the rapidity of change. Take schedules. We used to have two schedules a year—a summer schedule from late April to late October, and a winter schedule for the rest of the year. The summer schedule in a given year closely resembled the summer schedule of the previous year, and the same with winter schedules. The aircraft type operated, routing of flights, their frequency, and even departure and arrival times were fairly stable. Today we hardly go a week without some schedule change somewhere in our system. The frequency of these changes is not all to the good; in more stable times travel agents and even frequent travelers used to know our flight numbers and departure times by heart, and this was an asset. These days schedule information is hard to keep up to date. Just the same, these changes are necessary for at least two reasons.

The first reason is cost. Fuel prices have skyrocketed and have made many flights marginal. The cost of new aircraft and financing has also risen sharply, and this has created a capacity shortage. Expensive fuel and scarce aircraft force carriers to fine-tune schedules almost continuously. The objective is a dual one: increasing aircraft utilization (the average number of hours per day the aircraft is in the air) and deployment of the equipment in the market in which it earns the highest return. In this regard, our industry has an advantage over most manufacturers in that the major component of productive capacity, the aircraft, can be shifted overnight from one market to another.

The second reason for the increasing frequency of schedule changes is the new environment that opens up new opportunities. Since our fleet is fixed in the short run, taking advantage of these opportunities by entering new markets also means cutting back somewhere else. Also, these new

opportunities are by no means limited to Pan Am. Indeed, we seem to acquire new competitors on our major routes at a frightening rate. Although
we are not easily frightened, competitive conditions on a route are bound to
affect your own decisions as well.

We have a similar situation with fares. IATA conferences used to set
fares for an area of the world for two to three years at a time, and that was
that. Now, pricing is as much a continuous year-round activity as it is in
supermarkets.

The historical framework of bilateral agreements, the cornerstone of international air transport, is also changing. The Bermuda-type agreement,
reigning unchallenged for three decades, is gradually giving way to new
types of arrangements.

The traditional or Bermuda-type agreement requires double approval.
This means that both governments have to approve a certain action before it
can be implemented. This arrangement has become less and less viable.
When multilateral agreements exist, they tend to override the bilateral ones.
Governments with close ties to the national carrier are less likely to act in an
impartial manner, even if the consumer interest is at stake. The necessity of
double approval also tends to discourage innovation. Finally, disagree-
ments between two governments can lead to protracted stalemates.

An alternative is the country-of-origin principle. With this, each country
has full and sole jurisdiction over traffic originating within its borders. This
eliminates some of the problems of double approval. Although a government
can still protect its national carrier, the specter of a stalemate is removed and
initiative is encouraged by requiring the approval of only one government.
Directional fares may result, but the possibility of buying one-way tickets
puts a limit on the directional differences the market could tolerate.

The third type of bilateral agreement is characterized as "double disapproval." It is the most permissive of the three, and indeed the most liberal
imaginable short of total deregulation. Only disapproval by both governments could stand in the way of a carrier-initiated action. Needless to say,
this is most conducive to innovation and experimentation.

Total deregulation, where carriers enter and exit markets, determine
frequency and capacity, and set fares free of government intervention,
would largely eliminate the need for the bilateral agreement itself. Although
such a regime is being phased in for U.S. domestic air transportation, it is
not yet on the horizon for international aviation.

The United States, while still tied to most countries by Bermuda-type
agreements, has a number of country-of-origin and double disapproval
agreements. As bilateral agreements come up for renegotiation, each new
agreement seems to be more liberal than the one it replaces.

Does that mean that the U.S. government unilaterally imposes deregulation on the small airlines of defenseless countries to secure a cushioned

existence for its large carriers? Nothing could be further from the truth, although repetition has given this view unwarranted currency.

First, the United States has not, does not, and cannot impose its will unilaterally on other countries. That we have certain arrangements in aviation with Japan, different ones with Germany, and still other kinds with Australia, Israel, Poland, and so on has resulted in each case from bilateral negotiations, not unilateral decisions.

Second, for every concession the United States has offered generous inducements—perhaps even too generous. I must say we do not agree with this method of "trading routes for rates," for, while rate concessions are transitory, routes become very permanent.

Third, the fear of domination by large American carriers implies economies of scale that do not exist. Study after study has shown that medium size is optimum for airlines and the largest ones operate less efficiently. The profitability of U.S. trunk carriers provides empirical evidence.

Finally, the United States and its privately owned airlines are taking a far greater chance slugging it out in a free market than are other countries and their national carriers. To appreciate this, we need not debate their ownership, management, objectives, or state support ranging from preferential treatment to subsidies. Whatever the particular arrangement, one thing is clear: mistakes and losses to public companies are a matter of inconvenience or embarrassment—to private ones, a matter of survival.

When I say this, I state facts without endorsing economic protectionism. I do not believe it serves anybody in the long run. From airlines it removes the incentive to improve efficiency. (The "infant industry" case can be made for the carriers of developing countries, but even there the diversion of scarce and badly needed resources is open to question.) Passengers and shippers typically have fewer options in a tightly regulated environment. Of course, nonflying taxpayers get by far the worst of the deal; although much poorer as a group, they are forced to subsidize the flying of their more affluent fellow citizens.

Relaxing regulation in international markets is neither pro-American nor anti-American, neither pro-big airline not anti-big airline. It is pro-competition, pro-efficiency and pro-consumer. I don't think we can turn the clock back, and I don't think we should try.

International deregulation should be given a chance. I am talking about true deregulation, of course, without artificial floors and ceilings on fares and rates, so that increases in input costs can be passed on instantaneously as in unregulated businesses.

There is always the elasticity impact, of course; when you have to raise prices, demand tends to suffer. Yet with rising costs we have no choice but to take our chances with elasticity. The present provides a good example. The combination of a weak economy and higher fares hurt volume as badly as at any time in recent memory. Yet the major problem of carriers is yield, not traffic. The traffic decline appears catastrophic only in comparison with what we in the industry are accustomed to. Other industries have survived no-growth or even negative growth years without the staggering losses we are suffering. This, too, points to yield as the main culprit.

The fact is, you can adjust to substandard traffic, within reason, to mitigate the damage, but you can't adjust to substandard yield when most of your input costs are beyond your control (fuel, landing fees, and even labor).

Liberalized regulation is not the panacea, as the domestic carriers are finding out, but it should help reduce the regulatory lag and this should lead to speedier cost pass through. You might say I am biased against regulation, but, as the executive of an airline that once lost $350 million and had to fight for its life, I have a hard time working up much nostalgia for the "good old days." Nor was our case unique; other international carriers fared little better. For us the changes are coming none too soon.

This new environment requires a new breed of airline managers, both analytical and entrepreneurial. Major functions of the airline will also change. Forecasting will be a key activity—far more important than today. Don't forget, if a steel manufacturer builds a plant at a certain location, he has little choice but to produce steel at that location. Airlines are different in that their major resource, aircraft, is portable; you can literally shift them overnight from one market to another. In the past it didn't make much sense for a carrier to analyze the profitability of a certain route he wasn't authorized to fly. Soon, all routes in this country will be fair game. If you multiply this by the number of possible options on aircraft type, frequency, schedule, service, and price, the number becomes astronomical. Spotting profit opportunities in this jungle and forecasting traffic, market share, and revenue accurately in a constantly changing environment will spell the difference between profit and loss.

Changes in the external environment may shape not only management styles and techniques, but organizational structures. The fresh challenges the airlines will be facing in the 1980s will probably move them toward less-centralized decision making. As it is, for their size, airlines are in a tiny minority of firms operated as single profit centers. Some carriers have started by decentralizing marketing; other carriers and other functions are sure to follow.

It may start out modestly. One carrier, exasperated in trying to set commission levels for thousands of agents centrally, may turn to a division head, saying, in effect: "Here's $10 million commission money, produce $100 million or more in sales with it. You will be judged on the results."

Another carrier may go one step further and allow its regional manager to use some of that money for advertising or sales promotion at his discretion, as long as he delivers his revenue quota. This is still a far cry from profit centers, of course, but it is a beginning. We at Pan Am have started moving in this direction with the appointment of product managers.

Quantitative methods will come into their own. Let me give you an example. In the past, a certain route was operated by the same carriers, using pretty much the same equipment, offering similar schedules and identical prices, year in, year out. This will drastically change. You will see monthly, even weekly, changes on major routes. These decisions will have to be made in the face of uncertainty and with imperfect knowledge.

Suppose you want to enter a market already served by one carrier. You might undercut his price by 10 percent but you don't know if he'll match you. You also know that a third carrier is considering entering the same market. You don't know if your going in first will keep him out or not. How do you estimate the profit or loss you will have on the route?

There are a number of ways. You could make certain assumptions, for instance, that the incumbent carrier will match your price but the third carrier won't come in. The result will be correct if your assumptions turn out to be right. Another way is to make a best case/worst case scenario. This would at least size your opportunity and risk. You can go a step further. You could estimate the probability of each of these unknown events: the incumbent matching the price and the third airline entering. These probabilities will be subjective but still very useful. Knowing the best and the worst that can happen is better than having a single estimate, but certainly if the best has a 10 percent chance of materializing and the worst 90 percent, you would want to know it. Also, there may be other possibilities between the best and the worst.

This is the kind of information the decision tree technique I am describing would bring out. You may find that you have a 30 percent chance for a $5 million profit, a 60 percent chance to break even, and a 10 percent chance for a $5 million loss. This is the kind of information you will need for intelligent decision making.

The way tickets are priced may also change beyond recognition. If some of our regulators have their way, what we call an air fare today may mean no more than the list price of a car or the suggested retail price of a color TV set. There are also some special issues in pricing that will have to be addressed.

The scheduled carriers faced a severe crisis in the early 1970s. The product they were selling had a lot of costly features built in, such as free stopovers, interlining, children's discount, and so on. Some passengers wanted and used these, others did not. Along came charter carriers who found that, by catering only to point-to-point markets, they could substantially undercut the price charged by scheduled carriers. They walked away with a large share of the profitable business of the scheduled carriers and left them with all of the unprofitable traffic. This pushed several major carriers to the brink of bankruptcy.

Unless we do something about it, we will face a similar crisis in the early 1980s. The only difference will be that this time the challengers are also scheduled carriers (although some of them are the same corporate entities that created the first crisis when they were solely charter carriers). Once again, they are offering low-cost, low-priced, point-to-point transportation, except this time on a scheduled service. In more and more markets in which liberal bilateral agreements permit it they will challenge incumbent carriers.

This will present a dilemma for established carriers. They will have to realize that they can't be price competitive in all markets. If they cut their fare to the minimum in the nonstop market to be competitive with the challengers, they will not be able to absorb the cost of interlining, circuitous routing, and additional stops. On the other hand, if they price their product to include these expenses, they will not be competitive with the new carriers for local nonstop traffic. The question is, which strategy makes more sense? For a variety of reasons, it seems to me that carriers would do better concentrating on being competitive in their primary markets. This is where most of their volume and all of their profits are.

There is another curious phenomenon. Airlines have become profit oriented in their scheduling decisions. They have shown less reluctance to allocate their scarce resource, the aircraft, to routes on which it earns the highest return. What is curious is that the same airlines that are willing to become completely uncompetitive in certain markets as a result of scheduling decisions would not consider making themselves even slightly less competitive in these or other markets as a result of pricing decisions.

I believe the time has come for us as an industry to rethink this question. The carriers may find that this is not a zero sum game; that is, one in which one can gain only what another loses. It may be that we could all come out ahead; while the total number of passengers may not change, we would each carry more profitable passengers and fewer unprofitable passengers. From the point of view of the economy as a whole, scarce resources could be saved by this kind of rationalization. Passengers, too, would benefit from getting an incentive to take the more direct routing. Travel agents certainly should welcome this move. They know that, contrary to common belief, it is not so much the number of fares or the number of seasons as the alternate construction of fares on multistop itineraries that makes fare quotation so incredibly complex, time consuming, and error inducing. Point-to-point pricing, the ultimate in simplification, would also make it feasible to computerize fare quotes.

What does the scoreboard show for airline performance under deregulation so far? Let me start with labor. Productivity will be the key to survival. Regulation was a greater leveler; competition is as much a challenge to unions as it is to management.

To justify high wages and benefits (not to a Civil Aeronautics Board this time, but to the marketplace), we must improve labor productivity. Over the years myriad work rules have become embedded in our contracts, some sensible, some that needlessly cripple efficient operation. The nonunionized labor of some U.S. carriers and the lower paid labor of many foreign carriers pose special competitive problems, as do carriers with more flexible unions. If we are to remain in business and stay competitive, we must reach a compromise on rules that mean little or nothing to the employee but cost the company dearly.

The hallmark of responsible and farsighted union leadership and membership will be recognition of common goals in the competitive environment. Such spirit of cooperation must not be reserved for crises; it must permeate day-to-day work.

We realize this is different from the traditional role of unions as perceived by them, and we do not expect miracles. But we will work hard to create incentives, material and other kind, and to develop a sense of participation.

Unions have not yet been tested by deregulation, but they will be shortly as contract renewals come up. The unions of the large, established carriers will have some important decisions to make. If they go the wrong way, many workers with highly remunerative and rigid contracts will collect unemployment insurance as exemployees of struggling or defunct airlines, while their counterparts with reasonable, moderate, and flexible contracts will find opportunities expanded and job security enhanced. I have faith in the wisdom of union leadership and membership.

Management will be judged primarily by the marketplace. In the past, airline management could not make any big mistakes even if it tried. The two most important decisions were determined by government: where you fly and what you charge. Variations in carrier profits were as much due to good lobbying in Washington as to good management. All this is changing.

While carrier profits have always followed the business cycle, they are likely to become more volatile. The competitive market rewards efficiency and sound management, and punishes the inefficient and undisciplined. It is no accident that carriers that responded to deregulation by overexpansion and indiscriminate fare cutting are not doing well. The bottom line is a harsher and more objective judge of your performance than any regulator.

If I had to grade management's performance in the initial stages of deregulation, I'd say it's a mixed bag. Surely the industry has taken full advantage of the newly won freedom in entering and exiting markets, experimenting with pricing and promotional schemes that we once thought were reserved for the cosmetics and used car business, and has shown remarkable ingenuity.

Discipline (and profit performance) is something else. With all the unfavorable external circumstances, the domestic trunks' leadership cannot entirely escape responsibility for current losses. Because the freedom is so new, it may take time to develop the discipline that will have to go with that freedom. It had better not take too long!

Let me elaborate on this all-important issue. The discipline I am talking about manifests itself mainly in three areas: the decision-making process itself, capacity, and pricing. Let me discuss each in turn.

Decisions that in any way affect competitive equilibrium have to take into account competitors' reaction. Any decision that assumes the status quo by competitors is doomed to fail. It is strange that executives who themselves would never leave a competitive action unchallenged, constantly make such assumptions, implicitly at least, about their counterparts.

In this new environment, the minimum test for a decision must be that it is profitable, even if all competitors in the market match it. I say "minimum" advisedly, for the competitive response often goes a step further than the initial action.

This test applies both to capacity and to pricing decisions; the two are often related. A carrier pursuing a recklessly aggressive fleet, route, and scheduling policy may have to cut fares to uneconomic levels in a vain attempt to fill unneeded capacity. I would say those behaving that way play a poker game; there are winners and losers. Here there are no winners and, therefore, a better analogy would be the life-and-death struggle of gladiators in ancient Rome.

One irony is that even the winner loses. In a closed entry system you could rationalize such predatory behavior by hiding behind the long run: once a competitor is removed, the extra profits pay for the short-run costs. In today's open entry environment, the carrier driven out could be replaced by another the next day, starting the losing struggle all over.

The other irony is that unwise expansion can leave carriers ultimately smaller than their original size. Invading a market and then suspending service does not leave you where you were. Operating losses coupled with huge start-up and exit costs make you far weaker, causing retrenchment elsewhere, as well.

The same lack of symmetry and reversibility occurs in pricing: slashing a fare in half can be accomplished overnight; climbing back may take months, as some carriers are finding out.

There is a lesson here that I dedicate to you as "Waltrip's law": carriers putting profits ahead of market share will have not only more profit but a larger share in the long run—carriers sacrificing profits for market share will eventually lose both.

It's still early in the game and hard to make predictions for an industry that has not been noted for its rationality. Although most of the excess capacity of earlier years has been squeezed out and the erratic cycles of aircraft acquisitions have given way to more fine tuned fleet planning geared to year-to-year traffic growth, only a reckless gambler would bet on a continued and uninterrupted era of sanity. Probably those predicting alternating periods of conservative capacity, scheduling, and pricing policy accompanied by good profits, on the one hand, and intermittent capacity, scheduling, and price wars with inevitable losses, on the other hand, are closer to the mark. Deciding between joining or sitting out these wars is a rather dim prospect for responsible carriers.

One emerging problem is the dilemma of balancing traffic and yield. In theory, of course, you adopt a pricing policy that maximizes revenue. In the short run, with capacity and schedules fixed, you try to maximize the revenue per aircraft-mile. The trouble is that pressure on traffic and pressure on yield are grossly uneven because of the way the company is organized.

To put it simply: traffic has a hundred fathers—yield is an orphan. The reasons for this are many. First, under regulation, differentials among fares were well organized. This permitted most management activities to be geared to traffic measurement. As a result, every airline has literally hundreds of people directly accountable for traffic at headquarters, divisions, regions, ticket offices, and airports. They may have one or two people forecasting yield, but even they cannot be held responsible for it since they do not make the decisions affecting it. Thus traffic is seen as created, yield is seen as happening; traffic is personal, yield is impersonal.

Second, traffic is immediate, visible, and concrete; yield is invisible and abstract. The ten passengers you lost because your fare was higher you can see walking over to the counter of your cheaper competitor. Nobody can see the additional revenue derived from the ninety passengers retained at a higher fare.

Third, you measure traffic a number of different times: prior to the flight on the basis of advance bookings, immediately after departure, then in daily, weekly, and monthly summaries—all on a timely basis and without any doubt about the accuracy. Yield you find out about only once, weeks later and subject to so many influences that, even after the fact, it is more correctly called an estimate than actual.

Fourth, traffic is measured in a number of different ways: passengers, passenger-miles, seat factor, market share, by sector, by origin and destination, by point of sale, and so on. Yield is measured only one way: cents per passenger-mile or, at best, also as dollars per aircraft-mile.

All in all, the balance between these two forces that should have equal weight is rather lopsided. In almost any conflict, traffic is the victor, with yield (and often revenue, too) second best. With slight exaggeration one could say that some airline executives slash fares, match lower priced competitors, liberalize or violate restrictions on conditions for 365 days a year, then on January first they ask: what happened to the yield?

This phenomenon has a greater potential for threatening the profitability and indeed the viability of our industry than any other single factor I can think of. Our new freedom carries with it the obligation to manage in a responsible way. What can be done to lick this problem?

I will tell you—as the milkman said in "Fiddler on the Roof," I don't know. But one thing that I think would help is what I alluded to earlier: less-centralized decision making. I said a minute ago that yield has no father—neither does loss in a market. The scheduler can blame too low fares, the pricing executive too much capacity, and the salesman both.

As it is, nobody has bottom-line responsibility for the profitability of a route. The scheduling executive does not control fares, the pricing executive does not control schedules, and the sales executive controls neither. The only person with authority over all three and full responsibility for the result is the chief operating officer.

This was fine in the era I described earlier, when important decisions were few and far between. Today, for a major airline there are dozens of such decisions every day and no one person can possibly review all the options and make all the decisions. What happens is that most decisions are delegated to functional executives.

I may be in a small minority, but I believe that the time will come when we will follow other industries and put the accountability and authority for all related decisions affecting a unit of the airline (route, region, and division) into the hands of one person. Deregulation will certainly accelerate this process.

Planning will take on an entirely new meaning in the deregulated environment. If I started out on this discourse by asking how you can plan routes for 1985 if you are not sure where you will fly next month, let me conclude by emphasizing the increasing importance of good planning and forecasting, especially in the short and medium term.

All you need to do is look around. Virtually the entire industry is suffering losses and is pointing to the recession and rising fuel prices as the reason. Were these predicted? Were they predictable? Were they closely monitored? Were there contingency plans? If so, were they put in effect as early as warranted? Is there an early warning system in place?

More is involved than timing. If you have six months to make certain adjustments, they will cost far less than if they have to be done in one month as an emergency measure. They will cost less not only in accounting terms—important as this is—but in human terms as well.

Detecting trends early, anticipating events, and taking corrective action promptly can arrest hemorrhage before it's too late. Each succeeding week and month diminishes your options until events manage you instead of you managing events. Crisis management may be fashionable, but it is second best to crisis prevention.

This requires a new kind of manager: flexible, analytical, open minded, and profit oriented.

Glossary

Airline Deregulation Act of 1978   Legislation signed into law in October 1978, that provided for the gradual economic deregulation of the domestic pasenger airline industry to be completed by January 1, 1985. The regulation of air cargo was eliminated in 1977.

All-cargo carrier   One of a class of scheduled airlines holding certificates of public convenience and necessity, issued by the CAB, authorizing the performance of scheduled air freight, express, and mail transportation over specified routes, as well as the conduct of non-scheduled operations, which may include passengers.

All services   Scheduled plus nonscheduled, or charter, services.

Available seat-miles (ASMs)   An available seat-mile is one seat flown one mile. For an airline's total system, available seat-miles are the sum of the seat-miles flown by all aircraft. It is a measure of an airline's total passenger capacity.

Available ton-miles (ATMs)   An available ton-mile is one ton of capacity flown one mile. For an airline's total system, available ton-miles are the sum of all ton-miles flown by all aircraft. It is a measure of an airline's total capacity.

Block hours   The hours from the moment the aircraft first moves under its own power for purposes of flight to the time it comes to rest at the point of landing.

Break-even passenger load factor   The point at which the percentage of seats occupied results in revenues equaling expenses. It is obtained by dividing the cost per available seat-mile by the revenue per passenger-mile.

CAB (Civil Aeronautics Board)   The CAB is an independent regulatory agency of the federal government that regulates carrier operations, including rates, routes, operating rights, and mergers. As a result of the passage of the Airline Deregulation Act of 1978, it is scheduled to be phased out of existence by January 1, 1985.

Cash operating costs   Total expenses less depreciation and amortization.

Capacity-related costs   Those costs associated with the operation of the aircraft, and resources required to maintain the facilities to operate the aircraft.

Cargo   Includes freight, mail, express, and excess baggage.

Certificated carriers   One of a class of air carriers holding certificates issued by the CAB authorizing the performance of scheduled air transportation over specified routes, and a limited number of nonscheduled operations. This general carrier grouping includes the passenger/cargo carriers and the all-cargo carriers. This group of carriers is often referred to as scheduled airlines, although they perform some nonscheduled service. The CAB must certificate a carrier before it begins operations. The process is not the same as FAA certification, which involves safety considerations only. The criteria for CAB certification is a finding that an air carrier be "fit, willing, and able" to provide its proposed service, and that such service is consistent with the public convenience and necessity. Prior to 1978, the "P.C. & N." provision was interpreted somewhat restrictively ("necessity" needed to be shown); since 1978, however, in keeping with the pro-competitive policy section of the Deregulation Act, the CAB has been much more liberal in granting certification.

Coach or economy service   Service established for the carriage of passengers at fares and quality of service below that of first class service.

Combination aircraft   An aircraft designed to carry passengers and cargo. All passenger aircraft carry some freight in the belly. Combination aircraft carry freight on part of the main deck, which in most aircraft is devoted solely to passengers.

Commuters   A carrier which does not operate large aircraft and performs at least five round trips per week between two or more points and publishes flight schedules that specify the times, days of the week, and places between which such flights are performed, or transports mails by air pursuant to contract with the United States Postal Service.

Direct operating costs   Also called aircraft operating costs. Includes all expenses directly related to flight operations; for example, cockpit crew salaries, fuel, insurance, direct aircraft maintenance, and depreciation and amortization. It does not include cabin costs (food and flight attendants), sales and promotion costs, and the like.

Domestic operations   In general, operations within and between the fifty states. As of January 1981, includes service between the United States and Puerto Rico and Virgin Islands.

DPFI (Domestic Passenger Fare Investigation)   The DPFI was initiated by the Civil Aeronautics Board in January 1970. It lasted five years and involved an exploration of various fare issues. The investigation consisted of nine separate proceedings as follows: (1) aircraft depreciation; (2) leased aircraft; (3) deferred federal income taxes; (4) joint fares; (5) discount fares; (6) load factor and seating configurations; (7) fare level; (8) rate of return; and (9) fare structure. As a result of the investigation, various standards were established; for example, load factor and return on investment.

Enplanements   The total number of revenue passengers boarding aircraft in scheduled service, including originating, stopover, and connecting passengers.

Equivalent ATMs, ASMs, RTMs, RPMs   Since freight traffic and capacity are measured in ton-miles, while passenger traffic and capacity are measured in passenger miles, respectively, it is difficult to aggregate freight and passenger statistics. Calculating equivalent RTMs is a way to overcome this problem by converting passenger traffic into its tonnage equivalent, thus allowing aggregation of freight and passenger data.

FAA (Federal Aviation Administration)   The FAA has a dual role in civil aviation. It is responsible for promulgation and enforcement of safety regulations, and it is responsible for the promotion of civil aviation, including aviation research and development. The FAA is also responsible for administering the federal air traffic control system.

First class service   Service established for the carriage of passengers at standard fares for whom standard or premium quality services are provided.

Flight equipment   Airframe, aircraft engines, and other flight equipment used in the in-flight operations of aircraft.

Foreign flag air carriers   An air carrier other than a U.S. flag air carrier engaged in international air transportation.

Freight ton-mile   One ton of revenue freight transported one mile.

Freighter   An aircraft designed exclusively to carry freight, express, and so on, rather than passengers.

Fully allocated costs   All costs including overhead.

Haul length, average   See trip length, average.

Hop length, average   See stage length, average.

International operations   In general, operations outside the fifty states, including operations between the United States and foreign countries. As of January 1981, excludes service between the United States and Puerto Rico, and Virgin Islands.

Local service carriers   A grouping used for many years by the CAB for data aggregation of U.S. scheduled airlines operating routes of lesser density between the smaller traffic centers, as well as between those centers and principal centers. The group consists of the following carriers: Frontier, Ozark, Piedmont, Republic, Texas International, USAir, and Hughes Airwest (now merged into Republic). It has not been officially used as a category since January 1981.

Majors   A new grouping, effective January 1981, by the CAB of large U.S. scheduled airlines used for statistical and financial data aggregation. It includes those carriers with annual revenues of $1 billion or more and consists of the following carriers: American, Braniff, Continental, Delta, Eastern, Northwest, Pan American, Republic, Trans World, United, USAir, and Western.

Marginal or incremental costs   Costs incurred in producing one additional unit.

Nationals   A new group of certificated carriers, effective January 1981, consisting of carriers with annual revenues of $75 million to $1 billion.

Net profit margin   Net income after taxes as a percent of operating revenues.

Nonscheduled service   Revenue flights, such as charter flights, that are not operated in regular scheduled service.

O&D (Origin and Destination) Survey   The CAB conducts, in cooperation with the U.S. scheduled airlines, a passenger origin and destination survey presenting statistics on passenger travel via the scheduled services of these carriers and showing passenger trip origin and destination and volume of traffic by routing in terms of carriers and transfer points. True O&D refers to the initial origin to the final destination of the trip.

Operating profit/loss The profit or loss from air transportation based on the differences between operating revenues and operating costs. Does not include interest charges, nonoperating revenue and expenses, extraordinary items, or income taxes.

Operating profit margin Operating profits as a percent of operating revenues.

Operating revenue Revenues received from total airline operations, both scheduled and charter, including passenger, cargo, excess baggage, and certain other transport-related revenue.

Passenger ton-miles One ton of revenue passenger weight (including all baggage) transported one mile. The passenger weight standard for both domestic and international operations is 200 pounds.

Public convenience and necessity The consideration of such questions as whether the new service will serve a useful public purpose, whether existing carriers can serve that purpose, and whether a new applicant will impair the operations of existing carriers contrary to the public interest.

Regionals A grouping used in the past to include local service carriers. Also has been used in the past by the CAB for data aggregation to include certain smaller carriers not included in the local service carrier group; for example, Air Midwest, Air New England, Cochise, and Sky West. The category was redefined in January 1981; under the new CAB categorization, regionals are all certificated (noncommuter) carriers with less than $75 million in annual revenues.

Return on investment Net profit plus interest expense (on long-term debt) divided by long-term debt plus stockholders' equity (net worth).

Revenue passenger load factor The percentage of seating capacity that is actually sold and utilized. Computed by dividing revenue passenger-miles by available seat-miles.

Revenue passenger-mile (RPM) One revenue passenger transported one mile. The sum of such RPMs is the customary measure for total airline passenger traffic.

Revenue ton-miles (RTMs)   Tons of revenue traffic (passengers, freight, mail, and express) multiplied by the miles the traffic is flown. RTMs are the customary measure of freight traffic and mail traffic.

Scheduled service   Transport service operated over the routes of a U.S. scheduled airline, based on published flight schedules, including extra sections.

SFFL (Standard Foreign Fare Level)   The International Air Transportation Competition Act of 1979 provided for a Standard Foreign Fare Level (SFFL) defined as the foreign fare level in effect on October 1, 1979, to be adjusted on a periodic basis by the changes in operating cost per seat mile.

SIFL (Standard Industry Fare Level)   The Airline Deregulation Act of 1978 provided for a domestic Standard Industry Fare Level (SIFL) defined as the CAB fare ceiling in effect on July 1, 1977, to be adjusted not less than semiannually by changes in operating costs. The Act also provided for some fare flexibility, giving the airlines latitude to set fares at 50 percent below the SIFL and up to 5 percent above the SIFL. In the years since passage of the Act the situation has become more complicated (see chapter 4 for a discussion of the SIFL).

Stage length, average   The average distance in statute miles covered per aircraft hop from take-off to landing. Derived by dividing the total aircraft-miles flown by the number of aircraft revenue departures performed.

Supplemental carriers   Air carriers holding certificates, issued by the CAB, authorizing them to perform passenger and cargo charter services supplementing the scheduled service of the certificated route air carriers. These carriers are also referred to as nonscheduled carriers.

System   The total operations of a carrier or carrier grouping (domestic and international operations).

Traffic-related costs   Those costs required to sell transportation and to process passengers and cargo.

Trip length, average   The average distance in statute miles covered by a passenger on a single enplanement. A round trip would count as two trips for this measure. Derived by dividing total revenue passenger-miles by total enplanements.

Trunks   A grouping by the CAB of large U.S. scheduled airlines used over the years for statistical and financial data aggregation. The group consisted of the following carriers: American, Braniff, Continental, Delta, Eastern, National, Northwest, Trans World, United, and Western. Some analysts included Pan American in this grouping.

U.S. scheduled airlines   Air carriers holding certificates of public convenience and necessity, issued by the CAB, authorizing the performance of scheduled air transportation over specified routes and a limited amount of nonscheduled operations. As of December 1980, there were sixty-three U.S. scheduled airlines in operation according to CAB data.

Utilization-average hours per day   Revenue aircraft block hours divided by aircraft days assigned service on carrier routes.

Yield   Revenue per passenger-mile or per ton-mile.

Index

Index

A-300 type aircraft, 253-255, 258, 277
Accounting rulings: legal, 81; payroll, 81
Administrative functions and officials, 8, 175, 234
Advance purchase bookings, ticket, 177, 291
Advertising: costs, 8; factor of, 8, 13-14, 281, 286; objectives, 24; programs, 246-247, 250
Aerodynamics, importance of, 197, 275
Aerospace companies, 258
Africa, flight patterns in, 148-150
Age groups, 23; 25 to 49 years, 25, 31
Agencies and agents: car rental, 23; government, 205; reservation, 8, 245; travel, 8, 11, 185, 196, 246 248, 250-251, 283, 288
Air Cargo Deregulation Act in 1977, 212
Air freight: companies, 211; domestic, 176; markets, 199-200; rates, 171, 175; tariff system, 176
Air Traffic Conference, 196
Air-traffic-control system, 107
Air Transportation Association (ATA), 9,17, 19, 21, 65, 86, 113, 201, 240; surveys and studies, 23, 34, 113-114, 125
Airline Fuel Corporation (AFCO), 109
Airport(s): access to, 206; capacity, 118; slots, 206; space, 198
Alaska, 24, 30, 32, 174
Albany, New York, 269-271
Allocation: controls, 102; of resources, 171; slot, 196
Amarillo, Texas, 272
American Airlines, 231-232, 237-251
American Samoa, 248
Amsterdam, Holland, 265, 282
Antitrust laws, 169, 176, 178, 181; immunity from, 172, 196

Agiropoulos, Kathleen O., cited, 99-112
Asia, flight patterns in, 148-150
Assets, disposal of, 81
Atlanta, Georgia, 152, 156, 158
"Auctioning" slots, policy of, 196
Australia, 248, 285
Austria, 282
Automation systems, capabilities of, 244, 248
Authority: Civil Aeronautics Board, 172-173; international, 180
Auxiliary power unit (APU), factor of, 107
Available seat-miles (ASMs), 67, 72, 74, 77-78, 107-108, 117-118
Available ton-miles (ATMs), 72, 78, 117-118, 186; cost of, 193

B-707 type aircraft, 240, 247
B-727 type aircraft, 39, 197, 232, 240, 247, 253-256, 273-275, 277-279
B-747 type aircraft, 78, 116, 232, 240, 253, 280
B-757 type aircraft, 197, 254-255, 273-275
B-767 type aircraft, 246, 273, 275
Baggage handling, problem of, 6, 246
Banks and banking practices, 8
Bargain hunters and air fare prices, 235
Bargaining power, use of, 194-195, 205
Basic economic theory, 173, 185, 206
Belgium, flight patterns in, 282
Bermuda-type air agreements, 284
Bilateral air agreements and negotiations, 147, 152, 214, 265, 284-285, 288
Birmingham, Alabama, 270
Boeing Commercial Airplane Company and aircraft, 54, 197, 279
Bogotá, Colombia, 275

About the Contributors

Kathleen O. Argiropoulos is Assistant Vice-President—Law and Secretary of the Air Transport Association. Her primary responsibility is in the energy area, as well as with aviation issues having a direct impact on consumers with equal employment matters. Ms. Argiropolous worked for the U.S. Consumer Product Safety Commission prior to joining ATA in 1974. She received a B.A. degree from Mary Washington College of the University of Virginia in 1970, and, in 1973, a JD degree from the George Washington University Law Center. She is a member of the District of Columbia Bar.

Melvin A. Brenner has been an independent transportation consultant (Melvin A. Brenner Associates, Inc.) since 1977. Before that he had worked for twenty-two years in the airline industry, as Vice President—Marketing Planning, first at American Airlines and then at Trans World Airlines. He also has extensive government experience related to transportation, having served at the Civil Aeronautics Board, the Bureau of the Budget, and the Commerce Department prior to joining American. Mr. Brenner holds a Bachelors Degree in Business Administration from the City College of New York.

William M. Caldwell IV is Senior Vice President of Administration and Finance of Van Vorst Industries. Prior to joining this company in February 1981, he was Vice President of Marketing for The Flying Tiger Line, and previously had served as Director of Financial Planning and Control for Flying Tigers. Before joining Flying Tigers, Mr. Caldwell was a senior associate with Booz, Allen and Hamilton. He holds a Bachelors Degree in International Relations from the University of Southern California. He attended Christ College in Cambridge, England, and then received a MBA from Wharton Graduate School at the University of Pennsylvania.

James W. Callison is Senior Vice President and General Counsel of Delta Air Lines. He has been with Delta in various legal positions since 1957, and was elevated to his present post in 1978. Prior to joining Delta, he practiced law with the firm of Pogue and Neal. Mr. Callison attended the University of Nebraska, the University of Michigan (AB), and the University of Michigan Law School (JD). He is Vice-Chairman of the International Law Section of the American Bar Association and a member of the association's governing council.

Mark W. Crandall is an analyst in the Financial Planning and Analysis Department of Morgan Stanley & Co., Inc. in New York. Prior to joining Morgan Stanley in June 1981, he was an economic analyst at the Air Transport Association, where he assisted on current economic and financial projects. He holds a BA degree in Economics from Swarthmore College.

Robert L. Crandall is President and Chief Operating Officer of American Airlines as well as a member of American's Board of Directors. As a Senior Vice President, Mr. Crandall headed American's marketing operations for six years and its finance operation for one year before being named President in 1980. He worked for six years at Trans World Airlines before joining American. Earlier, he held finance positions with Eastman Kodak and Hallmark Cards. Mr. Crandall holds a BS from the University of Rhode Island and a MBA in finance from the Wharton School of Business.

Charles L. Glass is Vice-President and Treasurer of Eastern Air Lines where he is responsible for the company's financial planning and analysis, cash management, and other financial activities. He joined Eastern in 1964 and was made an officer of the company in 1970. Before moving to Eastern he was a staff auditor for Price Waterhouse. Mr. Glass holds a BBA from Duke University.

Raymond T. Glembocki is Director-Market Research and Forecasting at the Air Transport Association. He prepares industry financial forecasts and market studies for the ATA. Previous to joining the ATA in 1976, he had been Senior Manager—Market Research at National Airlines, and Assistant Manager—Planning at Douglas Aircraft. Mr. Glembocki has a BS from Michigan Technological University and a MBA from Pepperdine University. He is also a doctoral candidate in political economy at Catholic University.

Carl D. Hart is Director of Financial Analysis at the Air Transport Association, where he conducts various financial and accounting studies for the airlines. He joined the ATA in 1967 after working in the finance department of Piedmont Airlines. Mr. Hart has a BBA from Wake Forest College and is a Certified Public Accountant.

K. William Horn is Assistant Vice-President—Research at the Air Transport Association. Before joining ATA in 1964, Mr. Horn held positions with the U.S. Chamber of Commerce and the Transportation Association of America, where he was a transportation analyst. Mr. Horn received a BS degree from the University of Tennessee and a MBA degree from the University of Maryland.

Lee R. Howard is Vice-President—Economics of the Air Transport Association. He is responsible for industry traffic and financial forecasts and economic studies in such areas as airline costs, productivity, and future capital needs. Prior to joining ATA in 1974, Mr. Howard held planning and economic positions at Pan American World Airways, Lockheed, Trans World Airlines, and Douglas Aircraft. Mr. Howard holds a BS degree from the U.S. Naval Academy and a MS degree from the University of Southern California.

Alan E. Pisarski is a Vice-President with the consulting firm of Gellman Research Associates. He joined GRA in 1978 after serving with the National Transportation Policy Study Commission. He has extensive experience in the transportation field, having worked for the Office of Transportation Planning at the Department of Transportation, and having held various positions in the Office of the Assistant Secretary for Policy at DOT. Mr. Pisarski received his undergraduate degree at the City University of New York, and has studied urban planning at the graduate level.

John R. Summerfield has been President of Summerfield Associates Inc., a transportation consulting firm, since 1972. Prior to that his airline experience included positions as staff Vice President—Economic Planning at Pan American World Airways, as Vice President—Economic Planning at Western Airlines, and as Corporate Economist at Douglas Aircraft. Dr. Summerfield holds a BS in mechanical engineering from the Massachusetts Institute of Technology and a MBA and PhD in economics from the University of California at Berkley.

David A. Swierenga is Director—Economic Analysis for the Air Transport Association. He develops financial and economic analyses for the U.S. airline industry concerning revenue, cost, traffic, and productivity trends and their relationship to U.S. economic trends. Mr. Swierenga joined ATA in 1977 after holding posts with the Airline Pilots Association and National Airlines. He received his bachelor's degree in economics from Calvin College, and has done graduate work in finance at De Paul University.

Russell Thayer is the Vice Chairman of Braniff International and a member of Braniff's Board of Directors. Mr. Thayer has more than thirty-years experience in the airline industry. He joined Braniff in 1970 as Senior Vice President—Corporate and Market Planning, having worked previously at Eastern Air Lines, American Airlines, and Seaboard World Airlines. Mr. Thayer is a graduate of Princeton University.

William H. Waltrip is President and Chief Operating Officer of the airline division of Pan American World Airways, Inc. His earlier executive responsibilities in Pan Am included market planning, pricing, international affairs, strategic planning, scheduling, and advertising and sales promotion. He joined Pan Am in 1972 as a staff Vice President after serving in various economic and financial posts at Eastern Air Lines, American Airlines, and the Air Transport Association. Mr. Waltrip received his BBA degree from the University of Oklahoma.

Harvey J. Wexler recently retired as Senior Vice President—Government Affairs for Continental Air Lines. Prior to joining Continental in 1965, he had worked as Director—International Services of the Air Transport Association, as a financial analyst for Bankers Trust, and as a teaching fellow (economics department) at New York University. Mr. Wexler received a BS in economics from New York University and a MBA in finance from the Harvard Graduate School of Business Administration. He was a Fulbright Scholar at Oxford University.

About the Editor

George W. James is Senior Vice-President—Economics and Finance of the Air Transport Association. His responsibilities include directing the development of airline industry economic data and analyzing economic trends and problems for the association. He also directs the operation of the Economics and Finance Council, composed of the senior vice-presidents of finance and economic planning of ATA airline members. Prior to joining ATA in 1966, he worked for the Battelle Research Institute, ARMCO Steel Corporation, and served ten years in the U.S. Air Force. Dr. James received the B.A. from Ohio State University, the M.A. from the University of Texas, and the Ph.D. from Georgetown University.

About the Editor